The Common Law Employment Relationship

The Common Law Employment Relationship

A Comparative Study

Gordon Anderson

Faculty of Law, Victoria University of Wellington, New Zealand

Douglas Brodie

University of Strathclyde, UK

Joellen Riley

Sydney Law School, University of Sydney, Australia

Edward Elgar
PUBLISHING

Cheltenham, UK • Northampton, MA, USA

Published by
Edward Elgar Publishing Limited
The Lypiatts
15 Lansdown Road
Cheltenham
Glos GL50 2JA
UK

Edward Elgar Publishing, Inc.
William Pratt House
9 Dewey Court
Northampton
Massachusetts 01060
USA

A catalogue record for this book
is available from the British Library

Library of Congress Control Number: 2017939800

This book is available electronically in the **Elgar**online
Law subject collection
DOI 10.4337/9781783479702

MIX
Paper from responsible sources
FSC® C013604

ISBN 978 1 78347 969 6 (cased)
ISBN 978 1 78347 970 2 (eBook)

Typeset by Columns Design XML Ltd, Reading
Printed and bound by CPI Group (UK) Ltd, Croydon, CR0 4YY

Contents

Preface

With the collapse of collective bargaining and union membership the individual common law contract of employment has increasingly come to dominate not only the legal foundation of the employment relationship but also the terms and day-to-day management of that relationship. While much has been written about the contract of employment in individual jurisdictions, there has been relatively little consideration of the way the common law perspective on employment has been shaped by domestic factors bearing on employment relationships – statutes, domestic industrial relations structures and domestic social and political influences – across jurisdictions. This book explores this question by taking a range of aspects of the employment relationship and considers the way the common law courts in the United Kingdom, Australia and New Zealand have approached the regulation of those aspects of employment in their different environments.

As with any academic work the authors wish to acknowledge the support of their host universities and their academic colleagues. Gordon Anderson would also like to thank the Law School of King's College London for hosting him while on research leave in 2016.

The authors would like to thank the editorial team at Edward Elgar and thanks particularly to Louise Grey, a then law student at Victoria University, for her invaluable work in the initial editing, proofing and reference checking of the book.

Table of cases

Table of legislation

AUSTRALIA

CANADA

NEW ZEALAND

UK

TREATIES AND CONVENTIONS

1. Introduction

David Marsden has argued that the rise of the modern business enterprise relies on two great innovations: limited liability for companies and the employment relationship or, more accurately in legal terms, the contract of employment.[1] This book provides a comparative study of the second of these two innovations, the contract of employment, in three common law jurisdictions: Britain, Australia and New Zealand. Our objective is to analyse the character of the common law of employment in those jurisdictions and in particular to examine the interrelationship between the contract of employment and the political, economic and social dynamics that have shaped the employment environment in each jurisdiction. These jurisdictions were chosen because they share a common English law heritage. Our intention is to explore the extent to which subsequent evolution has been homogenous and, insofar as it has not, why a variance has developed.

The contract of employment, Marsden argues, 'revolutionized the organisation of labour services, providing firms and workers with a very flexible method of coordination and a platform for investing in skills'.[2] The need for the flexible coordination of labour in industrial enterprises was not, however, new. Historically, that need had been met by punitive legislation, the immediate predecessor to the contract of employment being the master and servant acts, 'one of the many legal ligaments that helped make the British Empire a thinkable whole'.[3] Hay and Craven argue that master and servant legislation had three common characteristics: first, that the employment relation was a matter for private contract; second, that the provisions of that contract were summarily enforced by lay justices or magistrates; and, third, that the uncooperative worker was punished by punitive sanctions rather than sanctioned through the usual

[1] David Marsden, *A Theory of Employment Systems: Micro-Foundations of Societal Diversity* (Oxford University Press 1999).

[2] ibid 3.

[3] Douglas Hay and Paul Craven (eds), *Masters, Servants, and Magistrates in Britain and the Empire, 1562–1955* (UNC Press 2004).

remedies for breach of contract.[4] While the antecedents of these acts may have a long history, Deakin and Wilkinson make the important point that the master and servant acts were not an attempt to retain a pre-industrial model of household employment. Instead, they 'were aimed to impose a more rigorous system of work discipline upon the growing number of labourers, artisans and outworkers employed in manufacturing'.[5] Deakin and Wilkinson also make the point that master and servant law did not stand alone but was the centrepiece of a web of criminal law designed to enforce labour discipline against a wide range of workers.[6]

While this punitive model of employment regulation had considerable advantages for employers, workers were less accepting[7] and, as they gained a political and industrial voice through the course of the nineteenth century, the use of criminal sanctions to enforce employment obligations became increasingly unviable. In the United Kingdom the master and servant laws were repealed in 1875, although the power to fine for breaches of employment obligations continued for some time under the Employer and Workmen Act 1875. In Australia the various state Acts slowly fell into obsolescence and disuse before repeal.[8] Attempts to enact domestic master and servant legislation failed in New Zealand.[9]

Following the repeal of the master and servant acts, the foundation of the employment relationship became the law of contract, but a contract of an unusual character as the common law courts took the 'leg' of private contract and supported it by incorporating into contract the key features of the master and servant acts. This new contractual basis of employment had two major advantages for employers. First, the legal subordination of

---

4 ibid 1.

5 Simon Deakin and Frank Wilkinson, *The Law of the Labour Market: Industrialization, Employment and Legal Evolution* (Oxford University Press 2005) 62.

6 ibid 63–5.

7 Hay and Craven (n 3); Christopher Frank, *Master and Servant Law: Chartists, Trade Unions, Radical Lawyers and the Magistracy in England, 1840–1865* (Ashgate 2010).

8 The Australian situation was more complicated as the various master and servant acts were enacted by the pre-Federation colonies and in some cases were not fully repealed until the 1930s.

9 John Henning, 'New Zealand: An Antipodean Exception to the Master and Servant Rules' (2007) 41 New Zealand Journal of History 62. Henning puts forward a number of reasons for this defeat, most notably the strong vision of New Zealand as a free-labour colony, but it is probably no coincidence that by the 1860s New Zealand had the most liberal franchise in the Empire.

the employee to the employer's control – ensured through the implied obligation that employees obey all lawful orders and unilateral discipline through the power to dismiss without reasons – remained intact. Additionally, freedom of contract meant that, in the vast majority of situations, employers could dictate standardized terms of employment tailored to their perceived needs.

These contractual developments were complemented and reinforced by the judiciary's creative use of the economic torts to restrict virtually any form of collective action by, now legalized, trade unions that might interfere with or result in breaches of the contract of employment.[10] Bargaining power was placed firmly in the hands of the first great innovation, the limited liability company.

Together these two developments delivered, to employers, a common law package that provided a continuation of the power dynamics of the master and servant era, albeit now using the vocabulary and techniques of private law rather than the criminal law. This book is largely concerned with the subsequent interplay between courts and legislatures in relation to these common law developments as each evolved their approaches in the light of domestic political, social and economic developments. Over time, the employment relationship became increasingly defined by this range of domestic influences, including the different statutory and collective bargaining regimes and the differing industrial relations and labour market structures of each country. Nevertheless, the contract of employment continues to provide the 'cornerstone'[11] of the law of employment in all three jurisdictions and is one of the legal ligaments binding what is now the Commonwealth, together.

Viewed in retrospect, this fundamental transformation in labour law in the late nineteenth century occurred during a brief period of about two decades when politics, the law and the British Empire were also in a fluid state. By the last quarter of the nineteenth century the former colonies in Australia, along with New Zealand, had become increasingly independent of Britain, and in 1900 the Australian colonies federated to form the Commonwealth of Australia. Moreover, within both Australia and New Zealand the political forces at work differed considerably from those of Britain. Politically universal adult suffrage was achieved in New Zealand in 1893 and within the next decade in Australia. This, combined with the demographic structures that differentiated the settler societies from

---

[10] Deakin and Wilkinson (n 5) 208.

[11] Otto Kahn-Freund, 'Legal Framework' in Alan Flanders and Hugh Clegg (eds), *The System of Industrial Relations in Great Britain: Its History, Law and Institutions* (Basil Blackwell 1954).

Britain and, to some degree, from each other, saw the pattern and platforms of political parties also become increasingly differentiated. These domestic influences made it almost inevitable that variations in the law would emerge as the legislatures and the judiciary in each country responded to their own legal, political, economic and social context.

These influences were particularly marked in the area of labour law. In principle, while all three jurisdictions share a similar body of law as a result of their common law heritage, unlike more established areas of the common law such as contract or tort, labour law at the end of the nineteenth century was in a nascent form. This, and the fact that labour law is sensitive to economic and social forces, meant that the development of the law was susceptible to the domestic influences peculiar to each of the three jurisdictions. A number of such influences can be identified. First, the period covered by the book begins at a time when the political and legal systems of both Australia and New Zealand were increasingly diverging from those of Britain as both countries sought indigenous solutions to their own economic and social problems. It was also the period during which the Australian colonies and New Zealand became increasingly independent politically, accentuated in the case of Australia by federation in 1901.

In the context of these more general influences, at least two major influences on labour law can be identified. First, as universal suffrage became the norm, increased democratization challenged the historically embedded ideology of the relationship between employer and employee and set the stage for an important interplay between the common law and statute. As workers gained political power, they sought to utilize it to improve their working lives and the legal regimes under which work was performed, although their ability to achieve such change was often subject to the different social and political constraints within each jurisdiction. Second, and partly as a consequence of democratization as well as of differing social attitudes in each jurisdiction, was the enactment of different legislative regimes regulating the collective determination of employment conditions. In particular, the enactment of the arbitration system in New Zealand in 1894 and, federally, in Australia in 1904 acted as a major constraint on the influence of the common law for the best part of a century. More recently, the rise of neoliberalism and the resurgence of individualized employment relationships has seen the contract of employment assume a more influential role in regulating employment relationships and driving industrial relations reform, although this varied significantly both in timing and extent in each jurisdiction.

Deakin and Wilkinson rightly claim that: 'Whatever its shortcomings the contract of employment remains at the core of the conceptual framework of modern labour law'.[12] This remained true for all three jurisdictions even when, for long periods, its role may have been, to a greater or lesser extent, overshadowed by various statutory and collective regimes that regulated collective action and through which the terms and conditions of employment for the majority of the workforce were determined. Throughout this period, the role of the contract of employment might be described as silent but effective. Whatever the statutory regime, the gateway to it was largely controlled by the common law – the common law courts defined the parameters for deciding whether or not a worker was an employee. While the terms and conditions under which employees worked may have been determined through some collective processes, the day-to-day control of their employment remained in the hands of management relying on the implied obligation of employees to obey lawful instructions and on the obligation of fidelity. And, of course, employment discipline was enforced by the right of arbitrary dismissal – the silence of the common law was not because of a lack of power but because its disciplinary exercise was arbitrary and rarely able to be challenged.

The objective of this book is to analyse this interplay of forces shaping the common law of employment and, in particular, the influence of, and interplay with, statutory law in key areas of employment. Our primary objective is to assess the extent to which the core values embodied in the contract of employment continue to shape the development of the contemporary employment relationship as that relationship has evolved over time in response to changes in the economic and industrial relations environments in each of the three countries. While it will cover a range of key issues including the constraints on the key implied terms, especially arbitrary dismissal, it will focus on some contemporary drivers and contradictions in employment relationships. For example, the common law courts have had, at least up until recently, considerable difficulty seeing beyond the commodity-based perspective that an employee is employed solely for the commercial purposes of the employer and should have no expectations beyond the agreed wage or salary. In recent years, judges have begun to recognize that the employment relationship is important to employees for a wider range of reasons, not all of which are pecuniary. In *William Hill v Tucker*,[13] in the context of the employee

---

[12] Deakin and Wilkinson (n 5) 108.

[13] *William Hill Organisation Ltd v Tucker* [1998] EWCA Civ 615.

seeking to be accorded the right to be given actual work to do, it had been argued by counsel for the employee that:[14]

> it is a guiding principle (not a universal rule) when construing a contract of employment that the employee's interest in doing his job, as well as being paid his salary, is now recognised; in particular in the case of skilled workers and others who benefit from practising their skills either because their remuneration depends on it or because their career prospects would be thereby advanced.

In finding for the employee, the Court of Appeal accepted that: 'as social conditions have changed the courts have increasingly recognised the importance to the employee of the work, not just the pay'.[15]

In a similar vein in *Blackadder*:[16]

> It may be that in modern times, a desire for what has been called 'job satisfaction', and a need for employees of various kinds, to keep and to be seen to have kept their hands in by actual work have a role to play in determining whether work in fact should be provided.

Whilst this recognition is to be welcomed, the key question is whether there has been any consequential impact on contractual doctrine. We will return to that question in subsequent chapters. It should also be said that the traditional perspective is, however, in conflict with the notion that an employee expects benefits such as skill development, career progression, and enhanced employability – the so-called 'psychological contract'.[17] This is especially the case when employees have funded high and expensive levels of education. Such education constitutes a considerable 'property' investment in employment that may be jeopardized by employer actions such as an unjustified dismissal or because of demand for flexible employment in professional and technical jobs that traditionally were 'for life'. Long-term employment, resulting in skills becoming more firm specific, potentially becomes a liability for the employee.

Additionally, labour markets do not remain static and labour law responds to changes, especially dramatic changes, in the labour market. One can see a contemporary contradiction with two pressures driving

---

14 ibid [12].

15 ibid [18].

16 *Blackadder v Ramsey Butchering Services Pty Ltd* [2005] HCA 22, [80].

17 Katherine W Stone, 'The New Psychological Contract: Implications of the Changing Workplace for Labor and Employment Law' (2001) 48 UCLA Law Review 519.

legal developments. The first is increasing flexible and precarious employment as employers seek to maximize their flexibility and shift risk onto employees. A second, and opposed tendency, is to treat the employment relationship as one that increasingly demands an expanding loyalty from the worker. This is illustrated by the courts allowing employers to intrude into an employee's private life, and in some jurisdictions to expand both the duty of fidelity and the scope of post-employment restraints. As is discussed in Chapter 2, the twentieth century saw the great majority of persons contracting to provide personal performance of work being combined into the single category of employees employed under a contract of employment. Contemporary developments present a major challenge to that categorization.

Hitherto contracts of employment, as with most commercial contracts, were, at heart, concerned with risk allocation. In the last 20 to 30 years, courts in a number of jurisdictions have accepted that an imbalance of power is a hallmark of employment relations. In New Zealand, for example, Sir Ivor Richardson has said: 'History tells us that in the absence of any organisation there is too great a risk of inequality of bargaining power, of exploitation of workers, and of damage to the social fabric'.[18] Against that backdrop, a question central to employment law is the extent to which the courts are prepared to intervene to prevent undue commercial/employment risk being transferred by the stronger party – the employer – to the employee. A number of related questions also arise such as whether the courts will, through devices such as implied terms, impose standards of behaviour in the workplace that align to contemporary thinking on how the parties to the employment relationship ought to behave.

Ideally, the law as a whole, whether the common law or statute, should reflect changing employment circumstances in answering such questions. The fact that the courts increasingly view the employment contract as 'relational' might be thought to be a positive step so far as employees are concerned. A relational contract might be defined as a 'contract that involves not merely an exchange, but also a relationship between the contracting parties'.[19] The employment contract is a paradigm instance of a contract of that nature and categorization as relational, in the eyes of some courts, facilitates implication of a term of good faith given the

---

[18] Ivor Richardson, 'The Role of the Courts in Industrial Relations' (1987) 12 New Zealand Journal of Industrial Relations 113, 113.

[19] Melvin A Eisenberg, 'Relational Contracts' in Jack Beatson and Daniel Friedmann (eds), *Good Faith and Fault in Contract Law* (Oxford University Press 1995).

values that such contracts are said to espouse.[20] An important question that then arises is whether categorization as relational will have any such impact on the law of the employment contract. It is, however, conceivable that the term 'relational contract' may come to be seen 'as no more than a "convenient phrase" in the manner of the tortious concept of assumption of responsibility in that the generality of language used can encompass the key features of the employment relationship but, at the same time, fails to offer the degree of specificity required to guide future developments'.[21] In the United Kingdom and New Zealand, the most significant development in the law of the employment contract that might have been expected to take place through categorization as relational actually predates judicial interest in relational contracts; that is, the implication of the mutual trust and confidence term.[22]

Recent changes in the law of the employment contract have been compelled by a number of factors such as recognition of the significance of inequality of bargaining power and the importance of the non-economic dimensions of the employment relationship. It is also the case that contract law in a number of jurisdictions is moving towards a position whereby good faith stands centre stage: this may represent the 'new commercial morality'.[23] In Canada, the Supreme Court in *Bhasin v Hrynew*[24] recognized that good faith constituted an overarching principle in the general law of contract, and this allows more specific developments within the employment contract to be mainstreamed. A law of contract where good faith played a central role would undoubtedly prompt further evolution in the law of the employment contract, although, as is demonstrated by the history of the statutory duty of good faith in New Zealand, the definition of such concepts can be crucial to their subsequent influence.

This book considers how the common law in three similar, yet different, jurisdictions has responded to these central questions and issues in employment law and how these jurisdictions will respond in the face of rapidly evolving working practices that are reshaping employment relationships.

---

[20] The United Kingdom Supreme Court took the view that an employment contract is relational in nature in *Braganza v BP* [2015] ICR 449.

[21] See Douglas Brodie, 'Relational Contracts' in Mark Freedland and others (eds), *The Contract of Employment* (Oxford University Press 2016).

[22] An employment contract may incorporate the mutual obligation of trust and confidence expressly.

[23] See Brodie (n 21).

[24] *Bhasin v Hrynew* 2014 SCC 71.

2. Development and character of the contract of employment

The principal objective of this chapter is to explain how and why 'one of the two innovations allowing the rise of the modern business enterprise',[1] the contract of employment (a contract between an employer and an 'employee'), achieved the pre-eminent position it occupies in modern employment law including its role in delivering aspects of social justice such as a minimum floor of employment conditions. This development primarily involved the legal creation of that ubiquitous concept of modern labour law – the 'employee'. Individuals can perform work through a wide variety of arrangements, but the consequence of doing so as an employee brings into play a largely unique set of legal rules defining the rights and obligations of that employment status. The development of the contemporary legal concept of an 'employee' has a long and complex history. While we need not refer to that history in detail, we will briefly review its salient features before moving to consider the principal characteristics of its correlative, the modern contract of employment.

HISTORY

The history of the evolution of the modern contract of employment has been well documented in both the United Kingdom and Australia and need not be described in detail here.[2] All three of our jurisdictions share

---

[1] David Marsden, *A Theory of Employment Systems: Micro-foundations of Societal Diversity* (Oxford University Press 1999) 3. The other is the limited liability of companies.

[2] See, in particular, Simon Deakin and Frank Wilkinson, *The Law of the Labour Market: Industrialization, Employment and Legal Evolution* (Oxford University Press 2005); Adrian Merritt, 'The Historical Role of the Law in the Regulation of Employment – Abstentionist or Interventionist?' (1982) 1 Australian Journal of Law and Society 56; John Howe and Richard Mitchell, 'The Evolution of the Contract of Employment in Australia: A Discussion' (1999) 12 Australian Journal of Labour Law 113. Little has been written on this aspect of

a common legal history up to the point of the settlement of the various antipodean colonies. From that point, their legal history begins to diverge, a divergence that was particularly apparent in the case of labour law. That being said, however, the underlying transformative process of labour law that took place in all three jurisdictions was broadly similar, although most apparent in the case of the United Kingdom and Australia. New Zealand was something of an outlier in these developments due to its later colonization in 1840 and as it never enacted a domestic master and servant act.[3] In practice, the law played little role in labour relations prior to the advent of the arbitration system in 1894. This was very different from the United Kingdom and Australia, where master and servant legislation played a major transformative role throughout the nineteenth century.

The Master and Servant Era

England has a long history of statutory regulation of both the price and mobility of much of the labour force. From the middle of the eighteenth century, the form of that regulation began to be transformed to meet the changing needs of capital in a rapidly industrializing economy. Deakin and Wilkinson identify three major facets of that transformation: the mobilization of labour through changes to the poor law system; increased restrictions on combinations of workers including craft workers aimed, among other things, at dismantling the producer control of manufacturing; and 'the generalisation of a model of employment based on the *personal subordination* of the worker to the employer, that is to say, a model incorporating an open-ended duty of obedience'.[4] The instrument for achieving these changes was a series of master and servant acts, the first enacted in 1747 and the last of which was not repealed until 1875. These acts were transported, along with convicts, to the Australian colonies and later gradually displaced by domestic regulation beginning in 1828.[5] The last of such acts were not repealed in Australia until the 1970s and appear to have remained influential until the 1960s.[6] While the

New Zealand law, but see Gordon Anderson, *Reconstructing New Zealand's Labour Law: Consensus or Divergence?* (Victoria University Press 2011) ch 2.

3 John Henning, 'New Zealand: An Antipodean Exception to the Master and Servant Rules' (2007) 41 New Zealand Journal of History 62.

4 Deakin and Wilkinson (n 2) 61 (italics in original).

5 Merritt (n 2) 60.

6 Howe and Mitchell (n 2) 117.

detailed environment in which these acts operated varied considerably, Merritt argues that the differences:[7]

> while seeming considerable on the surface were in large matters of detail which did not detract from the basic conformity of the socio-economic systems – both were capitalist economies, undergoing an intensification of industrialisation, under the regulation of a legal code creating and enforcing similar work relationships.

She argues that the effect of the acts would be to produce 'the patterns of employment current today and the law attached thereto'.[8] The driving force for the acts was economic – industrial employers required 'a more integrated and disciplined workforce ... Workers had to be converted into "hands"'.[9] A similar point is made by Deakin and Wilkinson, who argue that the master and servant legislation:[10]

> aimed to impose a more rigorous system of work discipline upon the growing numbers of labourers and outworkers employed in manufacturing, as well as maintaining control of the agricultural labour market at a time of considerable upheaval.

They later conclude that the Acts 'gave expression to the subordinate status of the worker within the employment relationship ... and were designed to remedy what were seen as some of its central deficiencies in disciplining the labour force'.[11] Deakin and Wilkinson also make the point that a major driver in this process was the evolution of the limited liability company and the subsequent development of new organizational and management structures that limited liability encouraged – the separation of ownership and governance and the development of modern forms of direct bureaucratic managerial control.[12] Indirect forms of control such as an internal contracting system became obsolete as new labour processes developed.[13] In some cases, at least, the driving force was not only

---

7 Merritt (n 2) 62.
8 ibid.
9 ibid 57.
10 Deakin and Wilkinson (n 2) 62.
11 ibid 106.
12 ibid 69.
13 ibid.

technological but financial as employers sought to 'keep all the decision-making, all the control, and all the subsistence of the workers in their own hands'.[14]

The process by which this transformation of labour regulation was achieved, described in detail by both Merritt and Deakin and Wilkinson, was in its essentials simple – a rigid and harsh penal system, punishing even the most minor of workplace breaches, was imposed on an ever widening group of workers eventually extending to the great majority of manual workers. Workers became liable for prosecution for a variety of breaches including failure to commence or complete often lengthy periods of service, unauthorized absences, misconduct at work, unsatisfactory performance of the work and loss or damage to the employer's property. Employers were liable for failure to pay wages or ill-treatment. Both Merritt and Frank report figures that make it clear that prosecutions for such disciplinary violations were common in both countries.[15]

More importantly in the longer term, however, was the expansion of this statutory disciplinary regime to an increasingly wide range of workers including skilled artisans and, in Australia at least, skilled agricultural workers, all of whom had previously enjoyed a strong degree of independence.[16] Merritt makes the point that traditionally there were three major forms of labour, these being:[17]

> quasi-servile relationship between a householder and his/her menials; second a principal-independent contractor relationship between manufacturer and artisan, farmer and skilled farm worker, purchaser and tradesman; and third, an emerging relationship between an 'employer' and a worker taking on some of the characteristics of the domestic or agricultural service relationship, and closely regulated by statute.

The effect of these new business practices and the master and servant regime was that, during the nineteenth century, Merritt's first two groups became merged into a common class. By the late nineteenth century, the key distinction for labour law had become that between (manual) workers

---

14 Sidney Pollard, *The Genesis of Modern Management: A Study of the Industrial Revolution in Great Britain* (Harvard University Press 1965) 39; cited in Deakin and Wilkinson (n 2) 67.

15 Merritt (n 2) 61; Christopher Frank, *Master and Servant Law: Chartists, Trade Unions, Radical Lawyers and the Magistracy in England, 1840–1865* (Ashgate 2010) 5.

16 For two different examples, see Deakin and Wilkinson (n 2) 70 and Merritt (n 2) 63.

17 Merritt (n 2) 57.

who came within the coverage of the acts, and white collar and professional 'employees' who did not.[18]

Contract, Collectivism and Legislation

The second phase of the evolution of the modern contract of employment took place in the late nineteenth century and through much of the twentieth. In essence, the twentieth century saw two developments – the judicial creation and development of what we would now recognize as the modern contract of employment and the continuing extension of the reach of that contract to bring clerical, managerial and professional workers into the homogenous category of 'employees'. With the repeal of the master and servant acts, new legal instruments were necessary to regulate the employment relationship. From the late nineteenth century through to the present day, regulation has been founded on contract but its substance was determined by a significant overlay of collectively determined processes and instruments and protective legislation. Over the course of the first half of the twentieth century, the interaction of these various facets of regulation broke down the traditional distinction between 'workers' and 'employees'. The traditional contract of service transmuted into the modern contract of employment as its coverage gradually extended to encompass white collar and professional employees. The new distinction that emerged was that between the expanded group of employees and independent contractors, a distinction increasingly based on economic-oriented tests.

Deakin and Wilkinson point to the emergence of a contractual model of employment in the nineteenth century, but its scope was limited by notions of social and economic status.[19] A servant and an employee remained in separate spheres of employment and were to continue to do so well into the twentieth century.[20] The distinction between servants/workers and employees was also adopted in protective legislation in the United Kingdom and strongly reinforced by decisions on the scope of such legislation.[21] This distinction seems to have been maintained until

---

18 It was this distinction, not the modern employee–contractor distinction, that was central to *Yewens v Noakes* (1880) 6 QBD 530, the seminal case stating the control test.

19 Deakin and Wilkinson (n 2) 79.

20 As late as *Marshall v English Electric* [1945] 1 All ER 642 (CA), the court regarded the employment of an industrial worker as consisting of 'little more than a bare exchange of work for wages': Deakin and Wilkinson (n 2) 85.

21 Deakin and Wilkinson (n 2) para 6.1.

the National Insurance Act 1946 (UK). The wider legislative coverage was carried forward into the protective legislation of the 1960s when, '[f]aced with this new situation, the courts abandoned the old distinction between low status and high status employees when seeking to identify the contract of service'.[22]

The distinction between workers and employees based on status remained important in common law and in statute in Australia[23] and New Zealand, but the most important driver of change in both those countries was the coverage of the arbitration system introduced around the end of the nineteenth century.

The situation in New Zealand was the least complicated as it did not have to contend with the complexities of a federal system and also because public servants, which of course included a substantial number of professional workers, were regulated by separate legislation.[24] Initially, coverage of the New Zealand arbitration system was confined to 'workmen' employed in an 'industry', but by 1925 a new definition of 'worker' had been introduced – 'any person … employed for hire or reward under a contract of service'.[25] That definition remains effective, although since 1991 it defines an 'employee' rather than a 'worker', a change that seems to have lagged well behind popular usage.[26] The critical point in New Zealand is likely to have been the amendments to the Industrial Conciliation and Arbitration Act[27] that permitted occupationally based awards, but any real distinction between workers and employees broke down relatively early.

The situation in Australia was more complex and, indeed, Howe and Mitchell suggest that it was not until 1983 that the High Court[28] 'finally accepted that all classes of employees could be engaged in industrial disputes'.[29] Decisions such as this were, however, focused more on jurisdictional boundaries between federal and state law[30] and the timing

---

22 ibid 95.

23 Howe and Mitchell (n 2) 114.

24 Jane Bryson and Gordon Anderson, 'Reconstructing State Employment in New Zealand' in Marilyn Pittard and Phillipa Weekes (eds), *Public Sector Employment in the Twenty-First Century* (ANU e-Press 2007).

25 Industrial Conciliation and Arbitration Act 1925 (NZ), s 2.

26 DL Mathieson, *Industrial Law in New Zealand* (Sweet & Maxwell 1970) 1.

27 Industrial Conciliation and Arbitration Act 1925.

28 Howe and Mitchell (n 2) 127.

29 *R v Coldham ex p. Social Welfare Union* (1983) 153 CLR 297.

30 Howe and Mitchell (n 2) 127.

of the merger between worker and employee would seem to have occurred, as in New Zealand, in the inter-war decades.

While this final phase of the transition varied in both time and process in all three jurisdictions, it seems reasonably clear that by the early post-war years the process of developing the uniform concepts of both an 'employee' and the contract of employment was largely complete. By the late twentieth century, the great majority of workers were employed in a legal framework that established and reinforced their subordinate status.

The Common Law Comes Into its Own

A final point to be discussed before considering the character of the modern contract of employment is its practical relevance in regulating employment relations. That, again, is a story of a major transformation. Until the 1980s, the contract of employment had relatively little impact for most employees – as Mathieson said of New Zealand, for workers covered by awards 'the common law merely plugs some of the gaps left by the relevant award'.[31] To a greater or lesser extent, this statement was also true for Australia and the United Kingdom. The differences both within and between jurisdictions were dependent on the degree of the collective determination of wages and conditions and on union strength, particularly on whether a union had sufficient strength to challenge or regulate not only an employer's negotiating strength, but also the employer's management of the day-to-day working of the employment relationship. Collective strength gave workers two critical powers: the power to have a voice in the determination of the terms and conditions under which work would be performed and the ability to constrain the two most important implied terms of the contract of employment – the employer's right to open-ended obedience and the right to dismiss without reason. For workers not protected by some form of collective instrument the contract of employment did play a more significant role, but even so there was relatively little employment litigation. The common law implied terms and, in particular, the exercise of the power to dismiss without reasons constituted the silent influence of the common law because in the great majority of cases, dismissed employees had no effective remedy as any action would be totally uneconomic, a factor that masked the law's influence. Effective remedies were dependent not on

---

[31] Mathieson (n 26) 1.

the law but on either collective support or statutory rights and, in their absence, an employee was likely to remain silent and seek new employment.

From the 1980s onward, however, the impact of neoliberal economic reforms allowed the contract of employment to come into its own as the principal regulator of the employment relationship for an increasing proportion of the workforce. As Merritt notes, 'the pivotal theories about the nature and obligations of the employment contract were the creation of the judges', on which organized labour had exercised at best only some limited indirect interest.[32] The impact of the neoliberal reforms varied from jurisdiction to jurisdiction, but overall union densities declined significantly[33] and, as collective bargaining collapsed, the contract of employment ceased to be largely the gateway controlling entry to collective and statutory rights and protections and became the controlling instrument of the employment relationship as a whole. One consequence of this development was that employment disputes increasingly lost their industrial character and became legal disputes, using the language and techniques of the law and, particularly, the law of contract. Amplifying this new role for the common law was the changing character of employment and, in particular, the growth of the service and creative sectors, in which employers increasingly sought to exploit not the physical labour of their employees but their creative and intellectual skills. And, again, as with the earlier move to integrated physical labour, the common law contract of employment provided the legal mechanism for new forms of employer control over the freedom for employees to utilize their intellectual capital. Much modern case law concerns expansions of the obligation of fidelity and attempts to constrain post-employment activities and associations.

---

32 Merritt (n 2) 80.

33 In the United Kingdom, trade union membership dropped from 13.1 million in 1979 to 6.5 million in 2013 (Socialist Review (2014) 396). According to the Australian Bureau of Statistics, trade union membership fell from 46% of employees in 1986 to 19% in 2007 (see ABS 4102.0: 'Australian Social Trends, 2008' (23 July 2008)), and according to the OECD, it had fallen further to 15.5% in 2014 (see https://stats.oecd.org/Index.aspx?DataSetCode=UN_DEN (accessed 9 January 2017)). In New Zealand, union density fell from about 60% to about 20% between 1990 and 2000 and subsequently has slowly declined to 18% ('Unions and Union Membership in New Zealand, Annual Survey 2015' (Centre for Labour, Employment and Work, Victoria University of Wellington 2017)).

THE DOMINANCE OF THE CONTRACT OF EMPLOYMENT

In accounting for the dominance of the contract of employment in modern employment relationships, two factors need to be considered; the nature and characteristics of the contract itself and the use of that contract as a government vehicle for the delivery of social and fiscal benefits. Indeed, as we saw above, there was a strong degree of mutuality in these developments – as governments broadened the coverage of legislation to cover wider groups of workers, the courts responded by abandoning the gap between manual workers and employees into a single class of employees.

The Character of the Contract of Employment

Following the repeal of the master and servant acts in the United Kingdom,[34] a new mechanism was required to regulate labour. With the repeal of the master and servant legislation, the employment relationship lost its statutory support, creating a lacuna that the common law courts were only too ready to fill. Employment had long been a matter of private contract, but this was only one of the three legs described by Hay and Craven.[35] The achievement of the common law was to take the leg of private contract and to expand it to fill the legal void left by the repeal of the master and servant acts, by incorporating into contract the key features of those acts. Essentially, the legal model for controlling and disciplining domestic servants in pre-industrial England was, over time, generalized and redefined in contractual terms to provide the underlying model for all workers employed under a contract of employment. A statement of that law made in 1860[36] that 'the servant is bound to obey all lawful orders of his master and to be honest, and diligent, in his master's business' and which gave four grounds for dismissal – wilful disobedience of a lawful order; gross moral misconduct, pecuniary or otherwise; habitual negligence, or conduct calculated to damage the

---

[34] Although criminal sanctions continued to be available under the Employers and Workmen Act 1875 until its repeal.

[35] Douglas Hay and Paul Craven (eds), *Masters, Servants, and Magistrates in Britain and the Empire, 1562–1955* (University of North Carolina Press 2004) 1. The other two legs were summary enforcement of employment obligations by lay justices or magistrates, and punishment.

[36] CM Smith, *A Treatise on the Law of Master and Servant* (2nd edn, Sweet 1860) ch 2; quoted in Deakin and Wilkinson (n 2) 73.

master's business; and incompetence or disability – would hardly differ from a modern statement of the law.

Fox's description of the process by which the common law assimilated traditional values of hierarchy and subordination into a contractual relationship may be regarded as over instrumentalist,[37] but is broadly accepted as accurate.[38] As Fox put it:[39]

> application of the contract system proper to the employment relation would have suggested implications alarming to property owners. Since no employment contract could anticipate all relevant contingencies ... the damaging implication of pure contract for the employer would have been that it could not allow him to be the sole judge of whether his rules were arbitrary or exceed the scope of his authority ... It followed that contract as the pure doctrine defined it could not be seen by the property-owning classes as an adequate foundation for governing the employment relation. Their needs were met by infusing the employment contract with the traditional law of master and servant, thereby granting them a legal basis for the prerogative they demanded.

Deakin and Wilkinson comment that:[40]

> hierarchal notions of the employee's duties of 'obedience' and 'loyalty' remain highly relevant to judicial interpretations, notwithstanding the repeal over a hundred years ago of the restrictive legislation in which they originated. It is the absorption of these statutory concepts into the common law which ensured their survival.

The inherent bias suggested in these passages continues to influence the modern law of the contract of employment. The judiciary continue to regard the contract of employment as a device allowing the owners of capital to utilize the benefit of that capital – it is, at heart, a contract primarily intended to further the interests of the employing party. This bias continues to strongly influence the interpretation of the employment contract and the application of contractual principles in labour law. This general argument has been developed by Griffith,[41] but has been supported by other writers. Forrest, focusing in particular on individual

---

37 Merritt (n 2) 58.

38 Deakin and Wilkinson (n 2) 701 describe the process as 'the assimilation by the common law of a hierarchical, disciplinary model of service'.

39 Alan Fox, *Beyond Contract: Work, Power and Trust Relations* (Faber 1974) 184.

40 Deakin and Wilkinson (n 2) 108.

41 JAG Griffith, *The Politics of the Judiciary* (4th edn, Fontana 1991).

employment, argues that this area of the law is every bit as political as collective labour law, and that:[42]

> the claim of the law to be impartial can only be understood within the context of a particular set of political values and political assumptions – assumptions about, for instance, the distribution of power in industrial relations, the respective rights of capital and labour, the validity of managerial objectives.

In more recent years, the courts have tended to take a somewhat more balanced view – as is evidenced by changes to the law of implied terms[43] – but, in the round, the contract remains very supportive of management prerogative.

The new contractual model provided the legal vehicle to ensure the perpetuation of ownership control of labour. Marsden made the point that, in particular, it provided the limited liability company a flexible method for coordinating work within an entity based on a hierarchical management structure and a centrally directed, vertically integrated production mode. The indeterminate nature of the contract allowed an employer to build a stable but flexible labour force available to work as required on changing tasks.[44]

First, the principle of freedom of contract meant that, in the great majority of cases, the employer could dictate standardized terms of employment tailored to the employer's perceived needs. This freedom may, in practice, have been constrained by the terms in collective agreements, awards or statutory requirements. In the absence of such constraints, a situation that has increasingly become the norm, employers have been able to rely on the standard principles of contract law to construct complex contractual arrangements, including the incorporation of unilaterally variable corporate policies, strongly favouring their own interests. In most cases where contracts were challenged, they could also rely on having the 'home advantage' in that the courts were generally reluctant to adopt interpretations that restricted managerial prerogatives.[45]

---

[42] Humphrey Forrest, 'Political Values in Individual Employment Law' (1980) 43 MLR 361, 361.

[43] See Chapter 7 of this book.

[44] David Marsden, *A Theory of Employment Systems: Micro-Foundations of Societal Diversity* (Oxford University Press 1999) 1.

[45] Freedland has made the legitimate point that 'the courts sometimes apply the accelerator and sometimes the brake': Mark Freedland, *The Personal Employment Contract* (Oxford University Press 2006) 166. Employees following the judges might, however, be less than impressed with their driving ability.

The second advantage that employers enjoy is that their control is critically reinforced through three fundamental terms that the courts imply into all contracts of employment and which clearly established the subordination of the employee to the employer's control. These terms, the clear legacy of master and servant law, were: first, the two open-ended and extremely flexible obligations on employees to obey all lawful orders and the employee's obligation of fidelity. Second, and reinforcing these obligations, and the employer's authority generally, was the employer's power to dismiss without reasons, a power reinforced by the rule in *Addis*[46] restricting the range of damages available for wrongful dismissal. This last term meant that, in the many cases where notice periods were extremely short, employment was for all practical purposes terminable at will. While this was true in other situations as well, the at-will element was mitigated to some extent by the requirement to give either proper notice or payment in lieu. In either case, however, the threat of dismissal, unemployment and reputational damage acted as a powerful disciplinary tool.

Merritt, writing in 1982, suggested that the contract of employment was a relatively new form of relationship and 'its implications have yet to be fully elaborated'.[47] Arguably, given developments since that time, with the decline in collective bargaining and the subsequent growth of individualized employment, considerable elaboration has occurred as the common law continues to take an increasingly active role in shaping the modern employment relationship in a much changed labour market. Indeed, over the last decade or so, the employment relationship in each jurisdiction has undergone significant change – change that is likely to be at least as significant for labour law, including the common law, as that which saw the emergence of the standard employment relationship that dominated the second half of the twentieth century and which continues to be at the centre of our conception of the contract of employment. The standard employment relationship has been under pressure for some decades. As women moved into employment in much greater numbers, the notion of the 'male breadwinner' model became increasingly challenged. More recently, notions of employment stability and the 'psychological contract'[48] have become increasingly threatened as jobs become

---

46 *Addis v Gramophone Co Ltd* [1909] AC 488.

47 Merritt (n 2) 57.

48 Katherine W Stone, 'The New Psychological Contract: Implications of the Changing Workplace for Labor and Employment Law' (2001) 48 UCLA Law Review 519.

less secure and as both the cost of employment and labour market risk are increasingly moved onto employees in the emerging 'gig' economy.

The Contract as the Gateway to Statutory Rights and Obligations

While the unitary values of the common law judiciary have had a strong influence in shaping the character of the common law cornerstone of employment law, the contract of employment and the employment relationship were not entirely shaped by the common law. The extension of the suffrage, and the subsequent growth of political parties strongly influenced by organized labour, provided a countervailing political influence that had significant implications for the character of the employment contract created by the common law. As the contractual era of employment took hold, labour law became increasingly influenced by legislation, much of which was specifically intended to mitigate negative consequences of the common law and augment the power of employees so that they had a realistic chance of influencing the conditions under which they were employed. The evolving contract of employment provided governments with a largely homogenous legal model of employment, a legal mechanism with which they could increasingly link the protections and demands of the modern social democratic state to the workplace and to the majority of persons contracted to provide personal services. While the coverage of such statutes was initially limited to manual workers, the tendency for them to apply more broadly became largely universal in the inter-war period.

At the risk of some simplification, there are broadly three, albeit overlapping, phases of statutory intervention. The first created a statutory floor of basic employment rights – initially legislation relating to workplace safety, workers' compensation and anti-truck legislation and, subsequently, and varying significantly between jurisdictions, a guaranteed minimum wage and public and annual holidays. More recently, this has extended to specific social and human rights – protection against discrimination and the right to parental leave. This generation of interventions did not significantly impinge on managerial prerogatives and other powers that the common law accorded to employers, and, at least until recently, these were regarded as having primarily a protective and welfare function, particularly for vulnerable workers.

A second phase of interventions beginning in the late nineteenth century enabled union organization and the joint determination of wages and conditions through either collective bargaining, as in the United Kingdom, or through the arbitration system, as in Australia and New Zealand. Such interventions, while more intrusive than the first in that they allowed joint determination of the terms and conditions under which labour was performed, and thus limited management's ability in relation to some aspects of work organization, did not directly impinge on day-to-day managerial prerogative. To the extent that such intrusion occurred, it largely took the form of the industrial resolution of workplace issues, that is, through formal or informal processes between unions and employers.

The third generation of interventions did, however, go directly to the heart of so-called management prerogatives and the claimed right of an employing entity 'to run its business as it thinks fit'. Such interventions are typified by unfair dismissal laws, which not only allow independent assessment of management decision-making in individual cases through either a legal or a quasi-legal process, but undermine the employer's unilateral power to determine disciplinary sanctions. However, such interventions are also characterized by legal, rather than industrial, solutions to workplace disputes. Indeed, in many cases, one of the objects of such legislation is to displace industrial remedies with legal ones. Inevitably, as both lawyers and the courts gain a foothold in such processes, they became increasingly influenced by common law values and rules, which may be less than sympathetic to the aims of the reform.[49] Periodic skirmishes between courts and legislatures over the direction of the law seem to be a defining characteristic of labour law in common law jurisdictions and, as employment legislation is largely predicated on the existence of the contract of employment, which often acts as the gateway to statutory coverage, it is necessary that employment legislation take into account the underlying structure and values in the contract of employment if such legislation is to achieve its objectives. The application of employment legislation, be it protective of individual employees or supportive of collective rights, is mediated by the judiciary's interpretation of that legislation. That interpretation is, in turn, influenced by the common law's assumptions on the respective roles of capital and labour.

JURISDICTIONAL INFLUENCES

While the common law is often spoken of as a monolithic system of law, that is misleading. The common law in all three jurisdictions we are

---

[49] Susan Robson, 'Policy Operations and Outcomes in the New Zealand Employment Jurisdiction 1990–2008' (PhD, University of Otago 2016).

considering does have strong English roots, but the courts are independent of each other. The decisions of the courts in any one jurisdiction, while they may sometimes be of considerable persuasive value, are not binding in another, and differing historical, social and economic contexts may result in the common law taking different paths in different jurisdictions, paths that may also be influenced by the issues that parties within each jurisdiction consider worth litigating. Such influences may be subtle, for example, a jurisdiction with significant financial markets may see greater litigation relating to post-employment constraints, or more obvious, as in the case of New Zealand, where the no-fault accident compensation scheme means that any litigation arising out of personal injury is extremely unusual.

The possibility of divergence in approach increases significantly when the statutory environment within which employment takes place comes into play. The law in both Australia and New Zealand diverged markedly from the United Kingdom with the introduction of the arbitration system in both countries. Subsequently, from the early 1990s, the law in Australia and New Zealand has also diverged significantly. Approaches to key issues of the employment relationship also vary significantly from jurisdiction to jurisdiction; each has a different approach to employment security, for example, and approaches to a floor of rights differ markedly. Such variations are likely to see differences in approach to the interpretation of statutes and in the way the common law interpretation of the employment relationship is applied.

It is to these issues we now turn, beginning with the perennial question of how the courts determine who is an employee.

3. Defining the employee

INTRODUCTION

The concept of an employee does not remain static. As economic and employment structures have evolved, the courts have incrementally expanded the scope of the concept from its initial focus on manual workers to encompass the full range of persons providing personal performance of work, including managerial and professional employees. At the same time, the courts have been required to categorize the increasingly complex range of legal techniques used to secure the personal performance of work outside the contract of employment.

Until relatively recently, the economic and social context within which such decisions were made was the form of employment that characterized much of the twentieth century – employment that was relatively stable, predominantly full-time and long-term, and which occurred within vertically integrated enterprises. While the grey zone between contractor and employee posed definitional problems for the law, alternative modes of employment remained limited and, to a large degree, clear cut.

Over the few last decades, however, contractual modes of employment have undergone a rapid transition as employers have sought to achieve greater organizational flexibility in their use of labour. These developments have been characterized by the use of alternative contractual structures to obtain the personal performance of work while avoiding statutory employment protections; to shift employment costs and labour market risks directly onto workers; and to minimize long-term commitments to the workforce. One consequence has been that the grey zone between contractor and employee has become increasingly crowded with practices such as triangular employment, short-term employment, zero-hours contracts and online bidding for work. The stable picture of an 'employee', which dominated labour law for many decades, is rapidly changing and poses major challenges for both the courts and legislatures.

Not only is the concept of employee increasingly challenged, but so is the concept of employer. The traditional, and usually limited, difficulty of identifying the actual employer within a group of closely held companies has become the more complex problem in dealing with the implications of the separation of the formal employer from the entity controlling and benefiting from the work performed – a consequence of the contractual rather than organizational integration of work.

In this chapter, we consider the manner in which the common law has been influenced by evolving employment practices when determining whether or not a worker was employed under a contract of employment. Chapter 4 will deal with the common law's response to the new modes of employment that increasingly challenge the common law's approach to employment.

Before discussing the common law rules, the critical policymaking role played by the courts should at least be noted. Given the 'gatekeeper' role played by the contract of employment, it is surprising that legislative intervention in this key area has been minimal, a point developed further below. The effect of this legislative silence has, however, been that the common law in all three jurisdictions, by defining both the character and range of workers formally categorized as 'employees', performs a major policy role in determining which workers enjoy access to the range of rights and obligations derived from statute. These include the right to engage in collective action, a range of statutory employment protections and fiscal and similar indirect obligations.

Finally, in approaching this aspect of the law it is apposite to consider the comment of Leighton and Wynn that:[1]

> [The] starting point is the postulation that the legal tests for classifying employment relationships as applied to temporary agency workers (temps), freelancers and other complex ways of working are flawed and inefficient, being based on outdated employment norms from the 19th century and a law of contract arguably intrinsically unsuited to the analysis of increasingly diverse, complicated and dynamic employment relationships.

DETERMINING WHO IS AN EMPLOYEE

A contract to personally perform work may take many forms and, given basic principles of freedom of contract, the parties are free to mutually agree on their employment relationship. The determination of whether a worker is an employee therefore involves two questions: first, have the parties validly determined the status of their relationship by mutual

---

[1] Patricia Leighton and Michael Wynn, 'Classifying Employment Relationships – More Sliding Doors or a Better Regulatory Framework' (2011) 40 Industrial Law Journal 5, 5.

agreement; and, second, if not, are the incidents of employment such that the worker can be said to be an employee?

The Intention of the Parties

While the intention of the parties may be informal, being assumed by employer or industry practice, it is increasingly the case that it will be stated in a formal contract.[2] Compounding this trend has been the decline in collective bargaining, as employment status is now much less likely to be defined by a collective agreement. The principle of freedom of contract and the rights of parties to make an agreement suitable to their own situation is fundamental to the common law. It is, however, a principle that on occasion must give way to the reality that a dominant party in a position to dictate the terms of a contract will do so to their own advantage and will seek to deny the weaker party access to rights and protections that might otherwise be available. This is particularly problematical in labour law, where most of the rights and protections available to workers are dependent on their status as 'employees'. A dominant party can attempt to avoid those protections by describing the relationship between the parties as something other than employer-employee, most usually employer-contractor, and drafting the contract to reinforce such a relationship through the use of terms that are not regarded as compatible with an employer-employee relationship.

Changing employment practices have resulted in such clauses becoming increasingly common – for example, negating the obligation of personal performance by allowing a substitute to perform the work or breaking mutuality of obligation by providing that there is no obligation to offer or accept work. A modern development, the implications of which have yet to be fully considered by the courts, is workers being required to provide their own equipment[3] or workspace – an employer cost-shifting exercise that doubles as a contractual reinforcement of contractor status.

The courts in all three jurisdictions have long stated that, in principle, they can look behind the formal characterization of the relationship. In *Massey v Crown Life Insurance Co*, Lord Denning stated that 'if the true relationship of the parties is master and servant … the parties cannot alter

[2] In *KiwiKiwi v Maori Television Service* (2007) 5 NZELR 6, [47] the Employment Court suggested that the absence of a formal contract was a strong indicator that the relationship was not one of employer-contractor.

[3] A classic example being Uber drivers, where employee–contractor status is a live issue. See *Aslam v Uber BV* ET 2202550/2015, discussed in Chapter 4.

the truth of that relationship by putting a new label upon it',[4] a statement later endorsed by the Privy Council in two Australian cases[5] and also by a full Federal Court.[6] In New Zealand, this position was long assumed but rarely articulated.[7] The leading case, *TNT v Cunningham*,[8] while accepting that the label given to a contract was not determinative, gave clear primacy to the stated intention of the parties – so much so that a full Employment Court took the case to mean that 'the clearly expressed contractual intentions of the parties prevailed over all other considerations ... if the contract was wholly reduced to writing, that was an end of the inquiry'.[9] This interpretation was later conceded to be 'too simplistic'.[10]

The *TNT* case would, however, seem to illustrate what appears to have been, until recently, the general approach of the courts in all three jurisdictions – while they may in principle agree that they may look beyond the stated contractual intention, in practice they have been reluctant to do so. This has been especially so where there is a formal written contract, or in the case of long-standing industry practice.[11] Until recently, the courts were also reluctant to look further where the form of

---

4 *Massey v Crown Life Insurance Co* [1978] 1 WLR 676, 679.

5 *Australian Mutual Provident Society v Chaplin* (1978) 18 ALR 385, 389; applied in *Narich Pty Ltd v Commissioner of Payroll Tax (NSW)* (1983) 50 ALR 417. *Massey* (n 4) was cited by the New Zealand Court of Appeal in *Telecom South v Post Office Union* [1992] 1 NZLR 275, 288 (CA), but on a different point.

6 *Building Workers Industrial Union of Australia v Odco Pty Ltd* (1991) 99 ALR 735, 755.

7 See the discussion in DL Mathieson, *Industrial Law in New Zealand* (Sweet & Maxwell 1970) 10.

8 *TNT Worldwide Express (NZ) Ltd v Cunningham* [1993] 3 NZLR 681 (CA).

9 *Koia v Carlyon Holdings Ltd* [2001] ERNZ 585, [25] (EmpC).

10 *Curlew v Harvey Norman Stores (NZ) Pty Ltd* [2002] 1 ERNZ 114, [35] (EmpC). The 'simplistic' interpretation was understandable, given that only one member of the court stated explicitly that an express contractual label was not determinative. Given s 6(3) of the Employment Relations Act 2000 (NZ), this aspect of *TNT* (n 8) has effectively been displaced by statute.

11 This has been consistently demonstrated in owner-driver cases. See the discussion in *TNT* (n 8) 684, where Cooke P relied on *Ready Mixed Concrete (South East) Ltd v Minister of Pensions and National Insurance* [1968] 2 QB 497; *Queensland Stations Pty Ltd v Federal Commissioner of Taxation* (1945) 70 CLR 539; *Humberstone v Northern Timber Mills* (1949) 79 CLR 389; and *Stevens v Brodribb Sawmilling Co Pty Ltd* (1986) 160 CLR 16 in support of His Honour's finding that the couriers were independent contractors. See also

contract was regarded as being incompatible with an employer-employee relationship.[12]

This judicial conservatism may, however, be slowly changing.[13] Since 2000 the courts in New Zealand have been specifically directed that, while matters that indicate the intention of the parties remain relevant, a court is 'not to treat as a determining matter any statement by the persons that describes the nature of their relationship'.[14] More recently, the United Kingdom Supreme Court judgment in *Autoclenz*,[15] developing on some earlier cases[16] and in contrast to the previous formalistic approach of the Court of Appeal,[17] provided an assertive judicial response to the reality that, in most contracts for the performance of work, the employer will be able to create, at least on paper, the form of employment that best suits the employer's interests: 'armies of lawyers will simply place ... clauses in employment contracts as a matter of form even when such terms do not begin to reflect the real relationship'.[18] Perhaps illustrating that the common law also drives convergence, the New Zealand Employment Court has commented that '*Autoclenz* affirms a very similar approach to the same essential question in the United Kingdom as is faced in New Zealand in applying s 6'.[19]

Additionally, in many cases the answer given by the courts will often be influenced by why the question is being asked. Attempts to exclude workers, clearly within the targeted group, from accessing protective legislation would appear to have been a significant factor in *Autoclenz*, where the workers sought to be paid the national minimum wage. A

O'Kelly v Trusthouse Forte plc [1984] QB 90 (CA) (casual waiters); and *Bryson v Three Foot Six Ltd* [2005] NZSC 34, [2005] 3 NZLR 721 (film industry).

12 *Express and Echo Publications Ltd v Tanton* [1999] IRLR 367 (CA); *Consistent Group Ltd v Kalwak* [2007] IRLR 560 (EAT); and *Firthglow Ltd (t/a Protectacoat) v Szilagyi* [2009] EWCA Civ 98.

13 Discussed further in Chapter 4.

14 Employment Relations Act 2000 (NZ), s 6(3).

15 *Autoclenz Ltd v Belcher* [2011] UKSC 41.

16 *Redrow Homes (Yorkshire) Ltd v Buckborough* [2009] IRLR 367; *Protectacoat* (n 12).

17 By *Autoclenz Ltd v Belcher* [2009] EWCA Civ 1046, the Court of Appeal had shifted position.

18 *Autoclenz* (n 15) 25; quoting Elias J in *Consistent Group Ltd v Kalwak* (n 12) [57].

19 *Atkinson v Phoenix Commercial Cleaners Ltd* [2015] NZEmpC 19, [20].

similar implicit policy was almost certainly influential in *Cashman*,[20] where the New Zealand Court of Appeal interpreted the term 'home-workers' very widely so as to include workers contracted on terms at or below national statutory minima. More recently the court has held that seasonal workers, although not employees within s 6 of the Employment Relations Act between engagements, may be employees for the specific purposes of s 82, which relates to the lockout of employees.[21] By contrast, the Australian Federal Court in *Odco Pty Ltd*[22] gave relatively little weight to arrangements circumventing award entitlements.

A different example is illustrated by the much-cited United Kingdom case, *Massey v Crown Life Insurance Co*, where the plaintiff unsuccessfully claimed to be self-employed for taxation purposes but an employee for compensation purposes.[23] This case was cited in *Telecom South Ltd v Post Office Union (Inc)*,[24] when Sir Gordon Bisson warned that those seeking to introduce tax advantages into their contracts might have to abide by the consequences of classifying themselves as being self-employed. This implicit policy is of significance in New Zealand, where a not insignificant proportion of cases are concerned with achieving employee status to challenge an alleged unjustified dismissal where there had previously been an ongoing mutually advantageous commercial relationship. Not surprisingly in such cases the courts have proved disinclined to overturn clear contractual arrangements.[25]

The why-factor also seemed particularly influential in the High Court of Australia's decision in *Hollis*.[26] In that decision, which concerned the employer's vicarious liability for personal injury caused to a third party by a bicycle courier, the court held that the courier was an employee of the courier company, Vabu Pty Ltd. This decision conflicted with an earlier decision relating to the same employer concerning the employer's obligations to pay minimum superannuation contributions. In that case, the New South Wales Court of Appeal held that the couriers, a group that

---

20 *Cashman v Central Regional Health Authority* [1997] 1 NZLR 7 (CA). This approach also allowed the court to avoid the question of whether the written contract would have prevailed if the workers had not been deemed employees.

21 *AFFCO (NZ) Ltd v New Zealand Meatworkers Union* [2016] NZCA 482.

22 *Odco* (n 6).

23 *Massey* (n 4).

24 *Telecom South* (n 5)

25 See, for example, *Curlew* (n 10); and also the comments in *Chief of Defence Force v Ross-Taylor* [2010] NZEmpC 22, [28]. In New Zealand, a major benefit for the 'employed' party is that, unlike the position for employees, contractor business expenses are tax deductible.

26 *Hollis v Vabu Pty Ltd* [2001] HCA 44.

included vehicle as well as bicycle couriers, were not employees.[27] In *Hollis*, the High Court was careful to limit its findings to bicycle couriers and to the specific point of vicarious liability. In a later case, it declined to extend vicarious liability to other contractors whose characteristics differed markedly from bicycle couriers.[28]

While the intention of the parties is an important factor, and one that may settle the issue, it seems that, increasingly, the courts may be persuaded to test challenged relationships where there is a clear statement of intention that runs contrary to the common law tests of employment status. It is to those tests we now turn.

Demarcating Employees: From Control to the Economic Relationship

In the absence of a clearly expressed intention, or where a court considers that the stated intention does not properly describe the relationship, the courts are left to determine employment status. To do so, they turn to a range of tests and indicia to determine the true nature of the relationship. It is not necessary for our purposes to discuss the well-known common law tests of employment in detail, although we will briefly discuss their evolution and development. Our primary focus is on the extent to which the application of the core tests of employment has varied in each jurisdiction. While these tests retain important common elements in all three jurisdictions, it is apparent that, in both their application and relative significance, they have also been influenced by domestic factors that, in aggregate, lead to noticeable variations in each jurisdiction.

That being said, however, the broad path followed in all three jurisdictions has been similar. The courts have long used a multi-factor test with a range of indicia to determine whether a worker is an employee or works in some other capacity. While the weight given to each of the indicia has varied over time and between jurisdictions, there has generally been a move away from the traditional control test to one focused on the factual and economic character of the relationship between the parties – the economic reality of the relationship.

---

[27] *Vabu Pty Ltd v Federal Commissioner of Taxation* (1996) 33 ATR 537 (NSWCA).

[28] *Sweeney v Boylan Nominees Ltd* [2006] HCA 19 (a refrigeration mechanic who contracted solely for Boylan. Among other reasons, the contractor was not presented as an emanation of Boylan).

The traditional control test, with origins going back to at least the nineteenth century, was developed for a different era of employment in which direct and detailed control was practically feasible and could, and did, extend to most facets of a servant's life. Even the classic modern formulation of the test, that of MacKenna J in *Ready Mixed Concrete*,[29] reflects the origins of the test in the law of master and servant and clearly indicates the high degree of subordination expected of servants:

> Control includes the power of deciding the thing to be done, the way in which it shall be done, the means to be employed in doing it, the time when and the place where it shall be done. All these aspects of control must be considered in deciding whether the right exists in a sufficient degree to make one party the master and the other his servant.

Even before 1968, the control test had long been problematical. As Deakin and Morris point out, the test was not developed as a test of employment but rather as a means of distinguishing manual and low status workers from higher status employees.[30] Indeed, Deakin and Wilkinson suggest that it was the transition from this model of employment to the modern notion of an 'employee' that was instrumental in the move from the 'excessively artificial' control-based test to one reflecting the economic relationship between the parties.[31] As the boundaries of the contract of employment were expanded to encompass managerial and professional employees, the ability to exercise effective control became increasingly illusory. At the same time, the move to vertically integrated contractual modes of business required businesses, especially in vertically integrated service industries where branding is important,[32] to exercise an ever-increasing degree of control over those providing the service, be they employee or contractor. In *TNT*,[33] for example, the Employment Court and Court of Appeal came to totally opposite conclusions when considering the weight to be given to the highly detailed level of control exercised over couriers. While the control test has become less dominant, it does remain relevant, especially where the

---

29 *Ready Mixed Concrete* (n 11) 515.

30 Simon Deakin and Gillian S Morris, *Labour Law* (6th edn, Hart 2012) para 3.26.

31 Simon Deakin and Frank Wilkinson, *The Law of the Labour Market: Industrialization, Employment and Legal Evolution* (Oxford University Press 2005) 95.

32 *Hollis* (n 26).

33 *TNT* (n 8).

focus is on an individual relationship rather than a widespread organizational requirement. In such a context, both traditional detailed control, and its converse lack of control or individual autonomy, continue to be regarded as indicators of status. In this sense, control might be seen as reflecting, in less loaded terms, the common law's perspective that subordination is central to the employment contract. In some New Zealand cases, for example, limited control seems to be a factor pointing to a non-employment relationship when a reasonable degree of independence is achieved, even if the fundamental test is prima facie being used.[34]

As the control test became increasingly unrealistic, it began to be displaced by an approach centred on the economic relationship between the parties; in essence, both the integration test and the economic reality (or fundamental) test ask the same question – whether or not the employment relationship is such that a worker has sufficient organizational and economic independence from the employer to break the employer-employee nexus. The criteria used for each test do, however, vary, so the different focus may result in a different conclusion.

The most influential modern statement as to whether or not a person is an employee is that of Cooke J in *Market Investigations*:[35]

> The fundamental test to be applied is this: 'Is the person who has engaged himself to perform these services performing them as a person in business on his own account?' If the answer to that question is 'yes', then the contract is a contract for services. If the answer is 'no', then the contract is a contract of service.

Cooke J went on to make the point that no exhaustive list can be compiled of the different considerations which are relevant in each case, nor their relative weight. Of control, his Honour said that, while control will always have to be considered, it could no longer be regarded as the sole determining factor. The key factors his Honour listed were primarily commercial: the degree of financial risk taken, the degree of responsibility for investment and management and the opportunity of profiting from sound management.

In *Lee Ting Sang v Chung Chi-Keung*, the Privy Council commented that:[36]

---

34 See, for example, the New Zealand cases cited in *Mazengarb's Employment Law* (online, LexisNexis) para ERA6.10.5.

35 *Market Investigations Ltd v Minister of Social Security* [1969] 2 QB 173, 184–5.

36 *Lee Ting Sang v Chung Chi-Keung* [1990] 2 AC 374 (PC), 382.

> despite a plethora of authorities the courts have not been able to devise a single test that will conclusively point to the distinction in all cases. Their Lordships agree with the Court of Appeal when they said that the matter had never been better put than by Cooke J in *Market Investigations Ltd v Minister of Social Security*.

While the *Market Investigations* test has been influential, the weightings given to it have varied. In New Zealand, the judgments in *TNT* and *Bryson* clearly recognized the economic reality test as the focal point of any consideration, but were also clear that a range of other factors could be considered and might, if appropriate, outweigh the test. In *On Call Interpreters*, the Federal Court of Australia described *Hollis* as applying a 'multi-factorial' approach, but with the 'focal point' being whether the services were being performed by a person in their own business.[37] However, Creighton and Stewart, writing in 2010, commented that 'most judges have traditionally been unwilling or unable to focus on the economic reality of the parties' relationship'.[38] While conceding that in *Hollis* there was some reference to the reality of the relationship, they conclude that 'there is nothing to suggest that the Court was intending to break new ground',[39] although they do suggest that this position may be shifting. The analysis in *On Call* would seem to support this shift.

It has been argued that the law in the United Kingdom appears to be more confused. Leighton and Wynn have suggested that:[40]

> [t]he recent history of judicial decision making in the area of employment status has been confusing and often unimpressive. Courts have at times placed emphasis on control, or on integration and at other times relied on more commercial tests.

This statement that the economic reality test provides a 'focal point' for a multi-factorial test is a sufficiently accurate summary of the situation in all three jurisdictions, but also indicates that the courts' preference is to allow themselves considerable flexibility in their decision-making in this area. This leaves them free to take into account factors such as industry practice or 'who wants to know?' – considerations reflecting that employment status has implications not only for the immediate parties

---

[37] *On Call Interpreters and Translators Agency Pty Ltd v Commissioner of Taxation No 3* [2011] FCA 366, [207].

[38] Breen Creighton and Andrew Stewart, *Labour Law* (5th edn, Federation Press 2010) para 7.54.

[39] ibid para 7.56.

[40] Leighton and Wynn (n 1) 22.

but also for third parties, including other employers and employees as well as revenue authorities or parties seeking to establish vicarious liability.[41]

Regardless of these caveats, the economic reality test provides a useful baseline against which to assess legal developments in our three jurisdictions and to assess the extent to which other factors influence decisions on employment status.

THE EVOLVING COMMON LAW

It can validly be argued that the common law has, using an open-ended multi-factor test, taken a broadly pragmatic approach that can adjust to rapidly evolving patterns of employment. While the common law tests of employment have been well established for many decades, their interpretation and relative importance has varied over time and from place to place in response to the differing balance of factors in each jurisdiction.[42] While the broad character of such developments is clear, there are some variations between jurisdictions, although it is not always easy to discern the precise extent of such variations. Courts can only decide those cases that come before them and the drivers behind such cases may vary, as may the train of logic used to decide them. Additionally, cases of this nature tend to be highly factual and often fact-based appeals are discouraged, thus limiting the opportunity for the higher courts to reconsider the law even if they considered that this was desirable in a particular case.[43] Nevertheless, the current legal position in both Australia and New Zealand has been the subject of relatively recent judgments that have examined the relevant law from a reasonably broad perspective.

The New Zealand Supreme Court had the opportunity to consider the law in *Bryson*[44] and the High Court of Australia had a similar opportunity

---

[41] See, for example, the Australian cases of *Vabu* (n 27) and *Hollis* (n 26).

[42] For example, in New Zealand, the question of vicarious liability for personal injury is of little relevance because of its no-fault accident compensation regime.

[43] In both the United Kingdom and New Zealand, appeals are restricted to a point of law only (Employment Tribunals Act 1996 (UK) 1996, s 21; Employment Relations Act (NZ), s 214). In Australia, appeals from decisions of the Fair Work Commission (FWC) require permission, which will be granted where the case concerns a question of 'public interest': Fair Work Act 2009 (Cth), s 604. Questions of law may be referred from the FWC (which is an administrative tribunal) to a full bench of the Federal Court: s 608(2).

[44] *Bryson* (n 11).

in *Hollis*.[45] More recently, the Federal Court in *On Call Interpreters* provided a detailed exposition of the law.[46] While the United Kingdom Supreme Court has considered the issue relatively recently in *Autoclenz*,[47] that decision was largely confined to the question of whether contractual documents accurately represented the relationship between the parties, and the tests generally were not reconsidered.

In *Bryson*,[48] the New Zealand Supreme Court's reconsideration of the law followed the enactment of section 6(2)–(3) of the Employment Relations Act 2000 (NZ), which instructed the courts to 'determine the real nature' of the relationship between the parties. In its decision, the court largely endorsed the approach developed by the Employment Court after 2000 and, in particular, Judge Shaw's summary of the relevant principles in the Employment Court decision in *Bryson*.[49] These were:

- The Court must determine the real nature of the relationship.
- The intention of the parties is still relevant but no longer decisive.
- Statements by the parties, including contractual statements, are not decisive of the nature of the relationship.
- The real nature of the relationship can be ascertained by analysing the tests that have been historically applied such as control, integration and the 'fundamental' test.
- The fundamental test examines whether a person performing the services is doing so on their own account.
- Another matter which may assist in the determination of the issue is industry practice although this is far from determinative of the primary question.

Judge Shaw added that '[t]he ultimate decision in a case such as this depends upon the entire factual matrix'.[50] The Supreme Court commented that 'the only criticism that might fairly be made' is that the list did not 'expressly direct attention to the substantive contractual terms'.[51]

While this may look like something of a checklist of matters to consider, it is clear from decisions both before and after *Bryson* that the

---

[45] *Hollis* (n 26).

[46] *On Call Interpreters* (n 37).

[47] *Autoclenz* (n 15).

[48] *Bryson* (n 11). The actual decision on the facts has been effectively overturned following the passing of the 'Hobbit Law', the Employment Relations (Film Production Work) Amendment Act 2010, which inserted subss (1)(d) and (1A) into s 6 of the Employment Relations Act 2000 (NZ).

[49] *Bryson* (n 11) [19] (citation removed).

[50] ibid [21].

[51] ibid [32].

primary test is the economic reality test, especially given that 'integration' is normally treated as one aspect of economic reality. In *Bryson* in the Court of Appeal, the court commented that: 'We think Parliament used the expression "real nature of the relationship" in a way that was at least consistent with Cooke J's "fundamental test" in the *Market Investigations* case'.[52] While this point was not addressed by the Supreme Court, it is consistent with the court's judgment and is well established in case law. As the authors of the leading commentary on employment law have stated: 'Of the various tests, the most significant in recent years has been the 'economic reality' test, with elements such as control and organisation being seen essentially as pointers to the autonomy – or otherwise – of the person concerned within this framework'.[53]

While the High Court of Australia's decision in *Hollis* is not as wide-ranging as *Bryson*, it does identify what the court viewed as the key principles. In particular, it refers to Windeyer J's statement that:[54]

> the distinction between an employee and an independent contractor is 'rooted fundamentally in the difference between a person who serves his employer in his, the employer's, business, and a person who carries on a trade or business of his own'.

On control, the court referred to *Stevens v Brodribb Sawmilling Co Pty Ltd*, where Mason J had stated, 'control is not now regarded as the only relevant factor. Rather it is the totality of the relationship between the parties which must be considered'.[55]

A detailed exposition of the law in Australia was given by Bromberg J in the Federal Court's decision in *On Call Interpreters*. After considering both academic and judicial sources and a reference to the statement in *Hollis* that 'the totality of the relationship' must be considered, His Honour stated:[56]

> Simply expressed, the question of whether a person is an independent contractor in relation to the performance of particular work, may be posed and answered as follows: Viewed as a 'practical matter':

---

52 *Three Foot Six Ltd v Bryson* [2004] 2 ERNZ 526, (2004) 2 NZELR 29, [102].

53 *Mazengarb's Employment Law* (n 34) para ERA6.5.3.

54 *Hollis* (n 26) [40]; citing *Marshall v Whittaker's Building Supply Co* (1963) 109 CLR 210, 217.

55 *Hollis* (n 26) [44]; citing *Stevens v Brodribb Sawmilling Co Pty Ltd* (1986) 160 CLR 16, 29.

56 *On Call Interpreters* (n 37) [208].

(i) is the person performing the work an entrepreneur who owns and operates a business; and,
(ii) in performing the work, is that person working in and for that person's business as a representative of that business and not of the business receiving the work?

> If the answer to that question is yes, in the performance of that particular work, the person is likely to be an independent contractor. If no, then the person is likely to be an employee.

While this test is effectively a restatement of the economic reality test, it is notable that it involves a two-step process: first, does the person operate their own business and, if so, is the particular task being performed as part of that business? The case concerned translators and interpreters employed for particular tasks, some of whom clearly had their own independent businesses when not employed by On Call.

While Leighton and Wynn have suggested that the law in the United Kingdom appears to be confused,[57] this comment may be too harsh as the courts, as in all three jurisdictions, have had to react to a wide variety of new contractual arrangements. The existence of more than one test can be helpful in this regard.

Those cases that have reached the higher courts have generally been focused on very specific issues and there appears to have been no general reconsideration of the law for many years. In part, the lack of clear guidance may be because the courts have been particularly robust in treating decisions on employment status as matters of fact and not therefore subject to appeal.[58] While the economic reality test, as affirmed by the Privy Council in *Lee Ting Sang v Chung Chi-Keung*,[59] seems to be a central element, it also appears that a pragmatic 'purposive approach'[60] looking at all the circumstances of the case may be the dominant approach. In *McMeechan*, Waite LJ approved earlier statements that the balanced approach required a court to:[61]

> consider all aspects of the relationship, no single factor being in itself decisive and each of which may vary in weight and direction, and, having given such balance to the factors as seems appropriate, to determine whether the person was carrying on business on his own account.

---

57 Leighton and Wynn (n 1) 22.
58 Deakin and Morris (n 30) para 3.20.
59 *Lee Ting Sang v Chung Chi-Keung* (n 36).
60 *Autoclenz* (n 15) [36].
61 *McMeechan v Secretary of State for Employment* [1997] ICR 549, 555.

The court added:[62]

> The empiricism of that approach does not preclude recourse to familiar touchstones which have been found useful over the years. *Harvey on Industrial Relations and Employment Law* gives a useful summary of them at paragraphs A10 to A53.

Those cases that have reached the appellate courts have, however, been focused largely on two issues: mutuality of obligation and the extent to which the form of contract should define the relationship.

Mutuality of obligation is important if a worker seeks to claim benefits dependent on a qualifying period, such as the right to challenge a dismissal. An early and highly influential case on mutuality of obligation, *O'Kelly v Trusthouse Forte plc*,[63] concerned the employment status of 'regular casuals', who in practice worked for a considerable number of hours each week and had priority in being offered work. The Court of Appeal, in a decision heavily influenced by both the strict terms of the written contract and the industry's practice of treating casuals as contractors, endorsed the tribunal's decision, which had seen the lack of mutuality of obligation to offer or accept work as fatal to any underlying contract of employment. The court also held that individual engagements to work were not contracts of employment but services performed as a contractor. The United Kingdom appellate courts have been robust in upholding the notion of mutuality of obligation,[64] although they have, albeit not in *O'Kelly*, been increasingly willing to recognize that one-off engagements might constitute employment. This does lead into interesting legal gymnastics to distinguish between a contract of general engagement and the contract of employment for a specific engagement. In *McMeechan*, for example, the Court of Appeal held that, while there was no ongoing contract of employment, such a contract did exist for individual engagements. Whether *Autoclenz*,[65] which signals the need for a much closer examination of the relationship between the terms of contract and the reality of the employment, will lead to a change in focus in United Kingdom case law remains to be seen.

The courts in Australia and New Zealand have not been concerned with mutuality of obligation, possibly because the arbitration system in

---

62 ibid; citing *Harvey on Industrial Relations and Employment Law* (LexisNexis 1991).

63 *O'Kelly v Trusthouse Forte plc* [1984] QB 90 (CA).

64 *Carmichael v National Power plc* [1999] 1 WLR 2042 (HL).

65 *Autoclenz* (n 15).

both countries meant that the concept of casual and seasonal employment was well-established in awards and could carry clear rights, such as seasonal re-employment.[66] With the abolition of awards in New Zealand and the move to modern awards in Australia, the situation has become a little more complex, but both countries have adopted a fluid approach to casual employment, accepting that ongoing employment obligations may arise and that individual engagements do not involve separate contracts. The United Kingdom law on mutuality seems to have had only a limited influence and is rarely discussed in judgments. One exception was *Jinkinson v Oceana Gold (NZ) Ltd*,[67] where mutuality of obligation was discussed at some length. The more accepted approach in New Zealand, however, while taking mutual obligation into account, is to rely on a factual evaluation of the 'regularity of work and continuity of employment'[68] and ask whether there is a legitimate expectation of ongoing work as a result of past practice.[69] The statutory injunction to determine the real nature of the relationship reinforces this approach.[70] It is likely, for example, that in New Zealand the facts of *O'Kelly* would be interpreted as a contract having evolved over time from casual to ongoing employment.

In Australia, 'casual' has both a general meaning and, in the context of awards, a more technical one.[71] The fluid character of casual employment was made clear in the *Public Service Assn* case,[72] where the Commission's identification of the characteristics of casual employment noted that, while it was characterized by 'informality, uncertainty and irregularity', it could also involve an ongoing contract but still with irregular and unrostered work.

---

[66] Recently affirmed in *AFFCO New Zealand Ltd* (n 21).

[67] *Jinkinson v Oceana Gold (NZ) Ltd* (2009) 6 NZELR 813. This case was unusual in containing a detailed discussion of the United Kingdom law.

[68] *Rush Security Services Ltd (t/a Darien Rush Security) v Samoa* [2011] NZEmpC 76.

[69] See, for example, *Barnes v Whangarei Returned Services Assoc (Inc)* [1997] ERNZ 626 (EmpC).

[70] See the discussion in *Rush Security Services* (n 68).

[71] On the technical meaning, see *Telum Civil (Qld) Pty Ltd v Construction, Forestry, Mining and Energy Union* [2013] FWCFB 2434.

[72] *Public Service Assn and Professional Officers Assn Amalgamated Union of NSW v Department of Justice* [2010] NSWIRComm 148.

COMMONALITY AND DIVERGENCE

Reviewing the approaches in our three jurisdictions it is unsurprising to find, at least at the general level, a common approach to determining who may or may not be an employee. The move from a control-based to an economic-based perspective reflects common trends in employment practice and the pattern of employment in modern labour markets. A second common feature is that, in all three jurisdictions, the question of who is an employee is regarded, in the great majority of cases, as a matter of fact rather than law. The consequence is that most decisions will be made by low level tribunals from which there are restricted rights of appeal usually limited to points of law. In New Zealand, where an authority decision may be challenged on the facts in the Employment Court, the court has stated that 'reliance on detailed factual comparisons with cases decided previously … is misplaced and unhelpful'.[73] It is perhaps not surprising, therefore, that courts are reluctant to fetter the necessary factual inquiry with rigid rules. The reluctance of courts to move beyond a multi-factor approach reflects the view that all cases must be decided primarily on their individual facts.

Different legal and labour market structures may, however, lead to the courts focusing on different aspects of the employment indicia. Looking at developments over the last four decades, New Zealand since the 1970s has differed from the other jurisdictions in two respects: first, its no-fault accident compensation scheme means that claims of vicarious liability are likely to arise only in unusual circumstances and in relation to professional liability; and, second, the personal grievance provisions allow a dismissal to be challenged from the point at which a contract becomes binding. The second characteristic, accentuated by the universal coverage of the personal grievance procedure introduced in 1991, has the consequence that many contractors, in the absence of an arbitration clause, will seek to challenge the termination of their employment by alleging that they were an employee. The focus of the cases has therefore tended to be on the individual concerned and whether the commercial arrangement they entered into was a contracting or employment arrangement, a question that tends, in spite of allusions to other indicia, towards whether the person was in business on their own account.

By contrast, the major Australian cases appear to be more concerned with issues of wider implications – vicarious liability in respect of third party injuries or the employer's liability for superannuation contributions.

---

[73] *Franix Construction Ltd v Tozer* [2014] NZEmpC 159, [41].

These issues have significant policy implications, with the answers given reflecting that position. This a point is illustrated by the two *Vabu* decisions, the first of which affirmed the traditional approach to owner drivers, while the second reflected that bicycle couriers had characteristics that merited a different approach and which, if anything, emphasized integration from a third party's perspective.[74]

Finally, the United Kingdom concerns seem different again, having a more particular focus on continuity of employment to be eligible for various employment protections. Most recently, this focus on actual practice as opposed to formal labelling, presumably in response to the increasingly obvious charade of some contracts, has resulted in a major turnaround in the case law, which leaves such contracts increasingly vulnerable to being reclassified.

---

[74] In particular, the courier being difficult to identify and the issue of insurance cover for third party injuries.

4. Changing and alternative modes of employment

INTRODUCTION

In Chapters 2 and 3 we traced how the common law courts dealt with the challenge of developing the modern concept of an 'employee' and the boundaries of that concept, especially that between a contractor and an employee. In this chapter, we turn to the challenges faced by the courts and legislatures in an era where modes of employment and both the economic and legal distance between workers and the beneficiaries of that work are changing at an accelerating rate. The composition of the labour market has changed beyond recognition over the last 30 or so years and those providing their labour are now much less likely to do so in the capacity of employee.[1] Indeed, inspired perhaps by Lewis Carroll, the judiciary tell us that it is erroneous to assert 'that because someone looks and acts like an employee, it follows that in law he must be an employee'.[2] It may be observed that, whilst this may be true where employment rights are concerned, a different stance is likely to be taken by the law of tort should the interests of third parties be involved. The labour market has witnessed a large growth in the number of agency workers, and the ranks of the self-employed have also swelled.[3] Others will offer their services through arrangements such as franchises, which will be viewed as commercial in nature. The extent to which workers are content to provide their services through a vehicle other than employment is often open to question: 'the self-employment figures may be concealing workers who have been forced to go it alone by a lack of viable alternatives – these are the "hidden unemployed", with no real desire to

---

1 See Simon Deakin and Gillian S Morris, *Labour Law (*6th edn, Hart 2012); Carolyn Sappideen, Paul O'Grady and Joellen Riley, *Macken's Law of Employment* (8th edn, Lawbook Co 2016).

2 *Tilson v Alstom Transport* [2011] IRLR 169.

3 See the growth of 'crowdsourced' work on digital platforms, described in the collection of essays published as *Crowd-sourcing, the Gig-Economy and the Law* in (2016) 37(3) Comparative Labor Law and Policy Journal.

take on the challenges of self-employment, and enjoying few if any of its potential benefits'.[4]

All of this is well known, but a question less often asked is: how has the common law responded? The judges have, without doubt, accepted that a response is necessary and have recognized that the changes in the labour market are unpalatable to many:[5]

> a significant move in the direction of the casualisation of labour and the growth of a two tier workforce, one tier enjoying significant statutory protection, the other tier in a legal no man's land being neither employed nor self employed, vulnerable, but enjoying little or no protection, may create social injustice and a festering sense of grievance which would not be satisfactory in the interests of an efficient workforce, a competitive economy, a healthy society or anything else.

Against this backdrop, there have been a number of modifications or developments of contractual doctrine and there has been a renewed focus on utilizing certain existing concepts that are seen as having particular contemporary relevance. Such endeavours are of note, but could not be described as radical and have had, and will continue to have, a limited impact. It is also the case that they are not invariably to the benefit of the worker; the concept of mutuality of obligation springs to mind at this juncture. Judicial caution is not surprising, as a bolder stance might go against public policy. The judges are very much aware that, not only is, for example, self-employment an utterly legitimate form of contractual arrangement, but it has been increasingly favoured by the government in all three jurisdictions for some years.[6] In *Smith v Carillion*, Elias LJ said, with reference to the position of agency workers, that:[7]

> It is also important to bear in mind that it is not against public policy for a contractor to obtain services in this way, even where the purpose is to avoid legal obligations which would otherwise arise were the workers directly employed ... That will frequently but by no means always be the reason why the employer enters into a relationship with an agency.

---

4 Izzy Hatfield, *Self-Employment in Europe* (IPPR 2015).

5 *James v Greenwich Council* [2008] IRLR 302, 308.

6 See discussion of the 'new economy entrepreneur' in Joellen Riley, 'A Fair Deal for the Entrepreneurial Worker? Self-employment and Independent Contracting Post Work Choices' (2006) 19(3) Australian Journal of Labour Law 246.

7 *Smith v Carillion* [2015] EWCA Civ 209, [2015] IRLR 467, [22]. It is also the case that government policy initiatives may be designed to promote self-employment.

The constraints imposed by public policy weigh particularly heavily on judicial thinking when expressed by way of a legislative instrument. It is also the case that the conservatism of common law doctrine may have a restraining influence on statutory protection.[8]

ADDRESSING BIFURCATION

One of the features of the contemporary labour market is an increased incidence of bifurcation of the employer's function. In cases such as those involving agency workers, the functions which are associated with acting as an employer are distributed across more than one entity.[9] As a result of this bifurcation, a worker will often be unable to demonstrate that they are party to an employment contract. This leads to obvious policy concerns. In Canada, this has prompted a significant modification of the traditional common law approach and, in the process, illustrated what is open to the judiciary by way of employment protection in the absence of legislative intervention. The Canadian position was expounded by the Supreme Court in *City of Pointe-Claire v Quebec*, where it was said that, in the case of a tripartite relationship, a modified approach to the traditional common law tests should be taken and the end-user may be held to be the employer even where control is shared, provided it has greater control:[10]

> when there is a certain splitting of the employer's identity in the context of a tripartite relationship, a comprehensive approach has the advantage of allowing for a consideration of which party has the most control over all aspects of the work on the specific facts of each case.

This approach requires a consideration of the factors relevant to the employer-employee relationship, including: the selection process, hiring, training, discipline, evaluation, supervision, assignment of duties, remuneration and integration into the business.[11] In such cases, the end-user may be found to be the 'real' employer for the purposes of the

---

[8] See S Anderman, 'The Interpretation of Protective Employment Statutes and Contracts of Employment' (2000) 29 ILJ 223.

[9] See Mark Freedland, *The Personal Employment Contract* (Oxford University Press 2003).

[10] *City of Pointe-Claire v Quebec* [1997] 1 SCR 1015, [48]. However, the relationship here was one in which two parties share the usual attributes of an employer.

[11] *Ontario Ltd v Sagaz Industries Canada* [2001] 2 SCR 983, [48].

claim in question, even though the extent of control might have been insufficient to demonstrate the existence of an employment contract in a traditional bilateral situation. The relationship is viewed as a tripartite one, in which one party is the employee and the other two parties share the usual attributes of an employer. The approach in *City of Pointe-Claire* is judicially favoured as a means of furthering legislative policy by ensuring that workers do not fall beyond the scope of statutory protection. An expansive approach to the concept of employment is more likely to be found in key areas, such as discrimination and human rights. In *Pannu v Prestige Cab*, for instance, this resulted in the workers concerned being able to bring a claim under section 7 of the Individual's Rights Protection Act 1972 (Alta), which provides that: 'no employer … shall refuse to employ … any person … because of the race, religious beliefs … of that person'.[12] The response in Australia, New Zealand and the United Kingdom has been much more modest.[13]

JOINT EMPLOYMENT

An employment market where bifurcation is one of the hallmarks has prompted interest in joint employment.[14] The United Kingdom case of *Viasystems v Thermal Transfer* provides a seemingly radical instance where the law of vicarious liability in tort is concerned, by holding that liability can be shared between the temporary and general employer.[15] Under a regime of shared liability, both employers are regarded as joint tortfeasors and, in line with general principles, the claimant can recover in full from either of them. At first glance, the decision in *Viasystems*, with the adoption of dual responsibility, appears to be a bold one. This is certainly true insofar as the treatment of the existing authorities was

---

12 *Pannu v Prestige Cab* (1986) 28 DLR (4th) 268, [3] (CA).

13 In considering this point, reference should be had to the relevant human rights legislation. The Human Rights Act 1993 (NZ), s 2, for example, defines an employer as including the employer of independent contractors and some triangular employment relationships.

14 Pauline Thai, 'Unfair Dismissal Protection for Labour Hire Workers? Implementing the Doctrine of Joint Employment in Australia' (2012) 25 AJLL 152.

15 *Viasystems v Thermal Transfer* [2005] EWCA Civ 1151, [2006] QB 510. See also Douglas Brodie, 'The Enterprise and the Borrowed Worker' (2006) 35 ILJ 87.

concerned.[16] That apart, we would argue that the decision is actually a remarkably conservative one. This becomes apparent once it is appreciated that the ratio of the decision is that dual responsibility can only arise when the right of control is shared. Matters would have been different had greater emphasis been placed on factual control. By way of contrast, in the agency worker case *Motorola v Davidson*, the Employment Appeal Tribunal had regard to control as a matter of fact. Lindsay J explained that: 'Although MacKenna J speaks of control, as we have noted, in terms of *rights*, there is ... no good reason to ignore practical aspects of control that fall short of direct legal rights'.[17] The conservatism of the approach in *Viasystems* means that temporary employers will normally avoid the burden of shared responsibility. However, the subsequent decision of the Supreme Court in *The Catholic Child Welfare Society v Various Claimants* regarded *Viasystems* as correctly decided, but refined the rationale and may beckon a more encompassing approach.[18] It was said that what one is looking for is:[19]

> a situation where the employee in question, at any rate for relevant purposes, is so much a part of the work, business or organisation of both employers that it is just to make both employers answer for his negligence.

The latter approach emphasizes the significance of integration into the employer's business and is much more akin to an enterprise liability type approach.[20] Since *Viasystems*, there has been a lack of subsequent cases, but it is worthy of note that the Supreme Court took the view that the facts of *Hawley v Luminar Leisure Ltd*[21] (discussed below) and *Biffa Waste Services Ltd v Maschinenfabrik Ernst Hese GmbH*[22] could have supported a finding of dual vicarious liability. Should subsequent cases focus on integration, *Viasystems* can be expected to take on a new lease

---

[16] At the time of the decision *Clerk and Lindsell on Torts* (18th edn, Sweet & Maxwell 2001) para 5.22 (n 93) expressed the orthodox view in stating that 'it is doubtful whether such a solution is open to the courts except where both employers are engaged in a joint venture'.

[17] *Motorola v Davidson* [2001] IRLR 4, 6 (emphasis in original).

[18] *The Catholic Child Welfare Society v Various Claimants* [2012] UKSC 56, [2013] 2 AC 1.

[19] ibid [43], quoting Rix LJ in the Court of Appeal.

[20] See *Bazley v Curry* [1999] 174 DLR (4th) 45; and see Douglas Brodie, *Enterprise Liability and the Common Law* (Cambridge University Press 2010).

[21] *Hawley v Luminar Leisure Ltd* [2006] EWCA Civ 18.

[22] *Biffa Waste Services Ltd v Maschinenfabrik Ernst Hese GmbH* [2008] EWCA Civ 1257, [2009] QB 725.

of life. *Viasystems* notwithstanding, the law of the employment contract in the United Kingdom has not taken on board joint employment in the sense that there is a shared contractual responsibility to the employee.[23] The courts have, however, been willing to explore the use of implied contracts in the case of agency workers and this is explored in the next section.

In Australia, the High Court cleaves to the traditional view and denies that dual responsibility can arise.[24] Similarly, suggestions that the law of contract, rather than tort, might recognize joint employment have yet to bear fruit. Admittedly, there may be scope in Australian law for a claim 'that multiple entities can jointly employ a person. Whether such a claim can be substantiated, either on particular facts or on the law following proper argument at a hearing, is a different question'.[25] The question is, however, far from straightforward and it would not be surprising if the courts awaited legislative intervention.[26] The New Zealand courts have been bolder and have found that, contractually, joint employment may exist, though the case law remains decidedly embryonic. The courts have focused on the relationship between two connected employers and those employers and the employee. In *Orakei Group v Doherty*, the court said that where the employers are concerned, what 'will constitute a sufficient degree of relationship will depend, in each case, on the details of such relationship, including such factors as individual shareholdings, corporate shareholdings, and interlocking directorships. The essence of that relationship will be the element of common control'.[27] The approach in *Doherty* is clearly driven by the position of companies that belong to the same corporate group and aims to restrain the use of the corporate structure to diminish employee protection. The requisite nexus with the employee will be present where control exists to a sufficient extent. In *Hutton v Provenco Cadmus Ltd (in receivership)*,[28] while it was accepted

---

23 There are minor exceptions.

24 *Oceanic Crest Shipping Company v Pilbara Harbour Services Pty Ltd* (1986) 160 CLR 626; *Day v Ocean Beach Hotel* [2013] NSWCA 250.

25 *Fair Work Ombudsman v Eastern Colour Pty Ltd* (2011) 209 IR 263, [78]. See also Rohen Cullen, 'A Servant and Two Masters? The Doctrine of Joint Employment in Australia' (2003) 16 AJLL 359.

26 See *Costello v Allstaff Industrial Personnel (SA) Pty Ltd and Bridgestone TG Australian Pty Ltd* [2004] SAIRComm 13, 29 March 2004 (DP Hampton), [135].

27 *Orakei Group v Doherty* [2008] NZEmpC 65, [57].

28 *Hutton v Provenco Cadmus Ltd (in receivership)* [2012] NZEmpC 207.

as 'common ground' that it was possible to have joint employers, it was held that no factual basis for joint employment had been established.

AGENCY

In the United Kingdom, the courts, for a limited period of time, were amenable to improving the lot of the agency worker by holding that an implied contract existed between the worker and the end-user. Such a conclusion was seen as permissible, even though an express contract was in place between the worker and the agency. A traditional approach would have denied any need for implication, given the existence of the express agreement, but the underlying policy considerations prevailed: 'many agency workers are highly vulnerable and need to be protected from the abuse of economic power by the end users'.[29] The key cases in this regard were *Dacas v Brook Street Bureau (UK) Ltd*[30] and *Cable and Wireless plc v Muscat*.[31] Enthusiasm for use of an implied contract analysis was short lived. It became apparent that there was a lack of judicial consensus in deciding when judicial intervention was legitimate and appropriate. Since *Dacas*, appellate judges have, in an approach also seen in *Johnston* and *Barker*,[32] increasingly cautioned against the application of such a 'policy driven judgment'. Dealing with the problems that the extensive use of agency workers throws up tends to be seen as predominantly a matter for Parliament: 'the common law can only tinker with the problem on the margins'.[33]

The judicial approach is now, again, one of conservatism; implication remains possible but, in practical terms, unlikely. The enactment of the Agency Workers Regulations 2010 (SI 2010/93) has played a part in this; the legislature has now pronounced on the issue and the scope for common law intervention has diminished. The conservatism of the current position is exemplified by the adoption of the commercial approach in *Aramis* in the employment context.[34] There, Bingham LJ took the view that a contract could only be implied where it was necessary to do so. It is debatable whether this is an accurate statement of

---

[29] *James v Greenwich* Council [2007] IRLR 168, 171.

[30] *Dacas v Brook Street Bureau (UK) Ltd* [2004] IRLR 358.

[31] *Cable and Wireless plc v Muscat* [2006] ICR 975.

[32] *Johnson v Unisys* [2001] UKHL 13, [2001] IRLR 279; *Commonwealth Bank of Australia v Barker* [2014] HCA 32.

[33] *James* (n 29) 171.

[34] *The Aramis* [1989] 1 Lloyd's Law Rep 213.

the position where the law of commercial contracts is concerned, and its extension to the employment context is both unnecessary and contrary to general principles.[35] After all, approaching the matter from first principles, it is far from axiomatic that failure to surmount the *Aramis* hurdle means that a claim that an implied contract exists must fail. It would be wholly consistent with general contractual principles to infer from the parties' conduct that they intended to enter into a contract without having to satisfy the test. The issue is simply one of determining what the parties intended to be inferred from their behaviour and if, on an objective basis, it appears that contractual relations were intended, a contract will come into being.

Initially, Australia was not attracted to an expansive approach to implied contract as a means of giving legal force to the working relationship between the agency worker and the end-user.[36] Given the existence of a contract between the agency and the worker, the view was taken that there was no scope for the implication of a further contract; the existing contractual position offered a more than adequate legal explanation of the working arrangements. The notion that the end-user or host organization should be treated as the worker's employer because the host exercised control over the worker's day-to-day work (according to the control test for determining employment) was answered by the finding that the agency employer had retained the ultimate power of control. It had merely delegated day-to-day control to the host, according to the terms of the commercial contract between the agency and the host.[37] In *Fair Work Ombudsman v Quest South Perth Holdings*, the Federal Court took a much more sympathetic approach to the use of implied contracts. Cases such as *Dacas* were perfectly consistent with Australian law:[38]

> In the context of triangular arrangements, the conduct of the parties may demonstrate that an initial contract made between a worker and an intermediary was ineffective or inoperative and that the existence of a contract of employment between the worker and the end user is to be implied from their conduct.

---

35 See Douglas Brodie, 'The Autonomy of the Common Law of the Contract of Employment from the General Law of Contract' in Mark Freedland et al. (eds), *The Contract of Employment* (Oxford University Press 2016).

36 *Wilton & Cumberland v Coal & Allied Operations* [2007] FCA 725. See also Andrew Stewart, 'Redefining Employment? Meeting the Challenge of Contract and Agency Labour' (2002) 15 AJLL 235.

37 See *Staff Aid Services v Bianchi* (2004) 133 IR 29, [25].

38 *Fair Work Ombudsman v Quest South Perth Holdings* [2015] FCAFC 37, [149]. See also *Homecare Direct Shopping v Gray* [2008] VSCA 111.

This must be correct, as the establishment of legal obligations through conduct has long been embedded in the common law. *Aramis* has not been allowed to cloud the waters. Nevertheless:[39]

> There will be limited scope for the implication of an employment contract between a worker and an end-user in a triangular setting, where the provision of a worker to the end-user is explained by the presence of a genuine labour-hire arrangement evidenced by the existence and performance of the hallmarks that such arrangements commonly bear.

New Zealand appears to be open to the implication of a contract in an agency case. In *McDonald v Ontrack Infrastructure* the court stated:[40]

> if an 'implied contract' is meant to cover the situation where all of the necessary incidents of a contract are established by implication from the parties' overt conduct rather than by reference to their expressed intentions, then we have no difficulty in accepting and applying that term as a tool to analyse the present situation.

In the United Kingdom, the enactment of the Agency Workers Regulations 2010 has acted as a deterrent to judicial creativity, but section 6 of the Employment Relations Act 2000 (NZ) has not had the same effect in New Zealand. The Act is of more general application; a more specific legislative intervention is much more likely to 'hobble' the common law. At the same time, the New Zealand courts have been anxious not to adopt a policy stance, but rather to present the issue as an 'intensely factual' one, and it has been suggested that it would be only in 'a rare case' that *McDonald* could be used to find that an employee has changed from one employer to another.[41]

Invocation of the concept of implied contract will avail employees little, unless the judges are of the view that policy points towards concluding that a contract of this nature exists and additional protection is afforded. It is always easy to fall back on traditional contractual thinking and deny implication. For instance, should the agency be responsible for payment of wages, it will be possible to maintain that an

---

[39] *Fair Work Ombudsman* (n 38) [167]. See also *Damevski v Giudice* (2003) 133 FCR 438. Where the host was once a direct employer, but seeks to outsource the role of employer to an agency without any practical change in working arrangements, Australian law will more readily recognize a continuing employment relationship between the host and the worker.

[40] *McDonald v Ontrack Infrastructure* [2010] NZEmpC 132, [39].

[41] Peter Chemis and Jennifer Howes, 'Tripartite Employment Relationships since *McDonald v Ontrack Infrastructure Ltd*' (2016) ELB 92.

absence of consideration prevents an implied contract arising with the end-user. A court would have to imply an obligation that a residual obligation to pay would arise should the agency default.

CONDUCT AND SHAM CONTRACTS

There is a tendency to place more emphasis on the way in which the relationship is conducted, rather than what is formally recorded. This trend recognizes the power possessed by the employer in their capacity as drafter of the contract and looks to what happens after the commencement of contractual relations as a means of scrutiny.[42] The employer may establish a working relationship in a particular way but, as time passes, whatever the original intention, the relationship may be conducted as if it were one of employment. Evidence of the conduct of the relationship is a means of establishing the parties' obligations: 'Evidence of how the parties conducted themselves in practice may be so persuasive that the tribunal can draw an inference that that practice reflects the true obligations of the parties'.[43] In *Carmichael v National Power*, the House of Lords admitted evidence of subsequent conduct to demonstrate what the parties thought they had agreed.[44] This allows the court to determine the terms of the contract from the way in which the parties have behaved towards each other. It was said that the relevant terms and conditions may be partly written, partly oral and partly established by a pattern of evolving conduct over time. *Carmichael* involves a departure from traditional principles in the treatment of subsequent conduct, though it does not apply (in the rare cases)[45] where the contract is formed wholly in writing.[46]

The approach in *Carmichael* has been accepted in New Zealand.[47] In the leading case of *Bryson v Three Foot Six*, the court said that:[48]

---

42 In *Borrer v Cardinal Security* [2013] UKEAT 0416, the principal issue was whether the claimant had a contractual right to work a guaranteed number of hours each week, namely 48 hours. The employer argued that he did not, as the written documentation provided that: 'Your working hours will be specified by your line manager'. The Employment Appeal Tribunal found for the claimant, given the way in which the contract operated in practice.

43 *Autoclenz Ltd v Belcher* [2009] EWCA Civ 1046, [2010] IRLR 70, 77.

44 *Carmichael v National Power plc* [2000] IRLR 43.

45 *Allen v TRW* [2013] ICR D3.

46 *TNT Worldwide Express (NZ) Ltd v Cunningham* [1993] 3 NZLR 681.

47 *Nisha v LSG* [2015] NZEmpC 171, [90].

48 *Bryson v Three Foot Six* [2005] NZSC 34, [2005] 3 NZLR 721, [32].

> 'All relevant matters' certainly include the written and oral terms of the contract between the parties, which will usually contain indications of their common intention concerning the status of their relationship. They will also include any divergences from or supplementation of those terms and conditions which are apparent in the way in which the relationship has operated in practice. It is important that the Court or the Authority should consider the way in which the parties have actually behaved in implementing their contract. How their relationship operates in practice is crucial to a determination of its real nature.

The New Zealand courts have generally been receptive to arguments that the nature of the relationship has evolved to something other than that stated in the original contract.[49]

In Australia, the traditional view was that subsequent communications could not be looked to as an aid in constructing a contract, but only as an aid in deciding whether a contract has been entered into at all.[50] There are now a number of decisions, particularly at lower tribunal levels, where the words of the contract are displaced by the actual reality of the relationship.[51]

Evidence as to conduct is of prime importance in sham contract cases, where there have been conceptual advances in recent years. It has always been the case that the courts have retained the right to determine the nature of the contract entered into by the worker. The 1914 High Court decision in *Curtis v The Perth and Freemantle Bottle Exchange Co* is one example.[52] A declaration of self-employment will be set aside if the obligations entered into indicate that the relationship is one of employment.[53] In *Bryson*, the court referred to section 6 of the Employment Relations Act 2000 (NZ), which provides that statements by the parties are not decisive of the nature of the relationship, although this provision reflects the earlier common law situation.[54] In *Massey v Crown Life Insurance*, Lord Denning stated that if 'the true relationship of the parties is that of master and servant under a contract of service, the parties

---

49 *Jinkinson v Oceana Gold (NZ) Ltd* [2009] NZEmpC 67.

50 *Australian Mutual Provident Society v Chaplin* (1978) 18 ALR 385; *Brambles Holdings Ltd v Bathurst City Council* [2001] NSWCA 61; *Pethybridge v Stedikas Holding Pty Ltd* [2007] NSWCA 154.

51 *Country Metropolitan Agency Contracting Services Pty Ltd v Slater* (2003) 124 IR 29; *Gothard v Davey* [2010] FCA 1163 provides an example in the context of identification of the actual employer.

52 *Curtis v The Perth and Freemantle Bottle Exchange Co* (1914) 18 CLR 17.

53 *Australian Mutual Provident Society* (n 50) 389.

54 *TNT* (n 46).

cannot alter the truth of that relationship by putting a different label upon it'.[55] In an attempt to circumvent such controls, employers may insert clauses into a contract which are inconsistent with the requirements of an employment contract, for example by conferring a right of delegation on the employee. The intention, however, will be that the relationship is to be conducted as if it were one of employment. Such exercises in manipulation have prompted the courts to revisit the concept of sham contracts.

The traditional approach to such contracts offered limited benefit to employees, as it assumed a common intent to deceive third parties rather than one to take advantage of the weaker party to the contract.[56] However, the position was advanced by the House of Lords in *AG Securities v Vaughan*, where it had to be determined whether the contract concerned was a lease or a licence.[57] The view was taken that clauses that were not intended to operate could be disregarded. *Vaughan* held that behaviour subsequent to the formation of the contract could be consulted to help determine whether a contractual provision was a sham.[58]

Vaughan paved the way for the Supreme Court decision in the employment case of *Autoclenz v Belcher*.[59] In *Autoclenz*, the contract provided that: 'For the avoidance of doubt, as an independent contractor, you are entitled to engage one or more individuals to carry out the valeting on your behalf, provided that such an individual is compliant with Autoclenz's requirements of sub-contractors as set out in this agreement'. It was found that the claimants were required to provide personal service under their agreements with the respondent, notwithstanding the substitution clause or that the clause did not reflect what was actually agreed between the parties. Designation as sham allowed the clause to be disregarded and the relationship to be treated as one of employment. The Australian courts have yet to pronounce on this issue

---

55 *Massey v Crown Life Insurance Co* [1978] 2 All ER 576, 579; *TNT* (n 46).

56 *Snook v London and West Riding Investments Ltd* [1967] 2 QB 786; *Ben Nevis Forestry Ventures Ltd v Commissioner of Inland Revenue* [2009] 2 NZLR 289, [33]; *Raftland Pty Ltd v Commissioner of Taxation of the Commonwealth of Australia* [2008] HCA 21.

57 *AG Securities v Vaughan* [1990] 1 AC 417.

58 See Alan Bogg, 'Sham Self-Employment in the Supreme Court' (2012) 41 ILJ 328.

59 *Autoclenz v Belcher* [2011] UKSC 41, [2011] ICR 1157.

(though the legislature has[60]), but *Autoclenz* has been said to reflect the law of New Zealand: the courts 'must make a realistic assessment of the reality in all the circumstances of work performed in a working relationship upon which significant rights and obligations will depend'.[61] The extent to which one may expect decisions such as *Autoclenz* to have an impact may be doubted, as it is far from difficult to set up an arrangement for the provision of work that does not involve a contract of employment.

The employment arrangements operated by Uber did, however, prompt intervention in the United Kingdom by the employment tribunal in *Aslam v Uber BV*.[62] The key question was whether the contracts concerned meant that the claimants were 'workers' for the purposes of certain employment protection rights. In the wake of *Autoclenz*, the tribunal clearly felt empowered to explore in depth the parties' relationship and ascertain the true meaning of what had been agreed. It was found to be contrary to reality to deny that Uber was in business as a supplier of transportation services, and the tribunal found that the claimants were workers. Moreover, the 'notion that Uber in London is a mosaic of 30,000 small businesses linked by a common "platform" is … faintly ridiculous'.[63]

The tribunal was also concerned that employers such as Uber might further enhance their already vastly superior bargaining power, given the nature of their lawyers' instructions. It appears that the efforts of lawyers to protect their clients from responsibilities that might otherwise arise through highly elaborate drafting and/or complex structures will, rather than protecting them, serve to prompt a searching inquiry. Resorting in corporate documentation to 'fictions, twisted language and even brand new terminology, merits … a degree of scepticism'.[64]

---

60 Fair Work Act 2009 (Cth) (Aus), s 357(1). See also Cameron Roles and Andrew Stewart, 'The Reach of Labour Regulation: Tackling Sham Contracting' (2012) 25 AJLL 258.

61 *Atkinson v Phoenix Commercial Cleaners Ltd* [2015] NZEmpC 19, [20]. In *Nisha v LSG* [2015] NZEmpC 171, it was not felt necessary to deal with *Autoclenz* (n 59), as the case concerned a sham contract in the strict sense.

62 *Aslam v Uber BV* [2017] IRLR 4.

63 ibid [87].

64 ibid [90].

MUTUALITY OF OBLIGATION

Judicial modification of contractual doctrine has not always been to the benefit of the worker in recent years. In the seminal case of *Ready Mixed Concrete (South East) v Minister of Pensions*, it was said to be a prerequisite of a contract of employment existing that the employee agrees to work in consideration of a wage or other remuneration.[65] This in itself is not controversial, but the evolution of this dimension of the law of the employment contract has been troublesome and has led to the emergence of the hugely controversial concept of mutuality of obligation, which requires 'the presence of mutual commitments to maintain the employment relationship in being over a period of time'.[66] This has posed acute problems for casual workers. On one interpretation, mutuality could prevent a short-term engagement from being a contract of employment (even of limited duration), given the absence of mutuality of obligation as to future performance.[67]

Should such an analysis be correct, protection of vulnerable workers would then require judicial will to translate the practical obligations flowing from the economic pressures on casual workers into legal ones. The parties' conduct would provide the basis for such a conclusion. However, the reported case law reveals a number of occasions where the courts elected for a no contract of employment analysis and made no attempt to correct market forces; there is:[68]

> a narrow line between the conclusion that the company were undertaking to offer work to the regular casuals undertaking to accept the work which was offered (i.e. a contract of employment) and the conclusion that there was no contract to employ and that the arrangement was simply the consequence of market forces (in effect, the dominant economic position of the company).

Matters have improved somewhat in the United Kingdom, in that the Court of Appeal, in *Cornwall County Council v Prater* accepted that mutuality of obligation as to future performance is irrelevant in the context of determining whether a specific engagement constitutes a contract of employment.[69] In the earlier agency worker case of

---

[65] *Ready Mixed Concrete (South East Ltd) v Minister of Pensions and National Insurance* [1968] 2 QB 497.

[66] Deakin and Morris (n 1) 164.

[67] *Airfix Footwear Ltd v Cope* [1978] ICR 1210, 1214.

[68] *O'Kelly v Trust House Forte* [1984] QB 90 (CA), [1983] ICR 728, 760.

[69] *Cornwall County Council v Prater* [2006] EWCA Civ 102, [2006] IRLR 362.

McMeechan v Secretary of State for Employment, the Court of Appeal held that undertaking an assignment resulted in a contract of employment for its duration. It was said that: 'When it comes to considering the terms of an individual, self-contained engagement, the fact that the parties are not obliged in future to offer – or to accept – their engagement with the same, or a different, client must be neither here nor there'.[70] The Court of Appeal has approved the stance taken in *McMeechan*. Nevertheless, matters remain problematic. Given that the Court of Appeal has since held, on more than one occasion, that the fact that a person supplying services is only doing so on an assignment-by-assignment basis may tend to indicate a degree of independence, or lack of subordination, in the relationship that is incompatible with employee status.[71] The validity of this approach is questionable, as all that should be relevant is the nature of the agreement entered into on any particular occasion. In any event, real difficulties remain should the worker wish to demonstrate that the relationship is ongoing.[72] It would be helpful to adopt Freedland's view that mutuality of obligation as to further performance, even on the assumption that it does form part of English law, derives from the law of consideration.[73]

Freedland goes on to suggest that a genuine commitment 'to maintaining an intermittent or casual work relationship' might be allowed to suffice.[74] This mirrors the position taken in the Australian case of *Swift Placements v WorkCover Authority of NSW*.[75]

The position is different in Australia,[76] where there is no concept of mutuality of obligation particular to the employment contract. As Freedland suggests should be the case in the United Kingdom, there is simply the standard requirement for consideration. In *Forstaff Pty Ltd v Chief Commissioner of State Revenue*, McDougall J stated that mutuality of

---

70 *McMeechan v Secretary of State for Employment* [1997] IRLR 353, 360.

71 *Windle v Secretary of State for Justice* [2016] EWCA Civ 459. See also Nicola Countouris, 'The Contract of Employment as an Expression of Continuing Obligations' in Mark Freedland et al. (eds), *The Contract of Employment* (Oxford University Press 2016). In New Zealand, the courts tend to avoid language such as 'subordination', preferring to use the language of 'control'.

72 ACL Davies, 'The Contract for Intermittent Employment' (2007) 36 ILJ 102.

73 Mark Freedland, *The Personal Employment Contract* (1st edn, Oxford University Press 2003) 100.

74 ibid 104.

75 *Swift Placements v WorkCover Authority of NSW* [2000] NSWIRComm 9.

76 See Sappideen, O'Grady and Riley (n 1) 180; quoting *JA & MB Bowden v Chief Commissioner* [2001] NSWCA 125.

obligation requires 'an obligation on the one side to perform work (or provide service) and on the other side to pay'.[77] Australia does not require a commitment to future performance before an employment contract can come into being. It is also significantly easier for an employee to demonstrate that employment is ongoing, despite there being periods of time when no work is undertaken.[78] The statutory framework, which is constructed so as to be inclusive of casual workers, may have helped to deter common law developments. In *Jinkinson v Oceana Gold*, the New Zealand Employment Court, in a general discussion of the law, referred to the approach in the United Kingdom, but the case was decided principally on the character of the employment in practice.[79] While an employee seeking to show that employment was ongoing, and not simply a discrete transaction, would have to be able to establish that there were mutual obligations that continued between periods of work, such cases are normally demonstrated by such practices as the employer creating ongoing rosters as was the case in *Jinkinson*. These practices can indicate that casual employment has morphed into permanent full-time or part-time employment.

Why have the courts in the United Kingdom acted as they have? The conclusion as to the fundamental elements of the employment contract is not compelled by general contractual principles – mutuality of obligation is a concept devised by, and restricted to, the law of the employment contract – and, indeed, contractual orthodoxy merely requires that consideration be present. At root, the cases on casual workers are about the extent to which the employer is obliged to take responsibility for workers with a limited or transient involvement with the business. Mutuality of obligation makes it easier to disavow casual workers, should it be convenient to do so. Deakin and Morris have argued that:[80]

---

77 *Forstaff Pty Ltd v Chief Commissioner of State Revenue* [2004] NSWSC 573, [90]; *Building Workers' Industrial Union of Australia v Odco Pty Ltd* (1991) 99 ALR 735.

78 In *Swift Placements* (n 75), [54], the employee was held to have an ongoing relationship where he 'was obliged under the contract to contact the appellant each day to ascertain whether work was available and once work had been allocated to him he had to attend the place nominated and undertake the work directed'.

79 *Jinkinson v Oceana Gold* [2009] NZEmpC 67.

80 Deakin and Morris (n 1) 167; and see also Christopher McCrudden, 'Two Views of Subordination: The Personal Scope of Employment Discrimination Law in *Jivraj v Hashwani*' (2012) 41 ILJ 30.

> The emergence of the mutuality test at a particular point in the evolution of modern employment law suggests that it should be seen as an attempt to refute the criterion of 'economic reality' and to reassert formal subordination as the basis of employment. Workers who do not make a long term formal commitment to the firm are viewed as having no claim to employment protection from it.

Where casual workers are concerned, employers have no interest in allowing a long-term commitment to be made. In relation to the content of the employment contract, the judges, through implication and interpretation, have acted to protect the vulnerability of the employee. However, they have been much more reluctant to challenge employer prerogative where the constitution of the relationship is concerned. Moreover, the ideology of freedom of contract that informs the common law is sympathetic to contracting out. For example, in *Stevedoring and Haulage Services v Fuller*, the employer had, in effect, been able to set aside the obligations he would otherwise have owed, by imposing express terms inconsistent with the requirements of mutuality.[81]

It should also be borne in mind that common law reasoning of this sort can serve to undermine the efficacy of statutory protection. In the United Kingdom, a number of statutory rights are extended to workers who are not employees, but who have entered into a contract whereby they undertake to do or perform personally any work or services for another party to the contract. The fact that this extension of protection adopts a contractual foundation means that elements of the common law doctrine – with the capacity to function in a manner at odds with legislative policy – may be found to be relevant. Thus, in *Byrne Brothers v Baird*, it was accepted that mutuality of obligation is a necessary element in the contract of a worker, as well as in a contract of employment.[82] Why should this be so? It was said that the requirement of mutuality is simply an element of the general law of contract. As we have seen, this is not, in fact, the case where mutuality of obligation is concerned. Its deployment in the present context was not inevitable, but the underlying contractual basis has meant that the common law doctrine has proved, yet again, to be beguiling.

---

81 *Stevedoring and Haulage Services v Fuller* [2001] IRLR 627.
82 *Byrne Brothers v Baird* [2002] ICR 667.

TESTING FOR AN EMPLOYMENT RELATIONSHIP

Judicial reticence to reform contractual doctrine is perhaps most clearly illustrated by the fact that the common law tests used to determine the existence of the employment relationship have remained fundamentally the same as they were when Fordist employment models dominated thinking about the organization of work: 'the emphasis on various matters has shifted in response to the changing way work, and society in general, is organised. However, the fundamental tests remain more or less constant'.[83] This is despite the fact that those tests have always made it relatively easy for the employer to constitute a relationship as one of self-employment – a state of affairs that is not lost on the judges: 'It is not difficult for employers to restructure a working relationship to emulate the legal characteristics of the independent contractor, that is to say, one who falls within the category of self-employed'.[84] The demarcation line between employment and self-employment will frequently be difficult to draw, and this allows the employer to mould the relationship to a form of their choosing. A significant number of relationships could be established, as the law is presently formulated, perfectly legitimately as either employment or self-employment. One consequence is that many workers who possess decidedly limited resources may be classified as independent contractors. The decision in *Vabu v Federal Commissioner of Taxation* is a good example.[85] In the United Kingdom, there 'is evidence to suggest that individuals facing labour market disadvantage are more likely to become self-employed as they struggle to find an employee job. As such, self-employment can provide a route into work for many disadvantaged unemployed groups, including women and mothers as well as migrants'.[86] The dramatic movement away from employment (and the consequential diminution in workers' rights) might have prompted the judiciary to question whether greater protection is required. However, the landscape remains largely the same and even in New Zealand, where there has been an element of statutory intervention, the adjudicator must still have 'regard to features of control and integration and to whether the contracted person has been effectively working on his or her own account

---

83 *ACE Insurance Ltd v Trifunovski* [2013] FCAFC 3, [38].
84 *Canada Post Corporation v Carroll* [2012] NBCA 18, [58].
85 *Vabu v Federal Commissioner of Taxation* (1996) 33 ATR 537.
86 Hatfield (n 4) 4.

(the fundamental test), which were important determinants of the relationship at common law'.[87]

It is arguable that the common law was less muted in the past. The integration test favoured by Lord Denning in 1952 in *Stevenson, Jordan & Harrison v MacDonald* sought to capture workers who were, in substance, employees, given their centrality to the functioning of the employer's business.[88] Should that approach be favoured, a finding of employment would be more likely. In *Ontario Ltd v Sagaz Industries Canada Inc*, the Canadian Supreme Court noted that, 'if the question is whether the activity or worker is integral to the employer's business, this question can usually be answered affirmatively'.[89] Crucially, in 1952, it was not erroneous to assert 'that because someone looks and acts like an employee, it follows that in law he must be an employee'.[90] The integration test has become influential in recent years where the law of tort is concerned. The judges see it as appropriate to cushion third parties from the changes in the labour market. The danger is that the use of agency or casual workers can circumvent the law of vicarious responsibility: 'An employer is vicariously liable for injury to others caused by an employee's carelessness, and is required by statute to insure against it; but an enterprise will have no such liability for harm done by somebody working for it who is not an employee'.[91] In *Hawley v Luminar Leisure*, the temporary employer was held to be vicariously liable in a context where third parties would have been unable to differentiate between borrowed workers and employees: 'there can be no doubt that any customer, passer-by or police officer seeing the doormen decked out in Luminar uniforms would have assumed they were Luminar staff. In effect this is what they were held out to be. The doormen were not recognisable physically as the employees of ASE'.[92]

The desire to protect third parties was also to the fore in *JGE v English Province of our Lady of Charity*, where the Court of Appeal was prepared to extend the categories of relationship for which a defendant is vicariously liable to include those 'akin to that between an employer and an

---

[87] The principles were laid out in *Bryson v Three Foot Six Ltd* [2003] NZEmpC 164, and were affirmed by the Supreme Court in *Bryson v Three Foot Six* [2005] NZSC 34, [2005] 3 NZLR 721, [32].

[88] *Stevenson, Jordan & Harrison v MacDonald* [1952] 1 TLR 101.

[89] *Ontario Ltd v Sagaz Industries Canada Inc* [2001] 2 SCR 983, [42].

[90] *Tilson v Alstom Transport* [2011] IRLR 169, 171.

[91] *Dacas* (n 30) 368.

[92] *Hawley v Luminar Leisure Ltd* [2006] EWCA Civ 18, 826.

employee'.[93] A court should seek to identify 'the broad characteristics of the employer/employee relationship' and ask whether the contract in issue 'bears a sufficiently close resemblance and affinity in character' to one of employment.[94] This approach was approved by the Supreme Court in *Various Claimants v Catholic Child Welfare Society*.[95]

Of late, the United Kingdom Supreme Court has again endorsed the foregoing approach in *Cox v Ministry of Justice*, where the prison service was held vicariously liable for the negligence of a prisoner.[96] In so doing, the Supreme Court spoke in terms strongly reminiscent of the integration test:[97]

> a relationship other than one of employment is in principle capable of giving rise to vicarious liability where harm is wrongfully done by an individual who carries on activities as an integral part of the business activities carried on by a defendant and for its benefit (rather than his activities being entirely attributable to the conduct of a recognisably independent business of his own or of a third party).

Cox can be seen as being predicated on the basis of enterprise liability, but it also has the potential to be highly inclusive. Individuals employed on a wide range of contracts could be said to be 'part of the business activity of the defendant', at least when carrying out the tortious activity in question. It is more than arguable that the reasoning is applicable to the self-employed, although, for the moment, the courts continue to display allegiance to the traditional orthodoxy that vicarious liability does not arise in respect of independent contractors. It is worth recalling, however, that in *Woodland v Swimming Teachers Association*, Baroness Lady Hale expressed concern that in 'today's world … large organisations may well outsource their responsibilities to much poorer and un- or under-insured contractors'.[98] *Cox* indicates that, akin to employment test notwithstanding, the employer is not responsible where 'a tortfeasor's activities are entirely attributable to the conduct of a recognisably independent business of his own'. This still leaves considerable scope for vicarious liability to arise in respect of individuals who would not be

---

93 *JGE v English Province of our Lady of Charity* [2012] EWCA Civ 938, [2013] QB 722, 767.

94 ibid 765.

95 *Various Claimants* (n 18).

96 *Cox v Ministry of Justice* [2016] UKSC 10.

97 ibid [24].

98 *Woodland v Swimming Teachers Association* [2013] UKHL 66, [2014] AC 537, 590.

regarded as employees in other contexts. In both Australia and New Zealand, 'employer' liability in health and safety legislation is now determined by whether the person is a person conducting a business or undertaking (PCBU) rather than on their status as an employer.[99]

It should be acknowledged that currently, whilst the overall picture tends to be one of conservatism, there are case law developments which could be built upon to provide a more effective approach, were the judiciary to be so inclined. *On Call Interpreters v Commissioner of Tax (No 3)* is worthy of note in this regard, as it operates on the premise that an independent contractor is a person who operates a business, and that a business will normally have assets.[100] Bromberg J observed that a business:[101]

> will usually involve the acquisition and use of both tangible and intangible assets in the pursuit of profit … A business typically has (or at least aspires to have) value (goodwill or saleable assets) beyond its physical assets … A common intangible asset of a business is its name, brand, reputation or goodwill.

This is a significant development. A stronger emphasis on the scale and extent of assets possessed by the worker would make it more difficult to establish that the relationship is one of self-employment.[102] The approach in *On Call Interpreters* can be seen as constituting a presumption against self-employment unless adequate resources exist. Any enthusiasm generated by *On Call Interpreters* must be tempered by doubts over whether it is reflective of the Australian case law more widely.[103] It is also the case that its approach is yet to be reflected in New Zealand and the United Kingdom.[104]

---

[99] See Work Health and Safety Act 2011 (Cth), s 5 and Health and Safety at Work Act 2015 (NZ), s 17.

[100] *On Call Interpreters and Translators Agency Pty Ltd v Commissioner of Taxation (No 3)* [2011] FCA 366.

[101] ibid [210].

[102] The existence of assets may count for less when dealing with professional workers providing a particular service: *Hall v Lorimer* [1994] IRLR 171, 175.

[103] Cameron Roles and Andrew Stewart, 'The Reach of Labour Regulation: Tackling Sham Contracting' (2012) 25 AJLL 258. See also *Tattsbet v Morrow* [2015] FCAFC 62, where it was held that the manager of a branch of a betting agency was self-employed.

[104] Hatfield (n 4) points out that in the United Kingdom, just 17 per cent of self-employed workers themselves employ staff of their own. This is said to be the lowest rate in Europe.

A STATUTORY SILENCE?

Even in an era where the basis of labour law has become increasingly regulated by statute, governments have been reluctant to intervene to define the category of persons who are subject to that law and instead have relied on the common law's concept of a contract of employment and of an employee. The common law has had to define the evolving boundaries of the contract of employment at a time when the contractual structures under which work is performed are rapidly evolving, usually to the detriment of those performing the work, as attempts are made to deny them the status of employees.

The inclination of governments to leave the problem of defining employees to the courts was apparent from an early stage. This inclination was particularly apparent in Australasia, where, given the adoption of the arbitration system in both Australia and New Zealand, it might have been expected that the parties to be covered by the relevant acts would have been defined. This was not, however, the case and both countries relied on the common law to define those workers who came within the coverage of the arbitration system. New Zealand's Industrial and Conciliation Act 1894 referred only to 'workmen'. The current definition of an 'employee' had its origins in the 1900 Act, which defined a 'worker' as 'any person of any age or either sex employed by any employer to do any skilled or unskilled manual or clerical work for hire or reward in any industry'.[105] In 1991, 'worker' became 'employee' and the core definition extended to add a specific reference to the work being 'under a contract for service'.[106] This addition was of little significance, as it had long been 'implicit' in case law.[107] Recently, the Supreme Court explicitly recognized the definition as reflecting the common law.[108]

The legislative position in Australia was even more straightforward. The 1904 Act referred to 'employee', without the term being further

---

[105] Subsequent refinements to that definition related to the expanding coverage of the arbitration system, rather than its core element of any person 'employed by any employer to do any work for hire or reward'. The definition was generalized in 1925 to cover 'any person of any age of either sex employed by any employer to do any work for hire or reward'. The reference to sex was removed in 1987.

[106] The current definition of an employee is 'any person of any age employed by any employer to do any work for hire or reward under a contract for service': Employment Relations Act (NZ), s 6(1)(a).

[107] DL Mathieson, *Industrial Law in New Zealand* (Sweet & Maxwell 1970) 1, citing cases dating back to 1917.

[108] *Bryson* (n 48) [31].

defined. The current Act, the Fair Work Act 2009, still refers only to 'employee with its ordinary meaning' as including 'a reference to a person who is usually such an employee'.[109] Bromberg J commented that Australian legislation has 'steadfastly avoided defining what is an employee'.[110] Similarly, the United Kingdom's legislative position is equally straightforward: the Employment Rights Act 1996 (UK), section 230 defines an employee as 'an individual who has entered into or works under … a contract of employment' and a 'contract of employment' is defined as 'a contract of service or apprenticeship'.

Apart from specific extensions for very specific purposes,[111] there has been little legislative enthusiasm for extending the definition of 'employee' to encompass groups that might fall outside the common law definition. The Industrial Relations Act 1996 (NSW), section 5(2), for example, lists a range of factors that do not prevent a person from being an employee, such as the fact that the person works on a labour-only basis or that the work is part time or casual. New Zealand has extended the definition to encompass 'homeworkers' and 'persons intending to work'.[112] The first extension, 'a person intending to work', defined in section 5 as 'a person who has been offered, and accepted, work as an employee', was because of a distinction drawn between contracts to employ and contracts of employment, with the contract of employment only coming into existence once work had begun.[113] The second, and only substantive, extension of 'employee' was to deem 'homeworkers' to be employees regardless of their formal contractual status.[114] A major review preceding the Labour Relations Act 1987 (NZ) had identified such

---

[109] Fair Work Act 2009 (Aus), s 15.

[110] In *On Call Interpreters* (n 100) [206].

[111] For example, the group of deemed employees in s 12 of the Superannuation Guarantee (Administration) Act 1992 (Cth), s 3 of the Workplace Injury Rehabilitation and Compensation Act 2013 (Vic), or the complex definition in s YA1 of the Income Tax Act 2007 (NZ).

[112] Employment Relations Act 2000 (NZ), s 6(1)(b).

[113] Early cases under the Industrial Relations Act 1973 (NZ) had held that termination of a contract after entering into it, but before work had begun, was not an unjustifiable dismissal: *Auckland Clerical etc Employees IUW v Wilson* [1980] ACJ 357 (EmpC). The new definition allows such employees to raise a personal grievance if they are dismissed before work commences: *Canterbury Hotel etc IUW v The Elms Motor Lodge Ltd* [1989] NZILR 958 (LC); *New Zealand Resident Doctors Assoc v Otago Area Health Board* [1991] 1 ERNZ 1206 (EmpC). See also *Gill v Cape Contracts Ltd* [1985] IRLR 499 (NIHC).

[114] Labour Relations Act 1987 (NZ), s 2.

workers as being particularly vulnerable to exploitation.[115] The government was not, however, prepared to further extend the meaning of 'employee' to encompass dependent workers generally,[116] a decision militating against more expansive interpretations of 'employee' in later cases.[117] The one clear exception to this conservative approach was the broad interpretation of 'homeworkers', that is, a person employed to do work 'in a dwellinghouse'. The Court of Appeal, in a case concerned with low-paid 'contractors' providing home support and carer relief to people living in their own homes, held that the term 'homeworker' included such non-occupant workers.[118] The Court described the workers in question as being very much the type of vulnerable worker, susceptible to manipulation, who needed the protection of the Act. It did, however, exclude 'those like artists, journalists or designers who choose to work from home, but in respect of whose place of work the other party to the engagement is indifferent'.[119]

New Zealand also seems to be unusual in excluding a specific group of workers that may well have been held to be employees – film production workers,[120] a decision made primarily to appease major film companies involved in the production of *The Hobbit* series.[121]

The United Kingdom legislation has broadened the coverage of at least some provisions of the Act by the use of the term 'worker', which covers not only employees, but also an individual who works under 'any other contract … whereby the individual undertakes to do or perform personally any work or services for another party to the contract whose status is not by virtue of the contract that of a client or customer of any profession or business undertaking carried on by the individual'.[122]

The statutory rights available to 'workers' include minimum labour standards, collective rights and rights under equality legislation. As we

---

115 *Industrial Relations: A Framework for Review* (Vol 2, Government Printer, Wellington, 1985) 88.

116 The government rejected the recommendations of the 1988 Committee of Inquiry into Dependent Contracting ('the Gerbic Committee'), which sought recognition for a new category of 'dependent and labour only contractor[s]'.

117 *TNT* (n 46) 694.

118 *Cashman v Central Regional Health Authority* [1996] 2 ERNZ 156.

119 ibid 167.

120 Employment Relations Act 2000 (NZ), s 6(7).

121 On this addition, see the articles in 'Symposium On The "Hobbit Law": Exploring Non-Standard Employment' (2011) 36 New Zealand Journal of Employment Relations.

122 Employment Rights Act 1996 (UK), s 230(3).

have seen, the meaning of 'worker' has not been without problems and common law thinking has been deployed to restrict its scope.[123]

Australia's Fair Work Act 2009 deals with the problem of sham arrangements and, in particular, focuses on steps taken by employers to move employees to contracts for services. A civil remedy is available where an employment contract is misrepresented as being one for services, where there is a threat of dismissal or actual dismissal in order to engage the employer as a contractor, or where misrepresentations are made in order to influence a person to enter into a contract for services for the performance of the same or substantially similar work.[124]

Legislatures have shown even greater reluctance to instruct the courts on how to determine whether a worker is an employee. The one exception is in New Zealand, where it is provided that:[125]

> (2) In deciding for the purposes of subsection (1)(a) whether a person is employed by another person under a contract of service, the court or the Authority (as the case may be) must determine the real nature of the relationship between them.
>
> (3) For the purposes of subsection (2), the court or the Authority –
>
> (a) must consider all relevant matters, including any matters that indicate the intention of the persons; and
> (b) is not to treat as a determining matter any statement by the persons that describes the nature of their relationship.

These provisions were enacted in the Employment Relations Act 2000 (NZ) as a reaction to the Court of Appeal's decision in *TNT*, which had been interpreted as an instruction that a court must give priority to the expressed form of the relationship, rather than its substance.[126] The debate around the final form of section 6(2)–(3) did, however, illustrate the policy and legal problems of attempting a statutory definition of employee.[127]

---

123 Deakin and Morris (n 1) 174–81.

124 Fair Work Act 2009 (Aus), Pt 3-1, Div 6.

125 Employment Relations Act 2000 (NZ), s 6(2)–(3).

126 *TNT* (n 46). While this interpretation may have been inaccurate (see *Curlew v Harvey Norman Stores (NZ) Pty Ltd* [2002] 1 ERNZ 114, [3] (EmpC)), it was understandable in the context of the strongly traditional contractual approach of the Court of Appeal at that time.

127 *Mazengarb's Employment Law* (online, LexisNexis) para ERA6.4.1. The majority of the Court of Appeal later described the s 6 amendment as being 'intended to nudge the law away from the position of almost absolute deference to party autonomy adopted in at least some of the judgments in the *TNT* case',

The reluctance of legislatures to intervene other than for limited and pragmatic reasons is understandable to some extent. Generally, the common law has shown that it is able to adapt the tests of employment to changing patterns of employment and work arrangements. However, the extent to which protection has been offered to those who are, in substance, employees is highly questionable. Legislatures in all three jurisdictions have tended to intervene only in limited circumstances. For example, in the United Kingdom, some employment rights are extended to the wider class of workers and, in all jurisdictions, legislation that has a central focus on employees may be extended to a wider group by defining specific groups to which the legislation also applies, a technique typically seen in regimes for the collection of tax or compulsory superannuation contributions.

CONCLUSION

The response of the common law has been decidedly timid in the face of wholescale changes in the labour market and employers' use of vastly superior bargaining power to impose working arrangements other than employment. Workers enter into such arrangements out of necessity rather than choice. The common law could choose to be more radical, though in fairness, public policy tends to favour the post-employment world. It should be remembered that the common law is immensely malleable and it is often the case that contractual doctrine can be applied or at least extended to allow the claimant to succeed. Much will turn on the view taken by the judges of the relevant policy considerations. Judges would do well to heed the advice expressed in *Fair Work Ombudsman v Quest South Perth Holdings Pty Ltd*: 'Whilst well known contractual principles are to be applied, an overly technical approach to contractual analysis is to be avoided'.[128] Certainly, greater scrutiny of contractual arrangements would not go amiss. The question posed by Robertson JA in the Canadian case of *Canada Post Corporation v Carrol* is a telling one and might usefully be posed more widely:

> Objectively and realistically speaking, does the claimant have the potential to gain more as an entrepreneur (independent contractor) than as an employee?

---

rather than representing a 'radical change in this area of the law': *Three Foot Six Ltd v Bryson* [2004] CA246/03, [113].

[128] *Fair Work Ombudsman v Quest South Perth Holdings Pty Ltd* [2015] FCAFC 37, [150].

> Alternatively stated, the underlying question is whether the working relationship provides the claimant with the opportunity to achieve economic security and success.[129]

After all, 'no reasonable person would go into business for herself or himself unless the potential benefits outweigh the loss of benefits which are presently available to employees under provincial and federal legislation'.[130] A major step forward would be to revitalize the tests used to identify the contract of employment, so that they guard against the inappropriate use of self-employment. The judges, however, regard the changes in the labour market as a fait accompli. They will modify contractual doctrine to take account of contemporary circumstances and will guard against abuse of power, but more fundamental measures are for the legislature. It appears to be accepted that the legislature has narrowed the scope of labour law.

The tradition of statutory silence notwithstanding, it may make more sense to look beyond the common law for solutions; greater use of legislation to address specific situations may be the way forward. For instance, in both New Zealand and the United Kingdom the use of fixed term contracts is now regulated by statute. Australia is clearly furthest down this road and there is a raft of measures that are directed towards protection of workers in a range of situations; these include unfair contracts legislation and instances of 'small business' regulation which traditionally would not have been viewed as labour law at all.[131] The Independent Contractors Act 2006 (Cth), for example, addresses exploitative practices where the claimants are party to a contract for services. More specific regulatory regimes exist to address risks associated with capricious termination of working arrangements, and access to affordable and fair dispute-resolution mechanisms in particular industries.[132] The subject matter is very much the bread and butter of labour law; the need is no less for workers who are not employees.

---

[129] *Canada Post Corporation* (n 84) [60].

[130] ibid.

[131] See Joellen Riley, 'Regulating the Engagement of Non-employed Labour: A View from the Antipodes' in Nicole Busby, Douglas Brodie and Rebecca Zahn (eds), *The Future Regulation of Work: New Concepts, New Paradigms* (Palgrave 2016).

[132] See, for example, road transport and the Owner Driver and Forestry Contractors Act 2005 (Vic).

5. Statutory and incorporated terms

Parties to employment relationships have always been constrained, to some extent, in their freedom to contract over terms and conditions of employment. Labour engagement is a field long regulated by statutory regimes, going back to the Statutes of Labourers of 1349 and 1350, which froze the wages of agrarian workers to protect feudal landowners from the inflationary effects of the Black Death. Until the late nineteenth century, highly prescriptive 'master and servant' and 'factories and shops' legislation played a significant role in determining employment obligations. The notion of employment as a freely negotiated contractual relationship is a relatively recent phenomenon.[1] A key concern for contemporary employment law continues to be the extent to which statutory schemes, and the instruments made under them, influence the content of employment contracts. This concern is coupled with the need to consider the role played by collective instruments, whether or not determined under a statutory scheme, and the increasing role played by employer issued policies, which are often broad and intrusive. This chapter interrogates the relationship between contract and these broader influences.

Not every legal employment obligation will become part of the employment contract. According to the Australian High Court, a meaningful distinction can be drawn between the employment relationship, which might be regulated by any number of kinds of law (many of them mandatory), and the employment contract, which is only one form of regulation determined, principally, by the choices of the parties themselves. This distinction was articulated in *Automatic Fire Sprinklers v Watson*,[2] and confirmed more recently in *Byrne and Frew v Australian Airlines Ltd*[3] and *Visscher v Giudice*.[4] It has been criticized in the United

[1] Simon Deakin, 'The Evolution of the Contract of Employment 1900–1950: The Influence of the Welfare State' in Noel Whiteside and Robert Salais (eds), *Governance, Industry and Labour Markets in Britain and France: The Modernising State in the Mid Twentieth Century* (Routledge 1998) 212.

[2] *Automatic Fire Sprinklers v Watson* (1946) 72 CLR 435.

[3] *Byrne and Frew v Australian Airlines Ltd* (1995) 185 CLR 410.

[4] *Visscher v Giudice* (2009) 239 CLR 361.

Kingdom. In *Societe Generale, London Branch v Geys*[5] Lord Wilson described the distinction between the employment relationship and the contract as 'unhelpful, indeed confusing'. Nevertheless, it provides a useful tool for our present purposes in explaining when, and how, certain terms mandated by, or arising as a consequence of, a statutory scheme (or indeed any other collectively determined instrument) will become binding upon the parties to the individual employment contract so as to attract contract-based remedies. Mandatory statutory regimes will create binding obligations upon employers and employees, but the remedies available for breach of those obligations will be determined by the relevant statute giving those obligations force. The availability of contract-based damages will depend upon whether the obligation has become part of the employment contract.

In this chapter, we consider the extent to which provisions arising from a range of sources have influenced employment contract terms. We consider terms and conditions of employment that have been established through processes of collective bargaining, and we also consider the codes of conduct and 'human resources' policies that commonly govern employment practices in large enterprises. As the court in *Edwards v Chesterfield Royal Hospital NHS Foundation Trust and Botham (FC) v Ministry of Defence*[6] opined, these kinds of governance tools are often adopted in organizations in order to manage compliance with statutory obligations, for instance, obligations to provide procedural fairness in disciplinary proceedings. A contemporary challenge for employment law is managing an expectation of 'coherence' between the demands of statutory regulation and the principles of common law.

MINIMUM EMPLOYMENT STANDARDS

The most obvious statutory constraint on the freedom of the parties to agree to such terms as they can negotiate is the statutory minimum standards that apply in all three jurisdictions. Such standards are set by legislation and breaches are enforced through remedies provided in the relevant statutes. The nature of these standards varies from jurisdiction to jurisdiction, but the matters covered are largely similar: they include at

---

5 *Societe Generale, London Branch v Geys* [2012] UKSC 63, [2013] 1 AC 52, [82]. In New Zealand an 'employment relationship' is defined in s 5 of the Employment Relations Act 2000 as meaning 'a contract of service'.

6 *Edwards v Chesterfield Royal Hospital NHS Foundation Trust and Botham (FC) v Ministry of Defence* [2011] UKSC 58.

least a minimum wage, minimum holiday provisions and protections as to the method of payment, but may also include minimum notice provisions, severance pay and controls on working time. Terms beyond these minimum provisions are more likely to be found in a collective instrument, for example, limits on the number or proportion of casual or fixed-term employees. This is not universally true, and in New Zealand, for example, there are statutory controls on the use of fixed-term contracts.[7] However, as these terms and remedies are statutory, it is not necessary to consider them further in this context.

TERMS INCORPORATED INTO THE CONTRACT

In all three jurisdictions, the employment relationship is likely to include at least some terms derived from outside the individual contract of employment. The two most common sources of such terms are the relevant terms of a collective instrument or terms incorporated by reference to documents external to the contract, typically the employer's policies and manuals on a variety of matters.

Terms from Collective Instruments

A major source of many employees' terms and conditions will be some form of collectively agreed instrument: in the United Kingdom a collective agreement, in Australia an award, and in New Zealand a statutory collective agreement. One might assume that the purpose of referring to these instruments is to configure their content as contractual obligations. However, in the employment context, there are often barriers to incorporation. The individualism of the common law looms large; the courts have tended to be unenthusiastic when it comes to taking on board the outcomes of a collective process and display a measure of reluctance in importing the outcomes of collective negotiations into the employment contract. The ambivalence of the common law towards giving legal recognition to collectively negotiated terms is seen in the courts' refusal to concede that collective agreements should be legally binding on their own terms.

---

[7] Employment Relations Act 2000 (NZ), s 66.

In the United Kingdom, at common law,[8] collective agreements are normally not legally enforceable by the collective parties.[9] They may be enforceable indirectly through the medium of the employment contract, although the courts have often found this dichotomy troublesome.[10] However, even where a collective agreement is expressly incorporated, any particular term will be incorporated only where it is apt to do so. The argument in the alternative would be that, because a source of terms has been expressly referred to in the contract, it must have been intended that those terms should have binding effect. There are, however, competing considerations, which are illustrated by *National Coal Board v National Union of Mineworkers*.[11] In 1946, an agreement had been entered into, which established a conciliation scheme under which the National Union of Mineworkers was given exclusive recognition. Two mineworkers contended that, under their contracts of employment, they were entitled to insist that the National Coal Board negotiate with the Union. This contention was rejected, and it was held that the reference in the contracts to collective agreements was to those agreements that contain substantive provisions regarding wages or conditions of service. The collective negotiating machinery was 'designed to be invoked and operated either by the NCB or by the NUM with the co-operation of the other. It simply does not lend itself to enforceability at the suit of an individual mineworker'.[12] The stance taken in the *National Coal Board* case makes good sense. Collective agreements are normally unenforceable as between the collective parties, given the statutory presumption to this effect, and to allow an individual to enforce a scheme such as the one in the *National Coal Board* case would be to circumvent legislative policy. Thus, where a clause is of a type that is collective in nature, it normally should not be given legal effect through the medium of the individual employment contract. While this problem is particularly acute for the United Kingdom, the issue is of less significance in Australia and New Zealand, due to specific statutory provisions.

---

8 This position has also been accepted in New Zealand, in relation to collective agreements made outside the statutory framework. See *Re Andrew M Paterson Ltd* [1981] 2 NZLR 289 (HC).

9 There is a statutory presumption to this effect: Trade Union and Labour Relations (Consolidation) Act 1992 (TULRCA 1992), s 179.

10 Andrew Wilson, 'Contract and Prerogative: A Reconsideration of the Legal Enforcement of Collective Agreements' (1984) 13 ILJ 1, 8.

11 *National Coal Board v National Union of Mineworkers* [1986] IRLR 439.

12 ibid 454.

In Australia, while an employment contract may make reference to an applicable 'modern award',[13] industrial awards are independently legally enforceable, as are collective agreements, so long as they have been approved.[14] The position is similar in New Zealand, where collective agreements are regarded as a creature of statute.[15] This approach also applied to the pre-1990 award system and the subsequent statutory provisions governing collective employment contracts under the Employment Contracts Act 1991 (NZ). The Employment Relations Act 2000 (NZ) defines an 'employment agreement' as meaning a contract of service and including 'an employee's terms and conditions of employment in … a collective agreement; or a collective agreement together with any additional terms and conditions of employment'.[16] The statute itself thus automatically incorporates the collective agreement's terms into the contract of employment. If a collective agreement expires, a question may arise as to whether terms that are collective in nature, as opposed to individual, form part of the ongoing individual contract, as this contract remains based on the expired collective agreement.[17] Additionally, if a collectively agreed document does not comply with the Act's formal requirements, including the need for formal ratification, it will be regarded as governed by the common law and not contractual in nature.[18]

The statutory context in New Zealand and Australia may provide an adequate explanation for the limited development of common law reasoning in employment. In the late nineteenth to early twentieth century, both countries enacted a system for conciliation and arbitration of industrial disputes by the making of industry-wide awards,[19] and created independent arbitral tribunals to enforce them. Until their abolition in New Zealand in 1991 and the Australian reforms of 1996, when

---

[13] See Fair Work Act 2009 (Cth) Pt 2-3.

[14] ibid Pt 2-4, Div 4; RJ Mitchell and RB Naughton, 'Collective Agreements and the Contract of Employment' (1989) 2 AJLL 252.

[15] *New Zealand Air Line Pilots' Assoc Inc v Air New Zealand Ltd* [2014] NZEmpC 168.

[16] Employment Relations Act 2000 (NZ), s 2.

[17] ibid s 61(2).

[18] *Re Andrew M Paterson* (n 8).

[19] Conciliation and Arbitration Act 1904 (Cth). For a thorough study of the early legislation, including the separate conciliation and arbitration systems in the Australian states, see Orwell de R Foenander, *Industrial Conciliation and Arbitration in Australia* (Law Book Co 1959).

legislation restricted awards to a bare safety net of basic terms,[20] these statutory instruments provided extensive prescription of minimum wages and working conditions. Few employment disputes involving award-covered employees came before the ordinary courts in either jurisdiction, as the relevant statutes provided independent, and more accessible, remedies.

In Australia, on those occasions when cases came to a court exercising common law jurisdiction, a threshold question would be whether the wages or other benefit determined by an award constituted terms of the worker's employment contract. It was held that contract damages were not available for breach of an award term unless parties had expressly incorporated the award into the employment contract,[21] although an entitlement to payment arising as a consequence of an award clause could provide grounds for a claim in debt.[22] Arguments that award clauses should be treated as terms implied by law into employment contracts ultimately failed. The courts saw no necessity to imply, because the award clauses already took effect according to the provisions of the statute, and had their own statutory remedies and enforcement mechanisms.[23] Contract remedies were reserved for those obligations that the parties had voluntarily assumed, and were held not to be available for breach of a mandatory award.

This history perhaps explains the decision in *Commonwealth Bank of Australia v Barker*, which reaffirmed the Australian High Court's resistance to development of the common law in a field populated by statutory regulation, even when the facts of the case itself did not require consideration of any statutory instrument.[24]

ESTABLISHING INCORPORATION AT COMMON LAW

With the dramatic decline in the significance of collective bargaining in recent times, cases concerning incorporation are now much less likely to

---

[20] The Workplace Relations and Other Legislation Amendment Act 1996 (Cth) reduced awards to a minimum safety net of 20 allowable award matters: see the former Workplace Relations Act 1996 (Cth), s 89A.

[21] *Amalgamated Collieries of WA v True* (1938) 59 CLR 417 had held that award clauses were incorporated in employment contracts regardless of the intentions of the parties, but this was effectively overturned in *Byrne and Frew v Australian Airlines Ltd* (1995) 185 CLR 410, 421.

[22] *Mallinson v Scottish Australian Investment Co Ltd* (1920) 28 CLR 66.

[23] *Byrne* (n 21) 421.

[24] *Commonwealth Bank of Australia v Barker* [2014] HCA 32.

involve collective agreements. Instead, attention is increasingly turning to publications such as staff handbooks and policy documents that are issued unilaterally by the employer. Perhaps not surprisingly, there are indications of greater judicial willingness to incorporate but, at the same time, there is a clear and strong countervailing tendency to view such publications as expressions of managerial prerogative that do not give rise to obligations in favour of the employee (as was the case in *Barker*).

The matter of incorporation of obligations located in an external repository is a two-stage process. First, there must be an intention to incorporate the term. Second, the term must be apt for incorporation. In Australia and the United Kingdom, it is recognized that not all of the provisions of a collective agreement or similar instrument are capable of operating, or can be properly construed as operating, as a term in an individual employment contract.[25]

An agreement or award that is relevant to the relationship between the worker and employer will not be incorporated unless it reflects the intention of the parties. The approach in contract law as a whole is applicable: 'What matters is what each party by words and conduct would have led a reasonable person in the position of the other party to believe'.[26] The position should be unproblematic where there is an express clause, but this is not always the case. In *Australian Workers' Union v BHP Iron-Ore Pty Ltd*, the question arose whether the terms of an industrial award were incorporated.[27] The employee had received a written offer of employment, which was accompanied by a document headed 'Joining Instructions to New Employees at Mt Newman'. The offer letter said that: 'In general, the terms and conditions of employment are as prescribed' in the award and other agreements, including an enterprise bargaining agreement. The joining instructions stated that, where there were inconsistencies, the conditions set out in the enterprise bargaining agreement would prevail. It was held that the words 'are as prescribed' did not indicate an intention to incorporate the terms of the award into an employment contract. This demonstrates how technical the interpretation of words becomes in the Australian system, which is so jealous of the independent operation of statutory instruments. Stating that the terms and conditions are 'as prescribed' distinguishes the mandatory terms of the statutory instruments from voluntary agreed terms in the

---

25 *Gramotnev v Queensland University of Technology* [2015] QCA 127.

26 ibid [47]; quoting *Toll (FGCT) Pty Ltd v Alphapharm Pty Ltd* [2004] HCA 52.

27 *Australian Workers' Union v BHP Iron-Ore Pty Ltd* [2000] FCA 39. The decision was overruled for different reasons on appeal ([2000] FCA 430).

contract. This is the case even though the phrase in question would seem to be sufficiently clear and precise to establish a close nexus between the award and the contract. A different conclusion was reached in *Moama Bowling Club Ltd v Armstrong (No 1)*, where it was provided that the agreement 'shall be deemed to incorporate the whole of the provisions of the award'.[28] The choice of wording distinguishes the two cases: one expression was held to describe the terms that bound the parties (by external prescription); the other expressed the parties' voluntary adoption of those obligations, by incorporation into their individual employment contract.

Establishing that an implied (as opposed to express) intention to incorporate is present is a more arduous proposition, and the pivotal decision in the United Kingdom in *Alexander v Standard Telephones (No 2)* is unsympathetic to incorporation.[29] One might have thought that a practice of contracting against a background of a collective agreement or collective bargaining machinery would be regarded as evidence of an intention to incorporate. Such an approach would sit readily with the contemporary contextual approach to construction contained in *Investors Compensation Scheme v West Bromwich*.[30] However, *Alexander* takes a diametrically opposed view, holding that 'there is no necessity to infer an intention to incorporate since collective agreements have a function and value of their own which exists wholly independently of any individual contract of employment'.[31] On one view, such a stance may be regretted on policy grounds, as incorporation of a collective agreement may fulfil broader policy objectives: 'the principal social function of the agreement as a code is the maintenance of wages and other standards in the interests of the workers'.[32] Collective bargaining seeks to 'convert formal into factual freedom of contract as between employer and workman, by raising the latter to a level of equality of bargaining power'.[33] The latter aim is thwarted where incorporation is not facilitated, especially if the enterprise bargain is not effectively enforceable by other means. The Australian context is clearly different, and *Byrne and Frew v Australian Airlines Ltd* explains why implication is unlikely:[34]

---

[28] *Moama Bowling Club Ltd v Armstrong (No 1)* (1995) 64IR 238.

[29] *Alexander v Standard Telephones (No 2)* [1991] IRLR 286.

[30] *Investors Compensation Scheme v West Bromwich* [1998] 1 All ER 98.

[31] *Alexander (No 2)* (n 29) 292.

[32] Otto Kahn-Freund, *Labour and the Law* (2nd edn, Stevens 1977) 132.

[33] Otto Kahn-Freund, 'Collective Agreements under Wartime Legislation' (1943) 6 MLR 112, 117.

[34] *Byrne and Frew v Australian Airlines Ltd* (1995) 185 CLR 410, 421.

> In a system of industrial regulation where some, but not all, of the incidents of an employment relationship are determined by award, it is plainly unnecessary that the contract of employment should provide for those matters already covered by the award. The contract may provide additional benefits, but cannot derogate from the terms and conditions imposed by the award and, as we have said, the award operates with statutory force to secure those terms and conditions. Neither from the point of view of the employer nor the employee is there any need to convert those statutory rights and obligations to contractual rights and obligations. There is, therefore, an insuperable obstacle in the way of the appellants' second argument that the terms of an award such as cl 11(a) are implied terms of the contract of employment.

Statutory context may proffer a good and sufficient explanation, but *Byrne* may contain a less noble motive: the 'contractual term propounded by the appellants would operate in a partisan fashion. It would favour the interests of the employee at the expense of those of the employer'.[35] Seen through United Kingdom eyes, it may be objected that the very purpose of collective intervention is to ameliorate the adverse consequences of a relationship underpinned by an inherent inequality of bargaining power. However, it should be borne in mind that awards and enterprise agreements come with their own remedies, and those remedies can include orders to comply. To that extent, statutory remedies may be more appropriate than common law damages.

In New Zealand, the distinction between contractual and statutory remedies has become less differentiated. The terms of a collective agreement form part of the individual employment agreement and, while the normal contractual remedies for breach of contract remain available, the statutory remedies – wage recovery actions, compliance orders and civil pecuniary penalties – are available for both contractual and statutory breaches.

A further indication of judicial antipathy is evident from a number of judgments that indicate that the fact that a significant part of the collective bargain is irrelevant to the individual employment relationship points against the agreement as a whole being incorporated. In *Alexander*, it was said that:[36]

> In this context, where none of the other clauses of the collective agreement are apt to be incorporated into the individual contract of employment, it would require some cogent indication in clause 6 that it was to have a

35 ibid [48].

36 *Alexander (No 2)* (n 29) 293.

> different character and to be incorporated into the individual contracts of employment.

The same line of reasoning was evident in the Australian case of *Dye v Commonwealth Securities*: 'Nor is it satisfactory to attempt to select some phrases and reject others as potential candidates for contractual terms, while putting aside the context provided by the whole document'.[37] *Alexander* was influential in the more recent United Kingdom decision in *Keeley v Fosroc International*, where the trial judge refused to incorporate because the terms of the redundancy policy were, in his Honour's view, 'marooned' among other provisions that were non-contractual: 'Few, if any, of the other parts of the section on redundancy would be apt for incorporation into individual contracts of employment'.[38] This is unconvincing, as it is highly questionable how much can be read into the overall content of an agreement. A collective agreement is likely to deal with both collective and individual obligations; similarly, a staff handbook will often deal with a wide range of matters. Where incorporation is concerned, the question must be: what is the function of the term in dispute? Is there an intention to create contractual obligations? In *Keeley*, the Court of Appeal rejected, rightly, the approach of the trial judge:[39]

> If put in clear terms of entitlement, it [a provision] may have a life of its own, not to be snubbed out by context immediate or distant in the document of which it forms part. Where the wording of the provision, read on its own, is clearly of a contractual nature and not contradicted by any other provision in the documentary material constituting the contract, context is not all.

These issues, and particularly the judicial hostility argument, seem to be of less relevance in New Zealand. As a collective agreement applies only to union members and is incorporated by statute into the member's individual employment contract, the issue of whether the parties agreed to incorporation does not arise. Additionally, because appeals beyond the Employment Court are not permitted in relation to the interpretation of either collective agreements or individual contracts of employment, the possibility of judicial hostility in the common law courts is minimized.[40] Where other documents are concerned, express incorporation by reference usually presents no difficulties, particularly when those documents

---

37 *Dye v Commonwealth Securities* [2012] FCA 242, [618].
38 *Keeley v Fosroc International* [2006] IRLR 961, 967.
39 ibid 967.
40 Employment Relations Act 2000 (NZ), s 214(1).

have been held out by the employer as part of an employment offer. The Court of Appeal upheld a decision of the Employment Court enforcing a 'key objective' of the applicant's remuneration policy, as set out in its policy and procedures manual, for the applicant to 'establish and maintain fair and competitive market remuneration'. The manual had been stipulated by the applicant to be part of the terms and conditions of employment between the parties.[41] A similar conclusion was reached where potential employees were told of a 'job and finish' policy allowing them to leave work when a particular operation was complete.[42]

THE EMPLOYER'S PUBLICATIONS

As noted above, the decline in collective bargaining and the growth in process-driven human resource practice, often to minimize employer risk in relation to statutory obligations, have seen a rapid growth in the adoption of employer policy manuals, codes of practice and the like. While such documents are generally structured to ensure employee compliance, it is also common for them to set standards for employer conduct, particularly in relation to process and enforcement. The question then becomes the extent to which such undertakings are legally enforceable by employers.

At present, at least in the United Kingdom, there appears to be a greater judicial willingness to incorporate documents issued unilaterally by the employer; *Briscoe v Lubrizol* dealt with the question of incorporation of a staff handbook.[43] The claimant's written statement of terms of employment made reference to an income-protection scheme, whose detailed terms were to be found in the handbook. The court noted that such a practice was a matter of common occurrence: 'It is of course frequently the case that details of an employee's contract and the benefit to which he is entitled by virtue of his employment are largely to be found in a handbook of the kind supplied to the claimant in this case'.[44] Against that backdrop of contemporary employment practice, the court expressed a desire to facilitate incorporation: 'For this purpose, and depending upon the circumstances, incorporation by express reference in

---

41 *Unisys New Zealand Ltd v Ruddlesden* [2004] 2 ERNZ 163, (2004) 2 NZELR 23 (CA).

42 *New Zealand Amalgamated Engineering etc Union Inc v The Christchurch Press* [2005] ERNZ 288 (EmpC).

43 *Briscoe v Lubrizol* [2002] IRLR 607.

44 ibid 610.

the statutory particulars of employment will not usually be required by the court'.[45] This is in marked contrast to the position taken in respect of incorporation of collectively agreed norms. The Australian decision in *Riverwood International Australia v McCormick* is in the same vein.[46] The court had to determine whether the claimant was entitled to a redundancy payment referred to in a policies and procedures manual. The contract provided that: 'You agree to abide by all Company Policies and Practices currently in place, any alterations made to them, and any new ones introduced'. As already discussed, determining whether or not the manual was incorporated required the court to ascertain the intention of the parties.[47] Importantly, the nature of the subject matter of the material sought to be incorporated was relevant to the determination of that question. Riverwood contended that, by agreeing to abide by the manual, the claimant agreed to comply with the obligations set out therein, but there was no corresponding obligation on the employer. It was held that the expression 'abide by' meant that the clause was intended to oblige the employee to comply with his obligations, and also to signify that the employer would comply with the obligations imposed by the manual.[48] An interpretation in favour of reciprocity of obligations was favoured. A decision to the contrary would have rendered entitlement to a redundancy payment a matter for the employer's discretion – an unappealing state of affairs.

Decisions such as *Riverwood* notwithstanding, it should be said that the courts can also be reticent when the question of incorporation of staff handbooks and the like is at issue. Publishing material of this nature is often seen as akin to issuing instructions to employees and a matter of managerial prerogative.[49] This stance overlooks the fact that the content of such publications will often include general statements expressing the employer's commitment to the wellbeing of the workforce, as well as more specific undertakings. By so doing, the employer seeks to achieve

---

45 ibid.

46 *Riverwood International Australia v McCormick* [2000] FCA 889.

47 *Foggo v O'Sullivan Partners (Advisory) Pty Ltd* [2011] NSWSC 501.

48 *Riverwood* (n 46) 107.

49 *Dye v Commonwealth Securities* (n 37). In *Westpac Banking v Wittenberg* [2016] FCAFC 33, [77], Buchanan J said that: 'At one level, a contractual requirement to comply with an employer's published policies (often expressed as compliance with the policies as they exist from time to time) is simply an agreed record of a basic contractual obligation imposed by implication on an employee – i.e. when performing work under the contract to always comply with the lawful directions of the employer'. An argument of this sort was rejected in *Romero v Farstad Shipping* [2014] FCAFC 177.

an enhanced performance from the employees. It does not seem unreasonable that the employer be bound as a result. The employer may use language that is not as specific as one would traditionally have expected in a contract, but will still seek to convey a sense of entitlement to key benefits and features of the working environment. More accessible language, and hence more effective communication, should not stand in the way of normative effect.

While manuals may not create contractual obligations, they may, in some jurisdictions, be at least partially enforceable though other means. In New Zealand, in particular, the combination of the statutory good faith obligation and the need for an employer to justify a 'disadvantageous action' are likely to influence a decision if employer commitments are disregarded.

TERMS APPROPRIATE FOR INCORPORATION

Irrespective of its source, a term will only be incorporated if it is capable of functioning as part of the individual contract. This is true, irrespective of whether the intention to incorporate was express or implied.[50] A term apt for incorporation is one within 'the ambit of the employer/employee relationship'.[51] Terms relating to the remuneration package are prime candidates for incorporation, and a broader view of what that may entail tends to be taken nowadays.[52] In *Keeley*, the Court of Appeal had no difficulty in regarding a term concerning an enhanced redundancy payment as apt for incorporation.[53] This was not surprising, given both the subject matter and the fact that the term was expressed in terms of an entitlement. It was also contained in the part of a staff handbook headed 'Employee benefits and rights'. The Court of Appeal in *Keeley* was at pains to stress that redundancy pay 'is now a widely accepted feature of an employee's remuneration package' and is part of what the employee

---

[50] The courts have taken the view that if a term was apt for incorporation then that would go towards inferring an intention to incorporate: *Lee v GEC* [1993] IRLR 383, 391.

[51] *Tadd v Daily Telegraph* [1983] IRLR 320, 328. In *Alexander v Standard Telephones* [1990] IRLR 55, 59, the distinction was drawn between 'terms in a collective agreement which are designed and intended to govern the relationship between the employer and the union, and those designed and intended to benefit individual employees'.

[52] The same cannot necessarily be said of clauses dealing with job security. See our discussion of *Kaur v MG Rover Group* [2005] IRLR 40 below.

[53] *Keeley* (n 38); and see *Lee* (n 50).

'undertook to work for'. Accordingly, such a term 'is particularly apt for incorporation by reference'.[54] This is made abundantly plain by the fact that provisions of this sort may still be apt for incorporation 'even if couched in terms of information or explanation, or expressed in discretionary terms'.[55] Such an approach is consistent with the contemporary approach to construction of employment contracts. Ambiguities are increasingly likely to be resolved in the employee's favour where the construction of the work-wage bargain is concerned, because of the importance of that element of the contract to the employee.

However, the position in general remains uncertain. *George v Ministry of Justice*, where a term in a collective agreement concerning prison officers was in issue, demonstrates that there may be an unwillingness to incorporate even obligations that go to the core of the employment relationship.[56] In *George*, a package of measures, agreed in 1987, resulted in a collective agreement on working practices, including the abolition of overtime and the introduction of time off in lieu (TOIL). This was designed to compensate officers who were required to work extra hours at the behest of the prison governor. The terms of the agreement were contained in what was called Bulletin 8. The dispute focused on clause 23 of the annex to Bulletin 8, which provided that 'accumulated TOIL will be granted as soon as operationally possible and within a maximum period of five weeks'.

The Court of Appeal held that incorporation of the agreement had not taken place and, in any event, the term in dispute was seen as inapt for incorporation, though the phrase 'within a maximum period of five weeks' could not be clearer or more definitive. Counsel for the employer argued that the relevant section of the Bulletin was manifestly of an aspirational nature, and so was not intended to be legally enforceable. Counsel submitted further that if TOIL was required to be provided within five weeks, even if it not operationally possible, it would have the potential for catastrophic consequences for the Prison Service. This argument on impossibility misses the point; if a contracting party enters into an undertaking that it later finds it cannot meet, then it will be liable in damages for the consequent breach. The law of frustration aside, contract law does not excuse on account of impracticability.

The Court of Appeal took the view that clause 23 was merely non-binding guidance. This was to overlook the language in which the

---

54 *Keeley* (n 38) 967.

55 ibid.

56 *George v Ministry of Justice* [2013] EWCA Civ 324.

clause was phrased and its significance to the agreement. The collective agreement put in place a new regime, under which the right to refuse to work beyond normal hours was surrendered, and with it the right to receive enhanced pay for extra hours worked. In its place, and in exchange for an obligation to work additional hours upon request, prison officers would be given TOIL. To deny effect to clause 23 was to make the obligations on the parties less reciprocal and thereby less equitable. If part of the clause, and hence the work-wage bargain, was apt for incorporation – that is the entitlement to require prison officers to work additional hours – it was difficult to see that other parts were not. This one-sided stance on reciprocity is similar to that taken in *Malone v British Airways*, which is discussed below.[57]

Similar problems relating to incorporation were considered in *Jensen v Attorney-General*,[58] a case concerning a corrections officer who had been subject to investigation after an inmate made a series of allegations against her, which were later found to be unproven. The employee sought damages for breach of contract in relation to the conduct of the investigation and, in particular, the employer's failure to publicly announce the findings and to clear her name by prosecuting the inmate for making a false allegation. Part of her claim for damages rested on establishing that the provisions of a number of the employer's codes and manuals were also express terms of her employment. The court held that this turned on whether the terms in question were contractual 'in the sense of being negotiated and settled between the employer and employee'. On this basis, it held that documents unilaterally produced by the employer, including a human resources policy manual and various codes establishing general standards of behaviour, could not be said to be contractual in nature. Another difficulty faced in *Jensen* was that a clause in the collective employment contract stated that the union and the employer had agreed that the employer had the right to plan, manage and organize 'operations and policies'. This clause was held to significantly narrow the range for incorporation of terms and conditions.[59]

---

57 *Malone v British Airways* [2010] IRLR 431.
58 *Jensen v Attorney-General* [2003] 2 ERNZ 36 (EmpC).
59 ibid [29].

PRESERVING MANAGERIAL PREROGATIVE: ASPIRATIONAL LANGUAGE

The language in which a clause is expressed can be of considerable significance. 'Non-contractual' or aspirational wording is said to point against incorporation. In *Kaur v MG Rover Group*, the court had to consider whether provisions concerning job security contained in a collective agreement were incorporated.[60] The agreement contained the statement that 'employees who want to work for Rover will be able to stay with Rover. Necessary reductions in manpower will be achieved in the future, with the co-operation of all employees through retraining and redeployment, natural wastage, voluntary severance and early retrial programmes'. This provision was regarded as inappropriate for incorporation on the basis that it espoused 'collective aims or aspirations'. The decision in *Kaur* notwithstanding, the Court of Appeal decision in *Briscoe v Lubrizol* sets out a more satisfactory approach and holds that what is at issue is the identification of rights and duties. In dealing with such questions, one should look to the substance of the matter in dispute. In *Briscoe*, the court observed that 'it is frequently the case that, in the employment context, the language of a handbook while couched in terms of information and explanation, will be construed as giving rise to binding legal obligations as between employer and employee'.[61] Such a substantive approach seems sensible. It is important not to lose sight of the context in which the language is used and the fact that, in an entirely different context (such as a commercial setting), language of that nature would not be regarded as giving rise to legal obligations is neither here nor there. Adopting the modern contextual approach to interpretation, it may be reasonable to conclude, where employment relations are concerned, that a contractual commitment has been made.

In the past, the Australian courts were also likely to regard aspirational language as incompatible with the creation of legal obligations. However, as in the United Kingdom, there has been something of a recognition that documents may be drafted in a more workplace-orientated manner that is intended to be readily understood by workers and their representatives, and which should not detract from an entitlement in law arising. Again, in an industrial relations context, a document that is styled as a policy may be a means of expressing and highlighting the employer's commitment to the workforce. In *Goldman Sachs v Nikolich*, the employer's staff

60 *Kaur* (n 52).
61 *Briscoe* (n 43) 610.

manual (called 'Working With Us', or WWU) was designed to serve several purposes:[62]

> One was to make it plain that GSJBW is an excellent place to work by reason of the pervasive nature of its "culture and 'family' approach" as reflected in WWU. In this way the firm no doubt held itself out as being more attractive to talented people who would value and respond to such a culture. Other purposes were to inform and to inspire employees.

A policy document of this sort engenders (as it is intended to) expectations on the part of the workforce of how they will benefit from the employment relationship. It does not seem unreasonable that those expectations should be sound in law. Otherwise, the employer's statement would be 'no more than an aspirational representation, imposing no obligation on the maker, it would be seen as an exercise in hypocrisy'.[63]

In determining whether a particular element of a policy is contractual, the Australian courts have resorted to general contractual principles: if a reasonable person in the position of a promisee would conclude that a promisor intended to be contractually bound by a particular statement, then the promisor will be so bound.[64] The fact that the language used differs from traditional contractual drafting should not be decisive. The key is what the likely impact on someone in the position of the worker would be. In *Nikolich* itself, the employer undertook to 'take every practicable step to provide and maintain a safe and healthy work environment for all people'. This was held to give rise to a contractual obligation. It might be suggested that a worker would also have made this assumption. It is true that the statement is in general terms, but at the same time appears to offer a clear commitment about a fundamental aspect of working life. The court in *Nikolich* was not deterred by traditional thinking:[65]

> The difficulty is that the statement in issue is not explicitly contractual in its language and could be seen as merely aspirational. It appears in a document of mixed content and purposes and, although these include contractual purposes, at least the primary repository of the employment contract is unambiguously elsewhere.

---

62 *Goldman Sachs v Nikolich* [2007] FCAFC 120.
63 ibid [30].
64 *Toll* (n 26) 179.
65 *Nikolich* (n 62) [30].

Validation of the approach in *Nikolich* might be thought to arise from the fact that implied terms in law, or statutory obligations, may be similarly framed:[66]

> It is true that some are expressed more generally than might be ideal in a contract identifying hard and precise obligations. However, the common law contractual obligation itself finds expression in the broadest possible terms, and I do not think that the absence of a hard and specific edge to the language used in WWU ought to be disqualifying in this respect.

Again, the language used is reminiscent of some of the obligations that are to be found in the Health and Safety at Work Act 1974 (UK).

It should be said that *Nikolich* has not been as influential as one might have expected or, at least, hoped. The subsequent case of *Zafiriou v Saint-Gobain*, for instance, cites *Keeley* and denies the benefit of procedural rights where the employer's policy indicated that employees would be treated 'with respect, in a courteous and professional manner and in accordance with the principles of natural justice'.[67]

Given the decision in *Nikolich*, it seems surprising that the court felt unable to give meaning to a fundamental legal concept such as natural justice. The court in *Zafiriou* had a degree of difficulty in justifying its position and was forced to concede that the phrase 'treatment in accordance with the principles of natural justice' could be read as conveying a legal obligation. However, incorporation was denied on the basis that the phrase was 'directed to non-lawyers and coupled with other general aspirations and expressed to be a policy'. This seems utterly perverse; an obligation will be denied legal effect not only when it is not sufficiently legalistic, but also when it is. One can also only wonder how many contractual documents would be denied legal effect on the basis that they were not couched in language that was comprehensible to non-lawyers.[68]

Nikolich also contrasts with the stance taken in *Bau v State of Victoria*, where a statement that the employer would aim to 'prevent inappropriate workplace conflict behaviours', and 'is committed to a workplace free from discrimination, sexual harassment and victimisation' did not give rise to contractual obligations on the basis that the language used was

---

66 ibid [328].

67 *Zafiriou v Saint-Gobain* [2014] VSCA 331.

68 The court also took the view that incorporation was unnecessary given the express terms of the contract.

aspirational.[69] It may be doubted whether the language in *Nikolich* was any more specific. It might also be said that a contemporary court would not find it difficult to say what amounted to sexual harassment. The court in *Bau* found that elements of the policy, such as statements that the employer 'will not tolerate inappropriate workplace behaviours', were concerned with the conduct that is expected of employees, rather than making promises about the conduct of the employer. This is something of a false dichotomy; to be meaningful statements in the latter category, they must be clear enough to give direction and, as a corollary, may well be sufficiently specific to be contractual in nature.[70] A key difference may be the fact that, in *Nikolich*, the employer's statement on health and safety was couched in terms not dissimilar to that which can be found in health and safety legislation; as a result, the employer was seen as importing long-standing wisdom on the meaning of the language used.

Much more recently, *Romero v Farstad Shipping* has provided a note of optimism.[71] One of the issues that arose was whether the employer's policy on workplace harassment and discrimination was contractual. Two dimensions of the decision call for comment. First, it concerned bullying and harassment where public attitudes have changed very considerably in recent years and, as a corollary, the expectations placed on the employer have become weightier. The court in *Romero* recognized this and translated those expectations into legal obligations. Second, in the court below, contractual status had been denied on the basis that the language was overly aspirational: 'there was some quasi contractual language in the Policy, in his Honour's opinion, it was insufficiently specific so as to amount to a binding contractual obligation'.[72] The Federal Court (Full Court) took a diametrically opposed view, though a more traditional

---

69 *Bau v State of Victoria* [2009] VSCA 107.

70 In *Gramotnev* (n 25) [113]–[114], it was said that the 'statement that all grievances would be dealt with in a supportive environment without victimisation or intimidation is intended as a statement of policy not a contractual promise of the outcome. The appellant's submissions focus on the text of the policy that states that all managers and supervisors have an obligation and responsibility or primary responsibility or the like. While these provisions may create an obligation upon a manager or supervisor as between the manager or supervisor and the respondent, in my view the appellant fails to recognise the difference between the obligation of the manager or supervisor to the respondent and a contractual promise by the respondent to each staff member that their manager or supervisor will perform the obligation'.

71 *Romero v Farstad Shipping* [2014] FCAFC 177.

72 ibid [16].

approach would have arrived at a conclusion to the contrary. Aspirational wording should not prevent obligations arising in law because:[73]

> In the case of the policy here in question, it is evident that the contract could not operate reasonably and effectively without such an implied obligation. It would make nonsense of the employee's ongoing obligation to act in accordance with what the policy required of him or her from time to time, if the employer had no obligation to act in accordance with what the policy required of it.

PRESERVING MANAGERIAL PREROGATIVE: SUBJECT MATTER

The range of subject matter viewed as inapt for incorporation is wide – an approach that has the consequence of preserving managerial prerogative. In the United Kingdom, the older case of *BL (UK) Ltd v MacQuilken*[74] denied that the terms of the collective agreement in issue gave rise to individual rights on the basis that matters of policy were at stake. A more recent example is provided by *Malone v British Airways plc*,[75] which demonstrates that, whilst judicial attitudes have changed, to some extent, a narrow view continues to be taken when considering whether a term is apt for incorporation. In addition, the courts are not slow to conclude that the nature of the language used is incompatible with a contractual obligation arising.

In *Malone*, a member of cabin crew maintained that, by virtue of terms derived from collective bargaining, she was entitled to expect to work on a flight staffed to a contractually prescribed level. She went on to argue that, because she now flew on flights with reduced complements, British Airways was in breach of contract – 'a state of affairs that would continue until the collectively agreed complement was restored or the reduction is satisfied by a further collective agreement'. The claimant was unsuccessful for a number of reasons, including the fact that the term in question was said to be inapt for incorporation. The key clause in the collective agreement in *Malone* was to be found under a heading

---

[73] ibid [43]; quoting *Foggo v O'Sullivan Partners (Advisory) Pty Ltd* (2011) 206 IR 87, [119].

[74] *BL (UK) Ltd v MacQuilken* [1978] IRLR 245.

[75] *Malone v British Airways plc* [2010] IRLR 431. The decision of the High Court was upheld by the Court of Appeal on different grounds: [2011] IRLR 32. See also R Russell, '*Malone v British Airways plc*: Protection of Managerial Prerogative?' (2011) 40 ILJ 207.

'Minimum Planned Crew Complements' and stated that: 'all services will be planned to the current industrially agreed complements for each aircraft type. Future crew complements will continue to take into account in-flight product and cabin crew rest requirements'. By way of elaboration, the section in question contained more specific information about complements and, for example, provided that there should be 15 cabin crew on a 747 flight.

It might have seemed that the degree of support that British Airways undertook to provide was very much a matter for the employment contract and, moreover, an individualized version of the collective obligation could have been formulated with ease. The court in *Malone* saw matters very differently. The following dictum of Auld LJ in *Keeley* was invoked:[76]

> a good way of testing ... is to ask whether, and subject to the issue of certainty, if the (relevant terms) had been set out in identical terms in (the employee's) statement of employment terms, it could seriously have been argued as a matter of construction that it was not apt for a contractual term and, on that account not part of the contract.

For Auld LJ, there was a clear correlation between the appropriateness of a term for incorporation and the degree of adaptation required (if any). A less nuanced approach was adopted by Sir Christopher Holland in the High Court. In his opinion, the collectively agreed clause could not be incorporated without redrafting, and that was fatal to the claim. Redrafting was not the function of the courts: 'this exercise of drafting underlines the unreality of a contention that the contract incorporates the relevant WSA provisions so as to render such legally enforceable'.[77] The fact that drafting would not have presented an intellectual challenge failed to assist the claimant.

The approach in *Malone* is unsatisfactory. Insufficient understanding was displayed of the fact that collective agreements serve to regulate both collective and individual relations. As a consequence, it is not surprising that meaningful incorporation may not be possible unless the court finds an alternative way of expressing the obligation in issue. It may be said that a better approach is to be found in the judgment of the Inner House of the Court of Session in Scotland in *Burroughs Machines Ltd v Timmoney*, where it was accepted that it is erroneous to incorporate the

---

[76] *Keeley* (n 38) [36].
[77] *Malone* (n 75) 437.

collective clause word for word into the employment contract.[78] Instead, the court should look to the purpose of the clause and devise appropriate wording. It is unfortunate that *Burroughs Machines* does not appear to have been cited to the court in *Malone.*

In New Zealand, the courts have suggested that, where a policy manual has never been regarded by the parties as having contractual effect, or where the parties were accustomed to the employer's extensive use of non-contractual policies and manuals, it may be difficult to maintain that a particular policy forms part of a contract or is subject to contractual rights. The ability of employers to impose detailed and far-reaching policies in such circumstances was illustrated by *New Zealand Amalgamated Engineering Printing and Manufacturing Union Inc v Air New Zealand*, where the employer proposed to introduce a drug-testing policy, including a requirement for employees to take random drug tests at work.[79] The union argued that this would amount to a unilateral variation of the employees' employment agreements. The court held that the parties were accustomed to the employer's extensive use of non-contractual policies, and that the employer had issued the policy in reliance on its right to manage and its duty to provide a safe workplace.[80]

JOB SECURITY

It is evident from cases on incorporation that the courts are not inclined to fetter managerial prerogative where dismissal is concerned. This may be changing to some extent where the context is disciplinary, given that the common law is placing increased emphasis on natural justice.[81] Terms concerning procedural matters are much less likely to be incorporated, particularly where they restrict managerial prerogative over dismissal. In the *Alexander (No 2)* case, the litigation concerned the part of the collective agreement that set out a redundancy procedure covering

---

[78] *Burroughs Machines Ltd v Timmoney* [1977] IRLR 404.

[79] *New Zealand Amalgamated Engineering Printing and Manufacturing Union Inc v Air New Zealand* [2004] 1 ERNZ 614, (2004) 2 NZELR 157 (EmpC).

[80] ibid [179].

[81] In *Edwards* (n 6) [29], Lord Dyson observed that if 'an employer has applicable disciplinary rules and procedures, they will normally have contractual effect'. See also Astrid Sanders, 'The Content of Contracts of Employment' in Mark Freedland et al. (eds), *The Contract of Employment* (Oxford University Press 2016) 465–8.

matters such as selection criteria.[82] Clause 15.5.1 provided that: 'In the event of compulsory redundancy selection will be made on the basis of service within the group'. It was held that the clause was 'not sufficiently cogently worded to give rise to an inference of incorporation into individual contracts of employment'. This is arguable. The wording of the clause seems clear enough and it would not be difficult to argue that individual rights were conferred on the basis of seniority. This was held to be inapt for incorporation, even though the provisions appeared to impact upon individual employment relations. The seniority provisions, for example, had 'the effect of benefiting employees who have been with the defendant for a long time and put at risk those that have not'.[83]

In *Kaur*, the applicant sought to show that she had a contractual right not to be made compulsorily redundant. It was the basis of her case that such a right was conferred by a collective agreement that had been expressly incorporated into the employment contract. The case turned on whether the language used showed that the terms in respect of job security were apt for incorporation. At the crux of the dispute was the following clause (paragraph 2.1):

> It will be our objective to ensure that the application of the 'partnership principles' will enable employees who want to work for Rover to stay with Rover. As with the successful introduction of 'Rover Tomorrow – The New Deal' **THERE WILL BE NO COMPULSORY REDUNDANCY**.

It should be noted that the wording printed in bold appeared in this way in the collective agreement itself.

For the trial judge, the inclusion of those words was highly significant and indicated that the parties intended to enter into a contractual commitment in respect of job security. The judge was also mindful of the question of reciprocity of obligation. Her Honour noted that the collective agreement also contained 'important provisions requiring flexible working, cooperation by avoidance of unconstitutional action, manpower effectiveness and a de-manning procedure, all of which provisions I find (and the claimant does not dispute) were apt for incorporation'.[84] Those provisions had been inserted at the behest of the company, as part of an attempt to compete more effectively. On one analysis, the consideration for their insertion was the undertaking in respect of job security.

---

82 *Alexander (No 2)* (n 29).
83 *Alexander* (n 51) 59.
84 [2004] IRLR 279, 286.

The Court of Appeal, however, held that the provisions in respect of job security were not apt for incorporation, and the court took a very different view over the issue of reciprocity, stating that 'the fact that paragraph 2.1 was not unilateral but part of such a package tells one nothing about its aptness for incorporation as a term of individual contracts of employment'.[85]

This is more than debatable, and it may be argued that the element of reciprocity would point towards both parts, or neither, being enforceable at the level of the individual employment contract; one could be said to be the counterpart of the other. Such a view having being taken on the reciprocity issue, the Court of Appeal then decided that the language of paragraph 2.1 was inconsistent with the existence of an intention to incorporate. The use of the word 'objective' in the first sentence of paragraph 2.1 was said to be aspirational in nature and pointed against incorporation. However, when the clause is read as a whole, it becomes apparent that the second sentence could not be clearer or more categorical; there is an unequivocal declaration that compulsory redundancy will not take place. Any doubt that may exist when the first sentence is read on its own is overwhelmed.[86]

The Court of Appeal also placed emphasis on paragraph 2.3 of the collective agreement, which explained how the employer intended to avoid the need for any compulsory redundancies. It stated that reductions in the size of the staff would be achieved 'with the co-operation of all employees', through routes such as voluntary severance and early retirement. However, the court found: 'it very difficult to see the reference to "no compulsory redundancy" as an enforceable term in each employee's contract of employment, both because of the vagueness of the language

---

[85] *Kaur* (n 52) [31].

[86] The court believed that its interpretation was reinforced by the opening words of the second sentence of para 2.1, which read 'as with the successful introduction of "Rover Tomorrow – The New Deal"'. This was said to 'suggest that the statement about no compulsory redundancy is to be seen as a repeat of the earlier position in The New Deal. Yet … the position under The New Deal was one where the statements about employees being able to stay with Rover were not contractual commitments': ibid [31]. Thus, the court took the view that the intention was merely to replicate the extent of contractual protection afforded under an earlier collective agreement. One may doubt whether that was the meaning intended by the parties, who would have been unlikely to have been unduly troubled by the legal status of an earlier undertaking. The real issue for them would have been the effectiveness, in industrial relations terms, of that undertaking. Against that backdrop, what was relevant was whether, as a matter of fact, compulsory redundancies had taken place.

of para. 2.3 and because any entitlement would depend on the activities of others in the workforce'.[87]

It may be admitted that paragraph 2.3 is imprecise as to how the company would, in a redundancy situation, avoid the need for compulsory redundancies, and hence unclear as to how the employer would discharge the obligation contained in paragraph 2.1. However, paragraph 2.3 can be seen as merely indicating how the employer anticipated being able to accomplish this, and the ease or difficulty with which a party anticipates being able to discharge a contractual obligation is not relevant to its enforceability.

The Australian judiciary appears to take a similar view, as *Byrne* demonstrates.[88] The issue was whether the following clause contained in an award was incorporated: 'Termination of employment by an employer shall not be harsh, unjust or unreasonable. For the purposes of this clause, termination of employment shall include termination with or without notice'. The answer given was no – although it had been observed in the court below that this went against a trend 'in the law to imply an obligation to afford natural justice to a person whose rights may be affected by a decision'.[89] Judicial concern over deprivation of livelihood came to the fore:[90]

> a dismissed employee is deprived of his or her livelihood. The deprivation is particularly severe in a time of persistent high unemployment. Its severity is increased if the dismissal is expressed to be on the ground of some alleged dishonest act; the disclosure that a person was dismissed from previous employment for such a reason will constitute a substantial barrier to gaining other employment. For these reasons, I am of the view that a clause such as clause 11(a) requires that an employer contemplating terminating the employment of an employee is obliged to afford procedural fairness to that employee. Not to do so would be 'unjust'.

Ultimately, however, it was held that the promise of procedural fairness was not contractual.[91] It arose from the application of a mandatory award term – a 'termination, change and redundancy' clause had been inserted into many industrial awards as a consequence of industrial arbitration.[92]

---

[87] ibid [33].
[88] *Byrne* (n 21).
[89] *Byrne and Frew v Australian Airlines Ltd* [1994] FCA 888.
[90] ibid [29], per Gray J.
[91] *Byrne* (n 21).
[92] See *Termination Change and Redundancy Case* (1984) 8 IR 34; 9 IR 115. Since 1993, these clauses have been replaced by a legislated entitlement to

Breach of the award was held to be susceptible to statutory remedies, but not to damages for breach of contract.

'COHERENCE'

A concern with 'coherence' between the common law and statute further complicates the decisions of courts confronted with arguments that employment contracts should be construed so as to include terms incorporated in or implied from collective agreements or codes of conduct. The arguments raised in *Johnson v Unisys*[93] that common law developments should not overreach limits set by Parliament's laws have taken on a special significance in cases involving allegations that employment contracts contain promises of procedural fairness. Remarkably, two Law Lords (Lords Dyson and Mance) decided, in *Edwards v Chesterfield Royal Hospital NHS Foundation Trust and Botham (FC) v Ministry of Defence*,[94] that even express clauses in an employment contract promising certain disciplinary procedures before dismissal did not have full contractual effect. They held that the employer had never intended that breach of those clauses should give rise to a right to common law damages, because the clauses had been included in employment contracts only in order to signal an intention to comply with statutory obligations to provide fair procedures. Breach of these clauses would only entitle the employee to seek an injunction requiring the procedures to be followed prior to dismissal, or, if the employee moved too late for an injunction to be granted, to seek statutory compensation for dismissal. Coherence arguments also persuaded the court in *Commonwealth Bank of Australia v Barker* to refuse to recognize any implied duty of mutual trust and confidence in Australian employment contract law – on the basis that extensive statutory regulation already provided for (and confined) certain obligations of fair dealing in employment relations.[95]

pursue a claim for unfair dismissal. See Fair Work Act 2009 (Cth), Pt 3-2 for the current federal provisions.

[93] *Johnson v Unisys* [2001] UKHL 13, [2003] 1 AC 518.

[94] *Edwards* (n 6).

[95] *Barker* (n 24).

CONCLUSION

The law of contract places greater emphasis nowadays on giving legal effect to the reasonable expectations of the parties. However, when one turns to expectations that are raised by the outcomes of the collective bargaining process, it is far from certain that they will find expression in contract law. Thus, we find that the contemporary judicial approach towards incorporation of collectively agreed terms appears to remain a cautious one. The common law is also clearly sympathetic to the maintenance of managerial prerogative, which is reinforced by the courts' approach to the aptness of terms for incorporation and the treatment of language deemed to be aspirational. In *Malone*, in upholding the judgment of the court below, the Court of Appeal was hugely influenced by 'the disastrous consequences for BA which could ensue if this term were to be individually enforceable'.[96]

Collective agreements, industrial awards and the like will serve more than one purpose. Judicial thinking is often not attuned to this and, as a result, the employment contract will often fail to give normative effect to the individual elements of the obligation in dispute. The style of agreements in dispute is often very different to that found in other contexts:[97]

> the ... [agreements] ... contain a great variety of provisions, some of which are clearly intended to be individually enforceable and some of which are clearly intended to be unenforceable. There are also provisions which I do not find to be clear either way. Even within the same section, there are enforceable and unenforceable provisions.

Such a backdrop tends to make the task of counsel for the claimant even more arduous. Where the legal status of the employer's policies is concerned, the courts, on some occasions at least, will subject the employer's drafting to close scrutiny to ensure that devices such as the use of aspirational language do not render the document non-contractual. This is important; key responsibilities should not be discretionary. However, claimants can be far from certain that their interests will be protected in this way.

One final observation is worth noting: when employers (or their legal advisors) include terms in employment contract documentation that expressly foreswear the contractual effect of workplace policies, courts

---

[96] *Malone v British Airways plc* [2011] IRLR 32, [62].

[97] ibid [53].

will give effect to those disclaimers. To the extent that any of the developing case law (including *McCormick v Riverwood International (Australia) Pty Ltd*[98] and *Nikolich v Goldman Sachs JB Were Services Pty Ltd*[99]) has given employees hope that the promises made in elaborate 'Working with Us' type manuals will be binding on employers, it remains within the power of employers to take that hope away, by simple contractual disclaimers.[100]

The solution to these attitudes of the common law will certainly require statutory reform. In the one jurisdiction where these problems seem less apparent – New Zealand – the combination of a statutory duty of good faith and the wide reach of the personal grievance procedure requiring employers to justify their actions appears to have had the result that the courts are more willing to be proactive in constraining management prerogative.[101] For example, in *Jensen*, discussed above, the plaintiff was suing for damages for breach of contract, but the court noted that, if, instead, she had pursued a personal grievance based on unjustifiable action, it would have been open to her to introduce the policy documents in the context, as one aspect of a wider inquiry into general questions of fairness and reasonableness.[102] In disciplinary cases, a policy is now probably to be regarded as part of 'all the circumstances' for the purposes of section 103A of the Employment Relations Act 2000 (NZ).[103]

---

98 *McCormick v Riverwood International (Australia) Pty Ltd* (1999) 167 ALR 689.

99 *Nikolich v Goldman Sachs JB Were Services Pty Ltd* [2006] FCA 784, (2007) 163 FCR 62.

100 See *Barker* (n 24).

101 This has recently been demonstrated in a number of cases relating to redundancy: see *Grace Team Accounting Ltd v Brake* [2014] NZCA 541.

102 *Jensen* (n 58) [30].

103 *Safe Air Ltd v Walker* (2009) 6 NZELR 761 (EmpC); and see the observations in *Butcher v OCS Ltd* [2008] ERNZ 367, [49] (EmpC) on the need for caution in relying on cases prior to the insertion of the test for justification by s 103A.

6. Fairness of the bargain and allocation of risk

Kahn-Freund, in his seminal work *Labour and the Law*, stated that: 'The relation between an employer and an isolated employee or worker is typically a relation between a bearer of power and one who is not a bearer of power'. The judiciary now subscribe to this view.[1] In *Russell v The Trustees of the Roman Catholic Church for the Archdiocese of Sydney*, Kahn-Freund's analysis was set out more fully:[2]

> Here then is an ancient tension in the system. For the common law assumes it is dealing with a contract made between equals, but in reality, save in exceptional circumstances, the individual worker brings no equality of bargaining power to the labour market and to this transaction central to his life whereby the employer buys his labour power. This *individual* relationship, in its inception, 'is an act of submission, in its operation it is a condition of subordination, however much the submission and the subordination may be concealed by that indispensable figment of the legal mind known as the contract of employment'.

This constitutes a remarkable transformation, given traditional common law thinking, but, from the perspective of the employee, the key question becomes whether we can expect to see a radically different approach in judicial law making. It seems fair to say that the recognition of imbalance in bargaining strength has been one of the principal driving forces behind a number of significant reforms at common law in recent years; the emergence of the implied obligation of mutual trust and confidence and the recognition of sham contracts are prime examples. The question addressed in this chapter is whether these developments mark at least the beginning of a trend to take greater account of this power imbalance, and

1 *Autoclenz v Belcher* [2011] ICR 1157 is one example.

2 *Russell v The Trustees of the Roman Catholic Church for the Archdiocese of Sydney and another* [2007] NSWSC 104, [91]; quoting Otto Kahn-Freund, 'Blackstone's Neglected Child: the Contract of Employment' (1977) 93 Law Quarterly Review 503.

the consequent imbalance of risk allocation between the parties to employment relationships.

Just as contract is used as a risk allocation tool between parties to commercial dealings,[3] the contract of employment is a mechanism for allocating risks between employers and those whom they engage to pursue their business interests. Some of those risks relate to operating in an uncertain universe. Who will bear the cost if an economic downturn makes the labour less valuable in the marketplace? Who will carry the cost of illness or injury to the worker? These kinds of risks have attracted the attention of legislatures, enacting statutes for minimum wages, leave entitlements, workers' compensation, and so forth, and tend to fall outside of the parameters of the parties' own control. There are risks, however, that are inherent in relationships of indefinite duration and that do fall within the parties' own influence. These include the risk to the employer that the employee will fail to perform to the expected or required standard, or that the employee's conduct will cause harm to the employer's reputation, or to the well-being of the enterprise and other employees. These kinds of issues are discussed further in Chapter 10.

A second kind of risk to the employer is that the employee will take the skills and knowledge developed on the job to another enterprise, perhaps by setting up in competition with the employer. This kind of risk is mitigated by reliance on the common law duty of fidelity, discussed in Chapter 7, and the way in which the common law permits the enforcement of certain post-employment restraints on competition, discussed in Chapter 9.

In this chapter, we consider the risk to the employee that the employer will abuse their superior bargaining power to dictate terms, or manage the employment relationship, in a way that imposes an undue or oppressive burden on the employee. After all, in choosing to accept employment from one employer, a worker often forecloses opportunities to work elsewhere. Employees accepting indefinite engagement in an enterprise often commit to the development of their own 'human capital' – their knowledge, skills and relationships – in the best interests of the employer's enterprise. These become 'sunk costs', in the terms favoured by economists. A person who has sunk considerable investment in a particular enterprise – and possibly built a life around the enterprise's needs – will lose a great deal if they are forced to abandon their position. It is not always easy for employees who have made this kind of

---

[3] See generally Stephen Waddams, 'The Price of Excessive Damages Awards' (2005) 27 Sydney Law Review 543.

investment to 'vote with their feet' when a position becomes intolerable. This chapter concerns the techniques by which the common law of employment has mitigated the risk of unfair bargains, and of capricious and arbitrary exercise of the employer's powers of management. To the extent that an abuse of power results in dismissal, these concerns are also revisited in Chapter 10. Here we focus principally on the development of principles of contract interpretation and construction that favour restraint on the capricious exercise of discretion.

POWER DISPARITIES AND FAIRNESS

Relationships formed against a backdrop of a disparity of power may well raise concerns about the fairness of the ensuing exchange. The fact that concepts of good faith and fair dealing are playing a more prominent role in the law of contract as a whole (including employment) might be thought to point towards greater judicial intervention. However, we run up against a deeply entrenched common law refusal (in the absence of a defect in process) to declare whether or not a bargain is reasonable – a position which tends to be replicated across jurisdictions. In *Commercial Bank of Australia v Amadio*, for example, the High Court of Australia made it clear that a contract will not be set aside on the basis of unconscionability merely because one side has exploited their superior bargaining power to conclude a one-sided bargain.[4] This was confirmed more recently in *ACCC v CG Berbatis Holdings*, where it was observed that: 'Many, perhaps even most, contracts are made between parties of unequal bargaining power, and good conscience does not require parties to contractual negotiations to forfeit their advantages, or neglect their own interests'.[5]

The position is the same in New Zealand[6] and the United Kingdom.[7] Such a position may seem out of keeping with trends in the common law more generally, but it is apparent that determining what fairness requires would be hugely problematic. It is suggested that the position adopted by the common law is a sensible one, as the challenges faced by an adjudicator would be manifold and almost certainly irresolvable in the absence of statutory intervention. For example, one would have to decide whether a term, prima facie unfair, is acceptable when other terms of the

---

4 *Commercial Bank of Australia v Amadio* (1983) 151 CLR 447.
5 *ACCC v CG Berbatis Holdings* (2013) 214 CLR 51, [11].
6 *Gustav v Macfield* [2007] NZCA 205.
7 *National Westminster v Morgan* [1985] AC 686.

contract are taken into account. An employer would be likely to maintain that the limitations in one element of the bargain were compensated for by generosity of provision in other respects. How might any such trade-off be evaluated? An initial difficulty is that the basis of the trade-off may not be apparent. It may not be clear which term(s) contribute to the quid pro quo.

Even where that is not the case, it may not be apparent how one evaluates the terms involved. In some cases, it may be possible to place a monetary equivalence on the terms being compared, but this will not always be so. In some cases, all that would be possible would be a very broad-brush approach. Some situations, of course, would be relatively straightforward. An employee may complain that they have arbitrarily been denied a pay rise granted to fellow workers. The Employment Appeals Tribunal held in *FC Gardner v Beresford* that this may amount to a breach of mutual trust and confidence.[8] The employee's complaint involved allegations of less favourable treatment than that afforded to workers in an analogous position within the same organization. The implied term was invoked to prevent abuse of discretion within those narrow parameters. Although Australian law does not recognize an implied duty of trust and confidence, a claim of this kind may succeed if it could be shown that the employer exercised a discretion in bad faith.[9]

Whilst the substance of the bargain remains beyond judicial challenge, the courts now hold that all discretionary clauses contained within the employment contract will be read subject to those fundamental implied terms that express the essence of the contract, in particular the obligation of trust and confidence, and in Australia, the obligation to cooperate.[10] It is acknowledged that, while the parties to an employment contract are likely to have conflicting interests, where:[11]

> the provisions of the contract effectively place the resolution of that conflict in the hands of the party exercising the discretion, it is presumed to be the reasonable expectation and therefore the common intention of the parties that there should be a genuine and rational, as opposed to an empty or irrational, exercise of discretion.

The subject of complaint has often been the exercise of a discretionary power by an employer, such as whether to pay a discretionary bonus and,

---

8 *FC Gardner v Beresford* [1978] IRLR 63.

9 See *Regulski v State of Victoria* [2015] FCA 206, [209].

10 See *Commonwealth Bank of Australia v Barker* [2014] HCA 32.

11 *Horkulak v Cantor Fitzgerald International* [2004] IRLR 942, 948.

if so, for what amount. The courts are determined to guard against abuse of power on the part of employers who seek to rewrite the terms of the bargain for their own benefit. Thus, in *Attrill v Dresdner Kleinworth*, the Court of Appeal held that the obligation of trust and confidence precluded the exercise of a unilateral contractual power to vary the terms of contracts of employment to allow the employer to withhold contractual bonuses in the event of a 'material adverse change'.[12]

The leading decision in the United Kingdom is *Braganza v BP*, where the employer formed the opinion that the most likely explanation for a seaman's disappearance was that he had committed suicide by throwing himself overboard.[13] Should that conclusion have been valid, it would have meant that his widow was not entitled to the death benefits provided for in his contract of employment. The contract provided as follows: 'For the avoidance of doubt compensation for death, accidental injury or illness shall not be payable if, *in the opinion of the Company or its insurers*, the death, accidental injury or illness resulted from amongst other things, *the Officer's wilful act, default or misconduct* whether at sea or ashore' (emphasis added in judgment). The Supreme Court acted to impose constraints on the employer's prerogative, and did so by applying the approach articulated in the famous judicial review case of *Wednesbury*:[14]

> The first limb focusses on the decision-making process – whether the right matters have been taken into account in reaching the decision. The second focusses upon its outcome – whether even though the right things have been taken into account, the result is so outrageous that no reasonable decision-maker could have reached it.[15]

The court concluded that the employer's decision was unreasonable in the *Wednesbury* sense, having been formed without taking relevant matters into account. The approach in *Braganza* was applied in *Bartlett v Australia and New Zealand Banking Group*, where the employer's

---

[12] *Attrill v Dresdner Kleinworth* [2013] EWCA Civ 394, [2013] 3 All ER 607.

[13] *Braganza v BP* [2015] UKSC 17, [2015] ICR 449.

[14] *Associated Provincial Picture Houses v Wednesbury* [1948] 1 KB 223, [24].

[15] *Braganza* (n 13) [24].

behaviour did not comply with the *Wednesbury* test because of deficiencies in the conduct of a disciplinary investigation.[16]

Given the importance of the work-wage bargain to the employee, it is not surprising that cases involving elements of the remuneration package often feature in litigation of this sort. The courts will act to protect employees where the employer is viewed as acting to expropriate any element of reward to which the employee has a reasonable expectation. In the bonus case of *Reinhard v Ondra*, it was found that the employer had failed to exercise its discretion properly: 'Having failed to give proper weight to what he had achieved and having improperly taken into account that which he did not achieve, … [the employer] … was in breach of contract'.[17] The decision was irrational or perverse.

Attempts by employers to free themselves of judicial regulation through the drafting of the contract may be unsuccessful. The courts are reluctant to surrender their supervisory role. In *Russo v Westpac Banking*,[18] the employer sought to exclude judicial intervention by maintaining that he held 'absolute discretion', whereas in *Silverbrook Research v Lindley*, it was said that decisions were at his 'sole discretion'.[19] Nevertheless, the courts held that a discretion of this nature should not be exercised capriciously, arbitrarily or unreasonably – the intention and ingenuity of the drafter being thwarted in both cases. The view was taken that, the literal meaning of the contract notwithstanding, the parties must be assumed to have bargained on the understanding that the relationship would be conducted on the basis of fair dealing. The courts may also favour a construction of the terms of the contract that reduces the scope of discretion. Thus, in *Bartlett*, the employer's power to summarily terminate depended upon the objective occurrence of 'misconduct', not simply the opinion of the employer that misconduct had occurred.[20] In arriving at this view, the importance to an employee of employment (both financially and otherwise) was fully taken on board. The limits of this approach are not altogether clear. *Bartlett* declined to place any implied restriction on the exercise of the notice clause.

Two general observations can be made about this line of case law. First, the extent of judicial scrutiny varies depending upon the nature of

---

16 *Bartlett v Australia and New Zealand Banking Group* [2016] NSWCA 30. *Patural v DB Services* [2016] IRLR 286 flags up concerns over *Wednesbury* (n 14) in the employment context.

17 *Reinhard v Ondra* [2015] EWHC 26, [445].

18 *Russo v Westpac Banking* [2015] FCCA 1086.

19 *Silverbrook Research v Lindley* [2010] NSWCA 357.

20 *Bartlett* (n 16).

the decision under consideration. Given the imbalance of power in the employment relationship, the courts will be more vigilant than they would be in the commercial context.[21] That said, the degree of scrutiny is not constant within the employment context. The courts are concerned to ensure that the employer does not 'snatch a bargain'; but, where remuneration is involved, the courts are cautious when it comes to second guessing the employer. The judiciary prefer to avoid determining what constitutes a reasonable or fair pay increase or bonus (which would be the inevitable consequence of holding that the employer's decision amounted to a breach). In *Commerzbank v Keen*, it was emphasised that:[22]

> it is not the function of the court to usurp the Bank's exercise of its discretion. It is for the Bank to decide whether to pay a bonus and, if so, how much, when and in what amount and form. The court is not entitled to substitute itself for the Bank.

Other aspects of the employer's prerogative are more likely to be subject to intervention. *Stevens v University of Birmingham* concerned a disciplinary investigation into allegations of misconduct, and it was found that there was no express obligation to hold a meeting with a person under investigation.[23] However, 'the overarching obligation of trust and confidence may require such a meeting to be held, because of the serious nature of the investigation and the potentially serious consequences for the person concerned'.[24] The judiciary are familiar, in a wide variety of contexts, with the requirements of due process and are much more inclined to intervene on this basis; such an intervention also accords with the common law value of natural justice.[25] It is also fair to say that the imposition of procedural requirements is seen as a more limited interference with managerial prerogative, as the substantive outcome may remain unaltered.

Second, and closely linked to the previous point, a variety of views have been expressed in the case law as to the appropriate test to apply. The underlying question here is the legitimate extent of intervention. Again, reflecting the discussion in the preceding paragraph, where remuneration is concerned, the judges tend to adopt an approach that has

---

21 *Braganza* (n 13), per Lord Hodge.

22 *Commerzbank v Keen* [2006] EWCA Civ 1536, [2007] ICR 623, [39].

23 *Stevens v University of Birmingham* [2015] EWHC 2300 (QB).

24 ibid [67].

25 See Dawn Oliver, *Common Values and the Public-Private Divide* (Cambridge University Press 1999) 60.

a strong resemblance to a public law one. In *Clark v Nomura International*, it was held that the correct test is one 'of irrationality or perversity (of which caprice or capriciousness would be a good example) that is that no reasonable employer would have exercised his discretion in this way'.[26] The Australian courts, in decisions such as *Silverbrook*, have applied the same approach.[27] This places a significant barrier in the path of claimants. The Court of Appeal in *Keen* went as far as saying that:[28]

> The burden of establishing that no rational bank in the City would have paid him a bonus of less than his line manager recommended is a very high one. It would require an overwhelming case to persuade the court to find that the level of a discretionary bonus payment was irrational or perverse in an area where so much must depend on the discretionary judgment of the Bank in fluctuating market and labour conditions.

In some other areas, the judicial approach may be much closer to a test based upon reasonableness. *United Bank v Akhtar* concerned a mobility clause.[29] It was held that, given the existence of mutual trust and confidence, lawful exercise of the clause required that reasonable notice be given of any move. It is salutary to remember that in the United Kingdom the underlying obligation will tend to be that of trust and confidence; good faith may perform the same underpinning function in other systems. In *Braganza*, despite the application of the *Wednesbury* test, Baroness Hale stated that: 'Any decision-making function entrusted to the employer has to be exercised in accordance with the implied obligation of trust and confidence'.[30] Demonstrating that mutual trust has been breached may, properly, involve recourse to different criteria depending upon the context.

STATUTE: CATALYST OR CONSTRAINT?

In recent years, there have been significant changes at common law that concern the fairness of the bargain – most notably where control of discretion is concerned. At the same time, there is nothing in the case law to suggest that the common law is likely to adopt a more radical

---

26 *Clark v Nomura International* [2000] IRLR 766, 774.
27 *Silverbrook* (n 19).
28 *Keen* (n 22) [59].
29 *United Bank v Akhtar* [1989] IRLR 507.
30 *Braganza* (n 13) [32].

approach to unconscionability. Might statute provoke a change in position? The answer may be very different depending upon the nature of the legislation concerned. Parliament, for instance, may legislate to provide minimum standards in respect of substantive employment rights. In such a case, where the employer has complied with such provisions, it would almost certainly be thought inappropriate to hold that a term was unfair.

In New Zealand, as in Australia and the United Kingdom, the common law position remains that the parties to an employment contract are free to agree on such terms as they see fit, a position made clear in section 65(1)(b) of the Employment Relations Act 2000 (NZ), which provides that an individual contract may contain such terms as the parties 'think fit'. This position, however, is mediated by two groups of statutory provisions. The first has the effect of requiring 'informed consent' to the contractual terms entered into, and the second allows an employee to raise an unjustifiable disadvantage personal grievance.

The guiding principle of the Employment Relations Act 2000 (NZ)[31] appears to be that, given the existence of a statutory floor setting minimum terms of employment, it is up to the potential employee to decide whether or not they are prepared to accept the terms offered by an employer. Such protection as there is comes through ensuring that employees have both an entitlement and an opportunity to seek independent advice on the offered terms. Section 63A(2) requires that an employer must provide the employee with a copy of the intended employment agreement;[32] advise the employee of their entitlement to seek independent advice about the agreement; give a reasonable opportunity to seek that advice; and consider any issues that the employee raises and respond to them. A breach of this provision does not invalidate the agreement,[33] but a failure to comply may constitute unfair bargaining under section 68 and, if so, a variety of remedies may be sought, including awarding of compensation; an order cancelling or varying the agreement; or 'such other order as [the Authority] thinks fit in the circumstances'.[34] Unfair bargaining includes being induced to enter the agreement by oppressive means, undue influence, or duress; and encompasses the employer's taking advantage of some form of diminished capacity or the employee's

[31] For a commentary on the more limited pre-2000 provisions of the Employment Contracts Act 1991 (NZ), see Gordon Anderson et al., *Butterworths Employment Law Guide* (4th edn, Butterworths 1998).

[32] The minimum terms that are required to be provided in writing are set out in Employment Relations Act 2000 (NZ), s 65.

[33] ibid s 63A(4).

[34] ibid s 69.

reliance on the skill, care or advice of a potential employer. There are also specific provisions relating to fixed-term employment[35] and trial periods.[36] Actions relating to individual agreements under section 68 are comparatively rare,[37] although there have been a number of cases where the courts have taken a strong line on breaches of section 63A.[38]

These statutory remedies displace the ability to challenge an agreement based on the ground that it is unfair or unconscionable,[39] but, given the range of categories in the section, this bar is of limited significance.

The second group of provisions are those relating to personal grievances. One category of grievance is a claim that:[40]

> the employee's employment, or 1 or more conditions of the employee's employment (including any condition that survives termination of the employment), is or are or was (during employment that has since been terminated) affected to the employee's disadvantage by some unjustifiable action by the employer.

Any disadvantage, whether material or otherwise, may form the basis of a personal grievance,[41] and the disadvantage need not relate only to terms of the contract but can extend to 'all the rights, benefits and obligations arising out of the employment relationship. The concept is necessarily wider than the terms of an employment contract'.[42] Examples have included transfers, non-promotion and demotions, suspensions from employment, withdrawal of discretionary benefits, unjustified or unfair disciplinary actions and the failure to protect employees from harassment

---

35 ibid s 66.

36 ibid ss 67A and 67B.

37 See e.g. *Warmington and O'Neill v AFFCO New Zealand Ltd* [2012] NZEmpC 19 (where an alleged reliance on a statement suggesting that restraint of trade clauses would not be enforced was rejected).

38 *Blackmore v Honick Properties Ltd* [2011] NZEmpC 152, (2011) 9 NZELR 306; and *Olsen v Carter Holt Harvey IT Ltd* (2008) 6 NZELR 318 (EmpC).

39 Employment Relations Act 2000 (NZ), s 68(4).

40 ibid s 103(1)(b).

41 *Alliance Freezing Co (Southland) Ltd v New Zealand Engineering Union* [1989] 3 NZILR 785 (CA).

42 *Tranz Rail Ltd v Rail & Maritime Transport Union (Inc)* [1999] 1 ERNZ 460, [26] (CA). This interpretation was supported by references to United Kingdom case law: see *BBC v Hearn* [1978] 1 All ER 111, 116; and *Universe Tankships Inc of Monrovia v International Transport Workers' Federation* [1983] 1 AC 366, 402.

and bullying.[43] However, while these cases are decided in terms of the statutory test, the common law remains influential. 'Justification' is judged, at least in part, by a consideration of contractual obligations such as fidelity and mutual trust and confidence.

A more interesting statutory model to consider might be the New South Wales scheme, where the Industrial Relations Commission has (up until amendments in 2006 that limited this jurisdiction to public servants[44]) possessed extensive regulatory powers under the Industrial Relations Act 1996 (NSW) in respect of unfair employment contracts. The scheme merits close attention, given its close focus on the fairness of the bargain and the open-ended powers of review bestowed. Decisions taken might stimulate fresh thinking at common law; deficiencies in the common law armoury may be highlighted and solutions may become apparent. It may, therefore, be worth speculating what impact, if any, the substantial body of jurisprudence that emerged from that jurisdiction during its most vibrant years might have on the common law – statute having the capacity to act as both a catalyst and constraint where the common law is concerned.

We would suggest that the impact of the New South Wales scheme is likely to be limited. In the first instance, the conferral of statutory authority did not diminish the difficulties in determining what is fair or unfair. This is reflected in the vague guidance that emerged in the case law:[45]

> In considering 'fairness', the determination is according to the common sense approach of a juryman by applying standards which appear to provide a proper balance or division of advantage and disadvantage between the parties who have made the contract or arrangement; in doing so, the conduct of the parties, their capability to appreciate the bargain they had made and their comparative bargaining positions when entering into the contract or arrangement will always have to be borne in mind.

The New South Wales legislation allowed complaints that went to the substance of a term to be addressed. For instance, it would have been possible to substitute a term of a manager's contract dealing with

---

43 Gordon Anderson and John Hughes, *Employment Law in New Zealand* (LexisNexis 2014) para 9.9.

44 See the Workplace Relations Amendment (Work Choices) Act 2006 (Cth), which foreclosed the operation of many state industrial laws in the private sector.

45 *Davies v General Transport Development Pty Ltd* [1967] AR (NSW) 371, 373–4 (per Sheldon J); *A & M Thompson Pty Ltd v Total Australia Ltd* [1980] 2 NSWLR 1, 13.

redundancy payments on the basis that it was not sufficiently generous when compared with the redundancy entitlements available to employers covered by collective enterprise agreements.[46] The fact that a term to that effect would not have been implied at common law was irrelevant. In *Payne v Foxboro*, the complaint was that the express terms on redundancy were not good enough.[47] The court noted that, while the benefits were on the low side for corporations of the standing and size of the respondents and their US parent corporation/s and, indeed, for many employers of lesser standing, they were not so low as to be unfair. A finding of unfairness was inappropriate 'in the absence of evidence of a higher and objective standard applicable to the circumstances of this case, or of some other comparative unfairness'. Such a cautious approach would be unlikely to give rise to common law radicalism and, indeed, there is no indication that it has.

It is striking that the substantive outcome in many cases was similar to what might have been expected at common law, even though the mechanism utilized might have been different. In a number of cases, actions were raised by highly paid employees with attractive remuneration packages, including items such as share options. The issue in such cases is often whether, on dismissal, such benefits can properly be expropriated. For example, in *Westfield v Helprin*, the employee had been granted share options but was dismissed before those options had vested.[48] Crucially, the employee had been dismissed without cause. In those circumstances, it was regarded as unfair that the options be forfeited in their entirety, when the scheme was intended to provide additional remuneration both for past performance and during its period of operation. At the point of termination, the employee had been employed for almost three-quarters of the qualifying period. The contract was varied so that, on termination other than for cause, the employee should have been entitled to exercise 73 per cent of the 40,000 options granted to him, proportionately reflecting his period of employment during the operation of the scheme. A similar outcome would have been likely at common law, though the route would have been different. For example, a court might have acted to protect the employee by way of an implied term in law. In *Briscoe v Lubrizol*, the English Court of Appeal accepted:[49]

---

46 *Moray Vincent v Merrill Lynch* [2000] NSWIRComm 160.
47 *Payne v Foxboro* [1998] NSWIRComm 360.
48 *Westfield v Helprin* (1998) 82 IR 411.
49 *Briscoe v Lubrizol* [2002] EWCA Civ 508, [2002] IRLR 607, [21].

> that it was an implied term of the claimant's contract of employment that the defendants would not terminate that employment save for a cause other than ill health so as to deprive the claimant of the continuing entitlement to the very disability benefit which it was the primary purpose of the defendant's scheme to provide for him until age sixty-five.

None of the judges in the Court of Appeal expressed any doubt as to the existence of a term along those lines (though they were not required to determine its precise formulation). Certainly, some such term was appropriate to prevent the terms as to sickness pay/benefits being unfairly undermined without conferring such a degree of protection that would distort the bargain between the parties.

One area where the New South Wales jurisprudence could usefully have an impact on common law development is in the realm of procedural fairness. This is an area where developments at common law are already taking place in the United Kingdom. In *Westfield v Helprin*, it was held that:[50]

> the contract of employment became unfair because the employer acted unfairly, harshly and unconscionably in terminating the services of the employee on grounds which were not made out, in failing to investigate the allegations against him, in failing to give him any warning, in refusing to give him an opportunity to answer the charges against him and in denying to him the employer's normal redundancy or severance benefits package which formed part of the overall employment arrangement.

Again, in *Burgess v Mount Thorley*, it was said that, in discussing any matter concerning the employee's conduct or performance with the employee, the company must provide full and complete particulars to the employee of the matters of concern in writing, and allow the employee a reasonable opportunity to respond to those concerns.[51]

Procedural fairness might be thought to be embedded in the values of the common law. The Australian courts have been much slower than the United Kingdom and New Zealand to move in this direction. Decisions such as *Westfield* might indicate a path forward in Australia, although more likely through the influence that such decisions have on employer human resources practices. Decisions from the unfair contracts jurisdiction in New South Wales may have influenced the development by employer HR managers of the policies for fair disciplinary procedures

---

50 *Westfield v Helprin* (1997) 82 IR 411, 431.

51 *Burgess v Mount Thorley* [2003] NSWIRComm 432.

that we have seen in cases such as *Romero v Farstad Shipping*.[52] When compliance with these policies is accepted to be an important part of the mutual promises in an employment contract, the common law can recognize obligations of fair dealing, even in a jurisdiction stubbornly resisting the recognition of an implied duty of mutual trust and confidence.

CONCLUSION

In this chapter we have considered the steps towards recognition of an obligation of fair dealing in the common law of employment. Given the imbalances of economic power between employer and employee, and the individualistic character of the common law and its predominant commitment to 'freedom of contract', any substantial amelioration of the employee's risk of unfair bargaining requires some legislative or third-party intervention. The latter usually takes the form of collective bargaining. In the absence of effective bargaining, which is only likely with some form of collective representation, individual employees are rarely able to manage risk through negotiating contractual terms. It is far from unusual for a dominant economic party to impose contractual terms that can be oppressive and unjust for the weaker party. This explains the high degree of statutory intervention to manage some of the most serious risks of unfairness to employees (in relation to minimum wages, maximum hours, leave entitlements, and safety controls, for example). The risk of capricious dismissal has been most effectively managed by statutory intervention (and this is discussed further in Chapter 10).

---

[52] *Romero v Farstad Shipping (Indian Pacific) Pty Ltd* [2014] FCAFC 177.

7. Fidelity, mutual trust and confidence and fair dealing

INTRODUCTION

A particular characteristic of employment law is the very significant role played by the terms that the common law implies in all contracts of employment – most significantly, the implied obligation of fidelity that restrains an employee's autonomy by requiring them to subordinate many of their own interests to those of their employer. Moreover, this obligation is largely undefined and open-ended. Until recently, an employer was not regarded as owing any similar constraints. As was said in one case: 'One finds little, in the older cases in which the law developed, to support the existence of reciprocal duties in the employer, to protect the employee's economic interests'.[1] That position changed somewhat with the development, in the 1970s, of the implied term of mutual trust and confidence and, more recently, the potential development of good faith obligations in the law of contract generally. Mutual trust and confidence is a reciprocal, albeit asymmetrical obligation, and significant differences in the development of the term are evident in different jurisdictions. Indeed, in Australia, the High Court has denied its very existence. Nevertheless, elements of commonality exist which may help to identify emerging core values of the employment contract, as norms of good faith and fair dealing become more significant in the law of contract as a whole.[2] In this chapter, we explore the interrelationship of the implied terms of fidelity and mutual trust and confidence and related obligations.

[1] *Re Schindler Lifts Australia Pty Ltd and Precision Elevators Pty Ltd v Milan Debelak* [1989] 89 ALR 275, 303.

[2] Douglas Brodie, 'Fair Dealing and the World of Work' (2014) 43 ILJ 29.

FIDELITY

The obligation of fidelity shares a common history across all three jurisdictions[3] and, historically, English law has been hugely influential. Formative English cases, such as *Hivac Ltd v Park Royal Scientific Instruments Ltd*,[4] *Robb v Green*,[5] *Wessex Dairies Ltd v Smith*,[6] and *Sanders v Parry*[7] have long been, and continue to be, cited, as until relatively recently, Australian and New Zealand case law has been sparse.[8] Perhaps the most significant common feature in all three jurisdictions is the width of the obligation and, as a corollary, the myriad of activities that are captured. The obligation of fidelity provides a powerful obligation that can be utilized to constrain a wide range of employee activities that an employer might consider detrimental to its interests. Over 80 years ago, the High Court in *Blyth Chemicals v Bushnell* summarized the position:[9]

> Conduct which in respect of important matters is incompatible with the fulfilment of an employee's duty, or involves an opposition, or conflict between his interest and his duty to his employer, or impedes the faithful performance of his obligations, or is destructive of the necessary confidence between employer and employee, is a ground of dismissal.

While the vagueness of the obligation has been judicially acknowledged,[10] the obligation presents a considerable challenge for the employee who wishes to know what they can or cannot do. The requirements derived from the obligation have been elaborated on in a variety of contexts and are expressed in terms capable of applying to a

---

3 AJ Geare, 'An Employee's Duty of Loyalty: New Zealand Law and Practice' (1999) 20 CLLPJ 283; Gordon Anderson, 'Good Faith in the Individual Employment Relationship in New Zealand' (2000) 32 CLLPJ 685; Bob Hepple, 'Employee Loyalty in English Law' (1999) 20 CLLPJ 205; Ronald McCallum and Andrew Stewart, 'Employee Loyalty in Australia' (1999) 20 CLLPJ 155.

4 *Hivac Ltd v Park Royal Scientific Instruments Ltd* [1946] 1 All ER 350; accepted in *Tisco Ltd v Communication and Energy Workers Union* [1993] 2 ERNZ 779.

5 *Robb v Green* [1895] 2 QB 315.

6 *Wessex Dairies Ltd v Smith* [1935] 2 KB 80.

7 *Sanders v Parry* [1967] 1 WLR 753.

8 *Sanders* (ibid) was accepted in *Morris v Interchem Agencies* [2003] NZCA 140.

9 *Blyth Chemicals v Bushnell* (1933) 49 CLR 66, 81.

10 *Hivac* (n 4) 174; *Schilling v Kidd Garrett Ltd* [1977] 1 NZLR 243, per Richmond P.

wide range of situations, not all of which have come before the courts. The outcome of any case is uncertain but, as we shall see, it appears that the courts are likely to incline towards the imposition of further constraints[11] and the rules developed to cover specific situations have tended to produce very similar judicial outcomes in all three jurisdictions. For instance, competition with the employer is not allowed but, prior to terminating the employment, limited preparatory steps are permissible.[12] While the courts have acknowledged that the development and application of the law in this area involves striking a balance between the interests of employer and employee,[13] judicial awareness of the existence of competing interests is unlikely to be of great benefit to employees. At its root, the obligation is predicated on the need to protect the employer's interests and, in so doing, impinges on the employee's autonomy and is 'not coterminous with the employee's normal working hours: they govern all the activities of the employee, whenever undertaken, which ... could materially affect the employer's business interests'.[14] For instance, public criticism of the employer, especially on social media, is increasingly recognized as a breach;[15] as are out-of-work commercial activities that annoy an employer's customers.[16]

Expansion of Constraints

In spite of at least one judicial view that 'the law of master and servant should not, in my view, necessarily be extended further in the direction of implying obligations on the part of the servant',[17] the range of obligations continues to expand. This expansion seems little affected by the advent of the obligation of mutual trust and confidence, which has had little impact on the content of the obligation of fidelity, other than to reinforce it. This is contrary to Lord Steyn's proposition in *Malik v Bank of Credit and Commerce International SA* that the 'implied obligation as formulated is apt to cover the great diversity of situations in which a balance has to be struck between an employer's interest in managing his

---

[11] The willingness of the courts to constrain employees, or to extend their employment obligations, was illustrated in *Sim v Rotherham Metropolitan Borough Council* [1987] Ch 216.

[12] *Kidd* (n 10); *Morris* (n 8).

[13] *Vestergaard Frandsen A/S v Bestnet Europe Ltd* [2013] UKSC 31.

[14] *Digital Pulse Pty Ltd v Harris* [2002] NSWSC 33, [21].

[15] See Chapter 8.

[16] *Tisco* (n 4).

[17] *Schindler Lifts* (n 1) 303.

business as he sees fit and the employee's interest in not being unfairly and improperly exploited'.[18]

This proposition might be thought to have had the potential for more general significance and to have led to a central organizing norm, whereby the employment contract takes full account of the fact that the interests of the employer and employee may legitimately diverge. There is nothing to suggest that this has occurred or is likely to do so. Cases such as *Sanders v Parry* remain good law.[19] For example, the New Zealand case of *Morris v Interchem Agencies Ltd* confirmed the rule in *Sanders* and held that, if a client approaches an employee with an offer of employment, the duty of fidelity obliges them to reject that offer of work and report it to the employer to allow the difficulties in the employer-client relationship to be addressed.[20]

The expansion of fidelity-based constraints is also seen, notwithstanding the decision in *Bell v Lever*,[21] in an expanding obligation on managers and senior employees to report a breach of contract on the part of other employees.[22] In the key English case, *Sybron Corporation v Rochem*,[23] it was held that an employee was under no duty to disclose to his employers his own misconduct, but was under a duty to disclose a fraudulent misconduct of subordinate employees, even though that disclosure would have revealed his own misconduct. The court held that, while there is no general duty to report a fellow servant's misconduct, the contract or the terms of employment or the status of the relevant employee may impose such a duty. It may also be the case that, depending on the employee's contractual obligations and so forth, there may be a duty to investigate.[24] It has also been suggested that 'one of the relevant factors will be the nature of the wrongdoing and its potential adverse effect on the company. Where … the alleged wrongdoing went to the very survival of the company, it is more likely that the court would imply a duty to report'.[25] Such a duty may require that the employee

---

[18] *Malik v Bank of Credit and Commerce International SA* [1998] AC 20, 46.

[19] *Sanders* (n 7).

[20] *Morris* (n 8).

[21] *Bell v Lever* [1932] AC 161. *Bell* held that employees do not come under a duty to disclose a breach of contract to their employer.

[22] *Rooney Earthmoving v McTague* [2009] ERNZ 240, (2009) 6 NZELR 774 (EmpC).

[23] *Sybron Corporation v Rochem* [1984] Ch 112.

[24] *RBG Resources v Rastogi* [2002] EWHC 2782 (Ch) [47].

[25] ibid [40].

report on the behaviour of either their superiors or inferiors, although such reporting may not only be futile but may also put the employee's job in peril.[26] *Sybron* has now been accepted as good law in Australia and New Zealand, and judges in both Australia and the United Kingdom have seen some merit in a more fundamental appraisal of the law of disclosure. In *Bank of Credit and Commerce International SA v Ali (No 1)*, Lightman J said:[27]

> there is indeed much to be said for relaxing the rule which exempts employers and employees alike from any duty to disclose to the other their breaches of duty, for disclosure may be essential to enable the other party to take urgent steps to cure, control or mitigate the consequences of such breach: such disclosure may be necessary to protect the other's 'physical, financial and psychological welfare'.

The price of any significant relaxation of the rule may, however, be a high one. A duty on an employee to disclose, for example, that they, or a fellow employee, took a day's sickness leave when not genuinely ill or used the employer's telephone or stationery for private use may be thought intolerable and may require standards that are extravagant and unattainable in the workplace.[28]

From Fidelity to Fiduciary?

The law has not reached the position where an employee is generally regarded as a fiduciary.[29] Notwithstanding this sentiment, however, fiduciary-like standards are increasingly expected of senior employees: 'The more senior the employee the more onerous is the duty of fidelity'.[30] Indeed, the Australian courts have held that a senior employee may owe fiduciary obligations to another company in the same group[31] if the employee is, for all effective purposes, even if not in law, an employee of that company.

One instance of increased responsibility can be found by looking to the application of the obligation of fidelity when 'poaching' of employees is

---

26 ibid [34].

27 *Bank of Credit and Commerce International SA v Ali (No 1)* [1999] ICR 1068, 1082. Subsequent proceedings did not shed any light on this point.

28 See *Hodgson v Barnes* [2012] VSC 94.

29 *Rooney Earthmoving* (n 22) [142]; but see also *Transnet NZ Ltd v Dulhunty Power* [2007] ERNZ 379, [33] (HC).

30 *Morris* (n 8) [45].

31 *Manildra Laboratories v Campbell* [2009] NSWSC 987, [69].

in issue. While an individual is not bound to inform their employer of their own plans to compete with the employer in the future, nor reveal that they have received a job offer from a rival, where the employer's business is threatened by an attempt to 'poach' staff, a manager may be obliged to report that threat to the employer.[32] The obligation to report in *Imam-Sadeque v Bluebay Asset Management* was not triggered by awareness of the misconduct of a colleague, but was implicit in the responsibility assumed by a senior employee who, by virtue of his position in the company, was required to put the employer's interests before his own and combat the threat to the business.[33]

This represents a significant extension of *Sybron* because, as discussed, an individual member of staff need not reveal that they have received a job offer. The Australian courts have confirmed that there is no general obligation on employees to inform their employer that they plan to take up employment with a new employer, and that a failure to do so does not constitute a breach of duty.[34] The New Zealand courts have also been reluctant to follow this expansion of liability and remain unpersuaded that:[35]

> the law has reached a point that the duty includes disclosing either one's own or one's fellow employee's intention to simply leave and compete. To so hold would be to undermine the freedom of movement of employees and be contrary to the authorities which allow preparatory competitive steps to be taken, provided these are not in breach of the obligation not to compete or to damage the employer, whilst the employee is still under the duty of fidelity, trust and confidence. The position of employees who are also directors may well be different.

In *Stoelwinder v Southern Health*, in the context of negotiations over a revised contract of employment, the court considered that it would be inappropriate to impose on the employee a duty of disclosure, as the employer, in such a situation, expects the employee to look after their own interests and it would be 'unjust because the result of imposing the duty would be to unfairly disadvantage the employee in the negotiations'.[36]

---

32 *Bank of Credit and Commerce International SA v Ali (No 1)* [2012] EWHC 3511 (QB).

33 *Imam-Sadeque v Bluebay Asset Management* [2012] EWHC 3511 (QB).

34 *Deeson Heavy Haulage v Cox* [2009] QSC 277.

35 *Rooney Earthmoving* (n 22) [142]; but see also *Transnet NZ* (n 29) [33].

36 *Stoelwinder v Southern Health* [2001] FCA 115, [47].

There is, however, clear scope for confusion regarding the obligations arising from a fiduciary relationship. This is partly a question of the language used. Elias J has referred to:[37]

> the use of potentially ambiguous terminology in describing an employee's obligations, which use may prove a trap for the unwary. There are many cases which have recognised the existence of the employee's duty of good faith, or loyalty, or the mutual duty of trust and confidence – concepts which tend to shade into one another.

It is also the case that the fact that, from time to time, the employee may come under fiduciary obligations may lead to the erroneous assumption that the employment relationship is fiduciary in nature. Matters have become further complicated because of an increasing tendency to accord fiduciary status to senior employees. In the seminal decision in *Canadian Aero Service v O'Malley*, the Canadian Supreme Court approved the view of Gower in his work on company law that fiduciary 'duties, except in so far as they depend on statutory provisions expressly limited to directors, are not so restricted but apply equally to any officials of the company who are authorised to act on its behalf, and in particular to those acting in a senior managerial capacity'.[38]

An individual who is caught by the *O'Malley* doctrine owes the full range of fiduciary duties. In contrast, ordinary employees can come under particular fiduciary duties, depending upon their specific contractual obligations. It is also important to appreciate that the class of employees who can be categorized as senior may be large. The Canadian case law warns us that the adoption of *O'Malley* can result in a very expansive approach, depending upon the definition adopted.[39] Key employees (who are not necessarily senior by any stretch of the imagination) have been held to be fiduciaries, on the basis that the employer is particularly vulnerable to competition upon their departure. It might be thought that such an expansion of obligation is undesirable; in part because the range of employees caught is far from clear, but also, more fundamentally, because the extent to which an employee must favour the employer's interests over their own is radically increased. Nevertheless, *O'Malley*

---

37 *Nottingham University v Fishel* [2000] IRLR 471, 483.

38 *Canadian Aero Service v O'Malley* [1973] 40 DLR (3d) 371, 606; quoting LCB Gower, *Principles of Modern Company Law* (3rd edn, Stevens Publishing 1969) 518.

39 The Australian case law is much less extensive, but early indications again suggest an expansive approach.

appears to be becoming increasingly influential. There is some suggestion that it will be followed in New Zealand,[40] and it has already been accepted in the United Kingdom.[41] The Australian case law is much less extensive, but the courts appear to be following suit as well. In *Hospital Products Ltd v United States Surgical Corporation*,[42] Mason J's suggestion that fiduciary status applied to the employment relationship might have overstated the position, but some decisions do incline to the broader view expressed by him.[43] Subsequent decisions, such as *Investa Properties v Nankervis*, have acknowledged that the *O'Malley* principles are relevant to senior employees.[44] In *Bayley v DBR Australia*, it was said that 'matters relevant to determining whether such a duty exists in any given employer/employee relationship include the following: How much latitude is the employee afforded by the employer and how great is the employer's vulnerability to the potential misuse of the position of power granted to the employee?'[45]

THE EMERGENCE OF MUTUAL TRUST AND CONFIDENCE

In the United Kingdom, one of the most interesting developments in the last 40 years has been the emergence of the implied obligation of mutual trust and confidence; the term emerged from employment tribunal jurisprudence in the late 1970s.[46] It can be seen as the progeny of *Western Excavating v Sharp*, where, in the context of developing the statutory law of constructive dismissal, the Court of Appeal opted for a contractual test rather than one based on reasonableness.[47] This made

---

40 *CE Elley v Wairoa-Harrison* [1987] NZHC 6; *RPD Produce Holdings v Miller* [2013] NZHC 705. See also Rob Batty, 'Examining the Incidence of Fiduciary Duties in Employment' (2012) CanterLawRw 10.

41 *Crowson Fabrics v Rider* [2007] EWHC 2942 (Ch), [2008] IRLR 288.

42 *Hospital Products Ltd v United States Surgical Corporation* [1984] HCA 64.

43 Andrew Frazer, 'The Employee's Contractual Duty of Fidelity' (2015) 131 LQR 53, 70.

44 *Investa Properties v Nankervis* [2015] FCA 1004.

45 *Bayley v DBR Australia* [2013] FCA 1341, [232].

46 The emergence of the term is well told in Bob Hepple, *Hamlyn Lectures – Rights at Work: Global, European and British Perspective* (Sweet & Maxwell 2005); and see Alan Bogg, 'Good Faith in the Contract of Employment: A Case of the English Reserve?' (2011) 32 CLLP 729.

47 *Western Excavating v Sharp* [1978] QB 761.

protection of employees contingent upon the creation of a corpus of implied terms that embodied contemporary expectations of modern employment conditions. The term is predicated on the basis that 'the nature of the contract of employment has been transformed. It has been recognised that a person's employment is usually one of the most important things in their life. It gives not only a livelihood but an occupation, an identity and a sense of self-esteem'.[48] The implied obligation of mutual trust and confidence forms a crucial part of that recognition process, and promotes the dignity and respect of employees. There is said to have 'been a fundamental change in legal culture',[49] given 'the changes which have taken place in the employer–employee relationship, with far greater duties imposed on the employer than in the past, whether by statute or by judicial decision, to care for the physical, financial and even psychological welfare of the employee'.[50]

The New Zealand courts were quick to adopt the term;[51] their Australian counterparts more hesitant. For the sake of clarity, it should be remembered that the term 'mutual trust and confidence' was not new in the employment context and may, for instance, have been synonymous with the implied obligation of fidelity. The old Australian case of *Blyth Chemicals Ltd v Bushnell*, illustrates this.[52]

Blyth Chemicals also invoked notions of cooperation and Hepple built on this skilfully in the United Kingdom by portraying the term as an instance of the traditional duty of cooperation, but crucially repositioning it as a positive version of that obligation.[53] This highly innovative step was, at the same time, aligned to the incremental approach to change favoured by the common law and has helped to facilitate acceptance at the highest judicial level.

---

48 *Johnson v Unisys* [2001] UKHL 13, [2003] 1 AC 518, 539, per Lord Hoffmann.

49 ibid 531, per Lord Steyn.

50 *Spring v Guardian Assurance plc* [1995] 2 AC 296, 335.

51 *Auckland Shop Employees Union v Woolworths (New Zealand) Ltd* [1985] 2 NZLR 372 (CA); and *Marlborough Harbour Board v Goulden* [1985] 2 NZLR 378 (CA).

52 *Blyth Chemicals Ltd v Bushnell* (1933) 49 CLR 66. In *Concut Pty Ltd v Worrell* [2000] HCA 64, [3], Kirby J remarked that the relationship of employer and employee is one 'importing implied duties of loyalty, honesty, confidentiality and mutual trust'. Australian case law also refers to the obligation of fidelity as one of good faith: see *Del Casale v Artedomus* [2007] NSWCA 172.

53 Bob Hepple, *Employment Law* (4th edn, Sweet & Maxwell 1981) 134–5, paras 291–2.

The concept of mutual trust and confidence has also been used traditionally (and continues to be) in deciding whether or not to grant equitable remedies.[54] The absence of mutual trust and confidence, as a matter of fact, went against the granting of an order to compel the employer to continue employment. This position helped to reinforce employer prerogative by, in effect, allowing the employer to determine (or claim) whether confidence still existed. This seems hugely anachronistic. Surprisingly, the relationship between the two lines of case law does not appear to have been judicially considered. The traditional usage looks to see whether, as a matter of fact, there is 'trust and confidence between the parties'; if there is not, then certain consequences may follow. On the other hand, the implied term obliges the parties to behave towards one another in a particular manner; it is prescriptive, rather than descriptive.

The initial reaction to the emergence of the term in Australia was reasonably favourable and, indeed, as time went on, whilst the dicta were by no means all one way, the trend appeared to be inclining towards acceptance.[55] It may be that, as in the United Kingdom, the difficulties posed by the relationship with statute did not become apparent until later. The statutory background did not provide a catalyst in precisely the same way as it had in the United Kingdom, but nevertheless it was 'the advent of statutory unfair dismissal protection that led to a rise in arguments that employees had been "constructively dismissed", and so became entitled to statutory compensation for unfair dismissal'.[56] Australian interest and, on occasion, enthusiasm was fuelled by the belief that the traditional judicial conception of the employment contract was no longer valid. It was said in *Burazin v Blacktown City Guardian*, with reference to *Addis v Gramophone*,[57] that the:[58]

> House of Lords treated contracts of employment as being the same as other commercial contracts, without reference to the interpersonal relationship that employment contracts establish or the fact that a breach of an employment contract, especially by an employer, may have a substantial effect on the other party's emotional well-being and self-esteem.

---

[54] It may well be losing something of its bite: *Australasian Meat Industry Employees' Union v G & K O'Connor Pty Ltd* [2000] FCA 627, [42].

[55] See Andrew Stewart, 'Good Faith: A Necessary Element in Australian Employment Law?' (2011) 32 CLLP 521.

[56] Joellen Riley, 'Siblings but Not Twins: Making Sense of "Mutual Trust" and "Good Faith" in Employment Contracts' (2012) 36 MULR 521.

[57] *Addis v Gramophone* [1909] AC 465.

[58] *Burazin v Blacktown City Guardian* [1996] 142 ALR 144, 148–9.

At the same time, a narrow approach was taken to the question of remedies:

> Although it might seem strange to concede the existence of an implied contractual term but deny its capacity to give rise to liability in damages, it must be remembered that the term is intended to bolster an ongoing relationship. To permit an action for damages during the currency of the employment relationship, it might be argued, would be antithetical to the reason for implying the term.

It might be said, by way of response, that the existence of effective remedies would encourage the parties to behave properly.

The Australian dalliance with mutual trust ended in 2014 when, in *Commonwealth Bank of Australia v Barker*, the High Court ruled that the term did not form part of the common law.[59] A negative response was given to the 'question whether the courts should take it upon themselves, by the development of the common law, to engage in law reform for a better social order'.[60] The High Court noted that the term could be seen as an expression of 'good industrial relations practice, embracing not only the material conditions of employment such as pay and safety, but also the psychological conditions which are essential to the performance by an employee of his or her part of the bargain'.[61] Denial was appropriate, as the term 'depends upon a view of social conditions and desirable social policy that informs a transformative approach to the contract of employment in law'.[62]

In New Zealand, mutual trust and confidence was seen as a very positive development. It was accepted in principle by the Court of Appeal in *Auckland Shop Employees Union v Woolworths (New Zealand) Ltd*[63] and confirmed in *Marlborough Harbour Board v Goulden.*[64] These decisions established mutual trust and confidence in New Zealand, although definitive approval by the Court of Appeal did not occur until *Auckland Electric Power Board v Auckland Provincial District Local*

---

[59] *Commonwealth Bank of Australia v Barker* [2014] HCA 32. On the decision in the court below, see Joellen Riley, 'Mutual Trust and Confidence on Trial: At Last' (2014) 36(1) SydLR 151.

[60] *Barker* (n 59) [324].

[61] ibid [39].

[62] ibid [41].

[63] *Auckland Shop Employees Union v Woolworths (New Zealand) Ltd* [1985] 2 NZLR 372 (CA).

[64] *Marlborough Harbour Board v Goulden* [1985] 2 NZLR 378 (CA).

Authorities Officers IUOW.[65] The employment contract was said to stand apart from other nominate contracts: 'a contract of employment is a special relationship under which workers and employers have mutual obligations of confidence, trust and fair dealing'.[66] One attraction of the term was its reciprocal nature. The traditional obligation of fidelity may be 'concerned with fair dealing and fair work during the existence of a practical working relationship', but the obligation imposed was one sided.[67] In the United Kingdom, concerns with abuse of power (more familiar in the public law arena) had helped to prompt acceptance of the term, and similar reasoning was evident in New Zealand: 'contracts of employment possess characteristics intrinsic to public law. In no other area of the law is the divide between private and public law less marked'.[68] However, the common law is now of limited relevance, as the Employment Relations Act 2000 (NZ) ensured that the employment relationship was underpinned by a statutory concept of good faith.[69] New Zealand now presents a picture of limited common law development, despite the jurisdiction being very much in the vanguard so far as acceptance of mutual trust and confidence is concerned. It is useful to bear in mind that it is a matter of complete irrelevance to an employee whether protection comes from statute or the common law. It is worth noting, however, that the Employment Relations Act was amended in 2004 to strengthen the good faith provisions, following two Court of Appeal decisions that gave a restricted reading to the original formulation.[70] Section 3 of the Act now provides that:

> The object of this Act is –
>
> (a) to build productive employment relationships through the promotion of good faith in all aspects of the employment environment and of the employment relationship –

---

[65] *Auckland Electric Power Board v Auckland Provincial District Local Authorities Officers IUOW* [1994] 2 NZLR 415. See also Anderson (n 3).

[66] *Principal of Auckland College of Education v Hogg* [1997] 2 NZLR 537, 552.

[67] *Kidd* (n 10) 256.

[68] *Aoraki v McGavin* [1998] 3 NZLR 276, 306.

[69] See Gordon Anderson, 'Transplanting Good Faith into New Zealand Labour Law: The Experience under the Employment Relations Act 2000' (2002) 9(3) MurUJEL 40.

[70] *Coutts Cars Ltd v Baguley* [2002] 2 NZLR 533; *Auckland City Council v New Zealand Public Service Assoc* [2003] 2 ERNZ 386; and see Anderson (n 3).

(i) by recognising that employment relationships must be built not only on the implied mutual obligations of trust and confidence, but also on a legislative requirement for good faith behaviour; and
(ii) by acknowledging and addressing the inherent inequality of power in employment relationships; …

This is reinforced by section 4, which requires that the parties 'deal with each other in good faith' and provides that the obligation of good faith requires parties in an employment relationship not to do anything, whether directly or indirectly, to mislead each other, or that is likely to mislead or deceive each other. Section 4 also states that the duty of good faith requires parties in an employment relationship to be active and constructive in maintaining an employment relationship in which the parties are responsive and communicative.

In the United Kingdom, the way in which the law of constructive dismissal developed played a big part in the emergence of mutual trust and confidence. In Australia and New Zealand, the stimulus tended to stem from a general recognition that the way the judges viewed the employment relationship was out of date. This more enlightened approach has perhaps been most cogently expressed in Canada: 'work is one of the most fundamental aspects in a person's life, providing the individual with a means of financial support and, as importantly, a contributory role in society. A person's employment is an essential component of his or her identity, self-worth, and emotional well-being'.[71] A key element in the change in attitude has been the recognition of the realities of employment relations, where it is almost always the case that there is a gross imbalance of power between the parties. A recent instance is the Canadian case of *Potter v New Brunswick*, where, in the context of a constructive dismissal claim, it was said that:[72]

> When faced with a unilateral change by the employer, the employee is placed in the unenviable situation of having to decide whether to accept the change or to resign and bring an action for constructive dismissal … This life-altering decision must be made in circumstances in which the information available to the employee is limited and there is an imbalance of power between the employer and the employee.

---

[71] *Reference Re Public Service Employee Relations Act (Alta)* [1987] 1 SCR 313, 368.

[72] *Potter v New Brunswick* [2015] 1 SCR 500, [66].

COMMONALITY

The foregoing section has revealed a number of significant differences between the three jurisdictions, but developments in all three also display interesting elements of commonality. It is suggested that the extent and strength of convergence provides a means of predicting how the common law will develop. It is apparent that, in all jurisdictions, procedural fairness is a core value. Thus, in New Zealand, mutual trust was seen as 'an application of natural justice to contemporary industrial relations'.[73] As a result, employers were obliged 'if conducting an inquiry into possible dishonesty by an employee, to carry out the inquiry in a fair and reasonable manner'.[74] In the United Kingdom, mutual trust has, from the earliest cases, displayed real affinities with natural justice.[75] *Gogay v Hertfordshire County Council*, in the context of allegations of child abuse, held that the punitive exercise of prerogative powers may be a breach of mutual trust in the absence of due process; the employer would not have lost in that case had they taken the trouble to establish that there was reasonable cause to suspend.[76] The commitment to procedural fairness is less evident in Australia. That said, it features strongly where employees can look to administrative law,[77] and *Russell v The Trustees of the Roman Catholic Church* suggested that a defect in process could constitute a breach of a term of mutual trust and confidence. The claimant's employment was terminated following an investigation into a complaint concerning his involvement in sexual misconduct. The claimant argued that the employer breached the implied terms of good faith and mutual trust and confidence by the manner of their investigation. No breach arose where the employer conducted a telephone interview of a principal witness rather than face-to-face: 'While a telephone interview may not be the best means of assessing credibility, the facts that Mr X lived on the other side of the country and was a police officer were material considerations in determining how to proceed'.[78] In *Hem, Re Coulco Trading Pty Ltd v Cant*, the employee was accused by his superior of being a thief, without justification.[79] The court accepted that

---

[73] *Auckland Shop Employees Union v Woolworths* [1985] 2 NZLR 372, 376.

[74] ibid.

[75] *Robinson v Crompton Parkinson* [1978] IRLR 6.

[76] *Gogay v Hertfordshire County Council* [2000] IRLR 703.

[77] *Jarratt v Commissioner of Police* (2005) 224 CLR 44.

[78] *Russell v The Trustees of the Roman Catholic Church* [2008] NSWCA 217, [37].

[79] *Hem, Re Coulco Trading Pty Ltd v Cant* [2007] FCA 81.

such conduct could constitute constructive dismissal, because it constituted conduct inconsistent with the mutual trust required for the employment relationship. It is difficult to resist the view that: 'Insistence on procedural fairness ... assists to protect the employee against the abuse or arbitrary exercise of the power in the hands of the employer'.[80] The consistency with which procedural fairness is imposed through the medium of mutual trust points towards it being a core value of the employment contract. Its centrality is not, however, contingent upon the existence of mutual trust, but finds expression through other common law devices and 'there are few, if any, relationships of employment, public or private, to which the requirements of fairness have no application whatever. Very clear statutory or contractual language would be necessary to exclude this elementary duty'.[81]

One might go on to argue that a relationship of mutual trust and confidence would militate against 'snatching a bargain'. A strong relationship is unlikely to emerge if the terms of the exchange are weighted heavily in favour of one side and the weaker party considers themselves exploited. There are no indications, however, that the traditional common law rules on unconscionability have been altered, or are likely to be.[82] This is despite the fact that the advent of mutual trust has thrown the issue into focus. In *Aoraki v McGavin*, the issue was whether the application of mutual trust could require the employer to pay redundancy compensation when none was provided for in the employment contract.[83] Whilst the answer was in the negative, attention was drawn to the 'manifest desire of the Tribunal and the Employment Court to secure fair treatment of such employees, particularly in the present climate engendered by restructuring and extensive dismissals, where redundancy payments have become commonplace in the major undertakings affected'.[84] The outcome in *Aoraki* is a sensible one, as deciding what constitutes fair terms is a task of such magnitude and complexity that legislative intervention would be required. However, the case is perhaps more notable for its strong endorsement of managerial prerogative and its restrictive approach to mutual trust and confidence.[85]

---

80 *Aoraki Corporation Ltd v McGavin* [1998] 3 NZLR 276, 305.
81 *Marlborough Harbour Board v Goulden* [1996] 1 NZLR 484, 492.
82 This issue is explored more fully in Chapter 6.
83 *Aoraki v McGavin* [1998] 3 NZLR 276.
84 ibid 289.
85 *Aoraki* (n 83); and see also *Brighouse Ltd v Bilderbeck* [1995] 1 NZLR 158.

Mutual trust is a default rule, and the possibility of contracting-out therefore arises. The judiciary have tended to view this prospect with disfavour, but have been reticent to prohibit exclusion on the basis of public policy. In the United Kingdom, this is at odds with the position taken in trade union membership cases, where the courts do not allow trade unions to disapply the rules of natural justice.[86] Writing extra-judicially, Lord Bingham said that attempts may 'be made to relax the obligations by express terms set out in a contract of employment, but I would not expect such terms to be sympathetically interpreted'.[87] Given that mutual trust put down such shallow roots in Australia, it is not surprising that there was little judicial discussion of the issue, but *Russell v Trustees of the Roman Catholic Church* approached the question of contracting-out from the premise that the implied obligation is an incident of the employment relationship: 'As a consequence, the duty not to destroy that relationship is a duty that cannot be excluded contractually, without changing the relationship to something other than employment'.[88] The soundness of this highly creative solution was never tested before the demise of the term in *Barker*, though the Supreme Court decision in *Autoclenz v Belcher* might be thought to lend support.[89] It may be contended that a clause that purports to exclude mutual trust in a contract that would otherwise be classified as one of employment should be set aside, as it is incompatible with the nature of the contract: 'the written contract does not represent the actual terms agreed'.[90] Mutual trust and confidence is an obligation which is fundamental to the employment relationship and expresses the essence of the bargain, and an attempt to set up an employment relationship without the term should be held to be a sham. In New Zealand, statute has intervened and this presents, by far and wide, the most effective solution.

---

[86] Douglas Brodie, 'Beyond Exchange: The New Contract of Employment' (1998) 27(2) ILJ 79.

[87] Tom Bingham, 'From Servant to Employee: A Study of the Common Law in Action' (2001) 13 Singapore Academy of Law Journal 253, 266; and see also Chief Judge Goddard in *Walden v Barrance* [1996] 2 ERNZ 598, 615 (EmpC).

[88] *Russell v Trustees of the Roman Catholic Church* (2008) 72 NSWLR 559, [127]–[128].

[89] *Autoclenz v Belcher* [2011] UKSC 41, [2011] ICR 1157. See also Alan Bogg, 'Sham Self-Employment in the Supreme Court' (2012) 41 ILJ 328.

[90] *Autoclenz* (n 89) [34]; quoting Aikens LJ in the Court of Appeal: *Autoclenz v Belcher* [2009] EWCA Civ 1046, [91].

The Role of Statute

Statute may act as a catalyst for common law expansion, though it may function as a constraint; it can also serve to consolidate or underpin judicial legislation. In the United Kingdom and Australia, the existence of a general scheme of statutory protection against unfair dismissal has served to ensure that the manner of dismissal remains beyond common law scrutiny. Had the common law been allowed to develop naturally, matters might have been different, as the majority in *Air New Zealand v Raddock* recognized:[91]

> we are content to leave open the possibility of a claim, for example where the right has been exercised in an unacceptable and damaging way, such as in a public and humiliating announcement of a notice of termination, designed to cause distress to the employee. There is a distinction to be drawn between the method of exercising a contractual right and the fact of exercising it.

In *Johnson v Unisys*, the essence of the claim was that a dismissal without a fair hearing constituted a breach of the implied term of mutual trust and confidence. The House of Lords was concerned that deciding in favour of the claimant would undermine the statutory scheme:[92]

> A newly developed common law right of this nature, covering the same ground as the statutory right, would fly in the face of the limits Parliament has already prescribed on matters such as the classes of employees who have the benefit of the statutory right, the amount of compensation payable and the short time limits for making claims.

It is notable that those concerns are premised on the basis that the mooted common law right would cover 'the same ground as the statutory right'[93] However, the claim was much more modest in scope and, once this is recognized, it may be doubted whether the concerns expressed carried much weight.[94] Prior to *Barker*, the Australian courts had followed the approach taken in *Johnson*.[95]

There are significant differences between the respective legislative schemes, but they do not make it any easier to justify a restrictive approach. Riley has argued that the Australian provisions 'do not

---

[91] *Air New Zealand v Raddock* [1999] 2 NZLR 641, 647.
[92] *Johnson* (n 48) 526.
[93] ibid.
[94] However, see Alan Bogg, 'Common Law and Statute in the Law of Employment' (2017) 69 CLP 67.
[95] *New South Wales v Paige* [2002] NSWCA 235.

expressly or even impliedly constrain the jurisdiction of courts of common law and equity in determining contract disputes'.[96] She has argued that the scheme is not directed to curtailing the employee's common law rights, but to the maintenance of minimum standards for low and middle income dismissed employees. It may be said that, if anything, the Australian courts are more reluctant to develop the common law in an age of extensive legislative intervention in employment relations. It might be argued that the Australian courts are unduly anxious to defer to the legislature, but it is probably fairer to say that the sheer extent of legislative intervention has inhibited the common law from regulating employment relations to a greater extent:[97]

> The common law in Australia must evolve within the limits of judicial power and not trespass into the province of legislative action. This Court and, to a lesser extent, intermediate appeal courts have a law-making function. That function can only be exercised as an incident of the adjudication of particular disputes.

The *Johnson* exclusion zone has given rise to difficult boundary issues. Nevertheless, of late, in *Edwards v Chesterfield Royal Hospital*, the Supreme Court extended the reasoning in *Johnson* in order that it should serve as a bar to a claim for damages by an employee for loss arising from the unfair manner of their dismissal in breach of an express term of their employment contract.[98]

The position in New Zealand illustrates a further form of interaction between common law and statute. In *Coutts Cars v Baguley*, against the backdrop of the enactment of the Employment Relations Act 2000 (NZ), the Court of Appeal did 'not see that the new statutory obligation on employers and employees to deal with each other in good faith introduces any significantly different obligation to that the courts have placed upon parties to employment contracts over recent years'.[99] This stance was regarded as too timid by the legislature, and in 2004 the Act was amended to make clear that the statutory concept of good faith was a broader concept than mutual trust and confidence.[100] The practical consequences have been described by Anderson in the following terms:[101]

---

[96] Joellen Riley, *Employee Protection at Common Law* (Federation Press 2005) 87, 92.

[97] *Barker* (n 59) [19].

[98] *Edwards v Chesterfield Royal Hospital* [2011] UKSC 58, [2012] AC 22.

[99] *Coutts Cars v Baguley* [2002] 2 NZLR 533, [42].

[100] Anderson (n 3) 711.

[101] ibid 720–21.

> that the personal grievance procedures provide the most likely cause of action for employees and the most effective remedies for employees it is here that the general good faith duty is likely to have its greatest impact. What does seem clear is that the duty has served to significantly reinforce the rights of employees raising a personal grievance. The courts have made it clear that good faith, including the clear consultation rights, is an essential component of justification. It is also likely that the right of employees to be consulted, including to be provided with proper information, will lead employers to make properly reasoned decisions. A failure to do so will be more apparent and hence the legal risk of a successful employee challenge greater.

The New Zealand approach is highly satisfactory; whilst mutual trust and confidence continues to flourish in the United Kingdom – the *Johnson* 'exclusion zone' aside – statutory embodiment and enhancement cannot be bettered.

The Limits of Statutory Constraint

The approaches of the courts in both the United Kingdom and Australia are similar in dealing with the interaction of common law and statute, although the Australian courts are perhaps more deferential to Parliament, given the greater extent of legislative intervention. In the United Kingdom, there has been a clear determination to ensure that the impact of the *Johnson* 'exclusion zone' does not impact on the development of the term more widely. Prior to *Barker*, there were indications that the Australian courts were taking the same view. Both systems seemed to accept that other aspects of the disciplinary process should remain subject to mutual trust, but if termination were to eventuate the employer's prerogative in respect of that decision would not be constrained. In *King v University of St Andrews*, the employer gave the pursuer notice of termination of the employment contract; prior to this, there had been hearings of a disciplinary nature.[102] The pursuer maintained that the obligation of mutual trust and confidence applied to the process of investigation and evaluation of the allegations against him. Lady Smith allowed the claim to go to trial. Counsel for the employee had submitted that *Johnson* could be distinguished on the basis that the alleged breach of the implied term related to the carrying-out of the investigations that preceded the decision to dismiss: 'a decision to dismiss and a decision to invoke an element of the disciplinary process are different in kind. This is because, during the operation of the employer's disciplinary procedures, the employer would

---

102 *King v University of St Andrews* [2002] IRLR 252.

have to have it as much in mind that the employee might remain in his employment as that he might not'.[103] As a result, if there:[104]

> was a decision not to dismiss then the implied duty of trust and confidence would obviously apply to the continuation of the ongoing working relationship between employer and employee. It is hard then to see how and why, bearing in mind the purpose of the implication of the duty, it should be regarded as suspended whilst the employer carries out the critically important task of assessing whether good cause for dismissal has been shown. For an employer to act in breach of that duty during an assessment which has the potential either to reinforce or to terminate the contract of employment would clearly be highly destructive of and damaging to the relationship between them.

Johnson makes clear that mutual trust does not apply to dismissal, but accepts that it would be unfortunate if 'fair dealing' was not required in respect of discipline and suspension. In Australia, *Rogan-Gardiner v Woolworths (No 2)* was to similar effect, but made clear that, before damages could be awarded, it would be necessary to identify an actionable breach that occurred independently of the termination of the contract.[105] An employee bringing an action on the basis of a right that has accrued prior to dismissal will often have difficult issues of causation to overcome.

THE FUTURE

This chapter now turns to look at what the future holds for mutual trust and, more widely, terms of the good faith variety. A number of specific issues will be examined, but particular focus will be given to the increasing role that norms of good faith and fair dealing are playing in the law of contract in general.

Doctrinal Considerations: the Basis for Implication

In the United Kingdom, policy considerations inform the creation of default rules or terms implied in law. There is now acceptance that 'to

---

[103] ibid 255.

[104] ibid. In his dissenting judgment in *Johnson* (n 48) 536–7, Lord Steyn said that mutual trust 'aims to ensure fair dealing between employer and employee, and that is as important in respect of disciplinary proceedings, suspension of an employee and dismissal as at any other stage of the employment relationship'.

[105] *Rogan-Gardiner v Woolworths (No 2)* [2010] WASC 290.

some extent at least, the existence and scope of standardized implied terms raise questions of reasonableness, fairness and the balancing of competing policy considerations'.[106] This has been clear since the decision of the House of Lords in *Liverpool City Council v Irwin*,[107] a decision that met with the approval of the High Court in *Byrne v Australian Airlines Ltd*.[108] This has allowed the courts, in cases like *Scally*[109] and *Watters v Commissioner of Police*,[110] to take greater account of the interests of employees and reflect the judicial conception of a modern employment relationship. In *Scally*, a contract negotiated by trade unions conferred on an employee a valuable right, contingent on him taking up the right in a prescribed manner. He was unaware of the right. The House of Lords held that there was an obligation implied by law as an incident of a contract of employment, as opposed to implied in fact, to bring the term to the notice of the employee. In New Zealand, the Court of Appeal in *Attorney-General v New Zealand Post-Primary Teachers' Assoc*,[111] in response to an argument that terms were more easily implied in the employment law context, held that no different approach was to be applied to the implication of terms in collective or individual employment contracts than was applicable to other contracts. This position has been reinforced in a number of subsequent cases. However, the courts do seem to apply some flexibility in approach. Applying the *Post-Primary Teachers'* case, the Employment Court has held that an implied term that the defendant would act reasonably in dealing with a sexual harassment complaint was 'so obvious that it goes without saying'. Further, it was held that the term was easily implied from a policy of the defendant that recognized the detrimental effect that such harassment could have on job satisfaction.[112] In *Everist v McEvedy*,[113] the High Court declined to imply a term that a staff solicitor was entitled to the benefit of the firm's professional liability insurance. It

---

[106] *Crossley v Faithful and Gould Holdings Ltd* [2004] EWCA Civ 293. In *Societe Generale, London Branch v Geys* [2012] UKSC 63, [2013] 1 AC 523, [56], Lady Hale endorsed this dictum: 'There is much to be said for that approach, given the way in which those terms have developed over the years'.

[107] *Liverpool City Council v Irwin* [1977] AC 239.

[108] *Byrne v Australian Airlines Ltd* (1995) 185 CLR 410.

[109] *Scally v Southern Health and Social Services Board* [1992] 1 AC 294.

[110] *Watters v Commissioner of Police* [2000] ICR 1064.

[111] *Attorney-General v New Zealand Post-Primary Teachers' Assoc* [1992] 2 NZLR 209 (CA). The facts of this case are unusual in that the alleged term concerned would have required a continuation of government expenditure.

[112] *N v Attorney-General* [2000] 1 ERNZ 717 (EmpC).

[113] *Everist v McEvedy* [1996] 3 NZLR 348 (HC).

did, however, hold that such a term arose on the different ground of being customary in the profession, unless specifically excluded.

Of late, there has been a significant change of position in Australia, as the rejection of mutual trust in *Barker* went hand in hand with the view that a test of necessity applies to implied terms in law as well as in fact.[114] It is important to note that the test was absent from some early decisions like *Burazin*.[115] This conservative position makes it much less likely that the courts will take on board policy concerns in developing the common law. More specifically, modern conceptions of the employment contract may be disregarded. It may not be easy to establish that implication is justified (particularly in the case of a modern detailed employment contract):[116]

> For obvious reasons the courts are slow to imply a term. In many cases, what the parties have actually agreed upon represents the totality of their willingness to agree; each may be prepared to take his chance in relation to an eventuality for which no provision is made. The more detailed and comprehensive the contract the less ground there is for supposing that the parties have failed to address their minds to the question at issue. And then there is the difficulty of identifying with any degree of certainty the term which the parties would have settled upon had they considered the question.

A note of caution is warranted, as one should be careful about placing too much significance on the basis of implication. Rather than viewing the different tests as conceptually distinct, it may make more sense to regard them as lying on a spectrum. In *Irwin*, Lord Wilberforce said that there are 'varieties of implications which the courts think fit to make and they do not necessarily involve the same process'.[117] He went on to acknowledge that the necessity test can be applied from a policy operated perspective, which involves a judicial search 'based on wider considerations, for such a term as the nature of the contract might call for'.[118] In the case of the employment contract, implication may not be necessary to allow the contract merely to function, but will be essential if it is to operate in a civilized way: 'These considerations are testimony to the

114 See Gabrielle Golding, 'Terms Implied by Law into Employment Contracts: Are They Necessary?'(2015) 28 AJLL 113.

115 Adrian Brooks, 'The Good and Considerate Employer' (2001) 20 UTas LR 2, 42.

116 *Codelfa Construction Pty Ltd v State Rail Authority of New South Wales* [1982] HCA 24, [6].

117 *Irwin* (n 107) 253.

118 ibid 255.

need for implied terms in contracts of employment protecting employees from harsh and unacceptable employment practices'.[119]

Reciprocity

Mutual trust is said to be a reciprocal obligation. It differs in this respect from some traditional obligations such as fidelity, which are inherently one sided. This dimension of the obligation appears to be contributing to an increase in the obligations borne by the employee. In New Zealand, it may have stimulated an expansion of the employee's obligation of fidelity. In *Tisco*, it was said that any:[120]

> conduct by an employee which is likely to damage the employer's business, for instance by impairing its goodwill, or to undermine significantly the trust which the employer is entitled to place in the employee, could constitute a breach of duty. The duty of fidelity and good faith carries with it a duty not to undermine the relationship of trust and confidence.

It is striking just how expansive this definition is. It bestows a very extensive discretion on the courts to extend the employee's obligations as they see fit. It is worth recalling that, historically, the obligation of fidelity has, in effect, amounted to a number of related but specific duties. The open-textured nature of mutual trust has led to employers in the United Kingdom coming under obligations in an extensive range of situations. In New Zealand, *Tisco*'s conflation of fidelity with mutual trust and confidence has had a similar impact on employees.

In the United Kingdom, mutual trust 'adds little to the employee's implied obligations to serve his employer loyally and not to act contrary to his employer's interests. The major importance of the implied duty of trust and confidence lies in its impact on the obligations of the employer'.[121] Instances of mutual trust, as such, increasing the burden on the employee are hard to find.[122] That said, particularly where senior employees are concerned, there has been considerable judicial activism to

---

[119] *Johnson* (n 48) 532.

[120] *Tisco* (n 4).

[121] *Malik and Mahmud v Bank of Credit and Commerce International SA* [1998] AC 20, 46, per Lord Steyn.

[122] In *Williams v Leeds United* [2015] EWHC 376 (QB), a breach arose on the part of a claimant who had used his work email to send a junior female employee an email with an attachment containing a number of obscene and pornographic photographs.

extend the duties owed.[123] Where disclosure is concerned, for example, an employee in a managerial position may come under a more extensive obligation than their colleagues; what is seen as incidental to the contract of employment may vary depending upon the employee's place in the structure of the organization.[124] Again, where the implied obligation of fidelity is concerned, more is now expected of senior employees than their junior counterparts. Much more radically, as we saw earlier in this chapter, the courts in Australia and England are moving towards the position adopted in Canada on the fiduciary status of senior employees.

Equitable Orders

The emergence of mutual trust serves to cast doubt on the traditional conception of mutual trust that is relevant to the granting of equitable orders. In *Nguyen v Vietnamese Community in Australia*, the Full Bench noted that the 'most common argument advanced in support of the proposition that reinstatement is inappropriate is the proposition, variously expressed, that there has been a loss of trust and confidence such that it would not be feasible to re-establish the employment relationship'.[125] Such arguments still tend to prevail in the United Kingdom, even though they might be thought to contradict the underlying rationale of mutual trust, which, by obliging the parties to behave well, seeks to engender a more trusting relationship as a matter of fact.[126] It is not, then, open to either side to opt out of a relationship constituted on that basis. The Australian courts have adopted a much more progressive position on this point than their United Kingdom counterparts:[127]

> Trust and confidence is a necessary ingredient in any employment relationship ... So we accept that the question whether there has been a loss of trust and confidence is a relevant consideration in determining whether reinstatement is impracticable, provided that such loss of trust and confidence is soundly and rationally based. In most cases, the employment relationship is capable of withstanding some friction and doubts. Trust and confidence are concepts of degree. It is rare for any human being to have total trust in another. What is important in the employment relationship is that there be sufficient trust to make the relationship viable and productive. Whether that standard is reached

---

123 See the discussion in this chapter at p 115.

124 *Sybron v Rochem* [1983] ICR 801.

125 *Nguyen v Vietnamese Community in Australia* [2014] FWCFB 7198. See also *Perkins v Grace Worldwide (Aust) Pty Ltd* (1997) 72 IR 186, 191.

126 Compare *Anderson v Pringle of Scotland* [1998] IRLR 64.

127 *Perkins* (n 125) 191.

> in any particular case must depend upon the circumstances of the particular case. And in assessing that question, it is appropriate to consider the rationality of any attitude taken by a party.

This approach is consistent with the implied obligation of mutual trust and also makes sense, given the realities of contemporary working life. It is:[128]

> difficult to say that a relationship of mutual confidence must exist in the case of every person employed by a large corporate enterprise. There are many occupations in such enterprises where the precise identity of the employee performing a particular job is immaterial to the collective management of the corporation.

FROM MUTUAL TRUST TO GOOD FAITH AND FAIR DEALING

In the United Kingdom, it is probably fair to say that the obligation of mutual trust and confidence is an obligation of the good faith type. There has been some suggestion that the Australian position is radically different, as it was said by the Court of Appeal in *Downer EDI Ltd v Gillies* that 'it seems to me that the duty imposed on a party to act in good faith is a duty that is fundamentally different from the mutual trust duty'.[129] However, this view was predicated upon the assumption that mutual trust could not apply to termination, whereas good faith might. There is, in principle, no reason at common law why mutual trust could not regulate termination. It has not been allowed to do so, given concerns that statute might be undermined. It should be said that *Johnson* and *Paige*[130] would have been decided in exactly the same way, had they been pled as good faith cases. It has, however, been claimed that the duties differ in nature in the following way: 'The duty to act in good faith is a duty imposed upon the manner in which a party exercises its rights under the contract and may apply to termination. The mutual trust duty is a substantive duty that applies independently of the express rights under

---

128 *Turner v Australasian Coal & Shale Employees Federation* (1984) 55 ALR 635, 648.

129 *Downer EDI Ltd v Gillies* [2011] NSWSC 1055, [204]. Compare *Russell v The Trustees of the Roman Catholic Church for the Archdiocese of Sydney* [2008] NSWCA 217, [32].

130 *Paige* (n 95); *Johnson* (n 47).

the contract'.[131] This is unconvincing as a basis of distinction, as it fails to recognize that mutual trust has more than one function – one of which is to regulate the exercise of discretionary powers.[132] It is, perhaps, understandable why the obligations would be viewed as distinct. At least in original conception, the obligation of mutual trust and confidence was employment focused. Whilst obligations of good faith have become increasingly prevalent in Australian contract law, it is fair to say that the two branches of law developed independently of one another. In New Zealand, *Bobux Marketing v Raynor Marketing* pointed against the establishment of a general duty of good faith, but this is of limited importance, given the Employment Relations Act 2000 (NZ).[133]

Matters are further complicated by the fact that, prior to *Barker*, some Australian decisions conflated the concepts of good faith and mutual trust.[134] Again, this is not surprising, as mutual trust can be depicted as an instance of good faith, which has been configured for deployment in the employment context.

In the United Kingdom, it appears that mutual trust and good faith have entered into a process of convergence; as a result, as notions of good faith become more pervasive at common law, the distinctiveness of the obligation of trust and confidence may become diminished. In *Braganza v BP*, Lord Neuberger found 'it difficult to accept that trust and confidence would require more than what in a normal commercial context would be expected' where discretion will be 'limited, as a matter of necessary implication, by concepts of honesty, good faith, and genuineness, and the need for the absence of arbitrariness, capriciousness, perversity and irrationality'.[135] In Australia, outside the employment contract, good faith is playing an increasing role in the law of contract. The position remains uncertain in the absence of an authoritative judgment from the High Court, although it may be that a general obligation of good faith will be recognized at the highest level and compensate for the absence of mutual trust or even prove to be more significant. In *Barker*, it was said that:[136]

---

131 *Gillies* (n 129) [205].

132 *United Bank v Akhtar* [1989] IRLR 507.

133 *Bobux Marketing v Raynor Marketing* [2002] 1 NZLR 506.

134 Sometimes they were both pleaded: Joellen Riley, 'Siblings but Not Twins: Making Sense of "Mutual Trust" and "Good Faith" in Employment Contracts' (2012) 36(2) MULR 521.

135 *Braganza v BP* [2015] UKSC 17, [104].

136 *Barker* (n 59) [42].

> The above conclusion should not be taken as reflecting upon the question whether there is a general obligation to act in good faith in the performance of contracts. Nor does it reflect upon the related question whether contractual powers and discretions may be limited by good faith and rationality requirements analogous to those applicable in the sphere of public law.

Australian cases since then suggest that, the caution expressed in the foregoing dictum notwithstanding, the courts will regulate discretionary powers in the employment context on the basis of fair dealing. The results will often be similar, if not identical. The compensatory function of good faith is demonstrated by decisions that have arisen since *Barker*, such as the bonus case of *Murphy v Westpac Banking Corporation*:[137]

> This was a bargained for bonus to be assessed against set objectives. Such a clause should receive a reasonable construction and not permit the appellant to choose arbitrarily or capriciously or unreasonably that it need not pay money the set objectives having been satisfied ... The discretion is to be exercised honestly and conformably with the purposes of the contract.

Key elements of the employer's prerogative, such as the power to unilaterally vary contractual terms, will therefore remain subject to judicial regulation.[138] The court in *Murphy* was at pains to stress that the position adopted was not contingent upon judicial recognition of an implied obligation of good faith. It should be said that the obligation in *Murphy* would go towards the establishment of the latter obligation if the courts wished to synthesize related developments in this way; the decision can readily be viewed as an instance of good faith. Prior to *Barker*, the Full Court in *Walker v Citigroup Global Markets Pty Ltd* declined to decide whether a term of good faith applied to employment contracts.[139] Since *Barker*, it remains a real possibility that some obligation of the good faith type will be part of the law of the employment contract.

Mutual trust and confidence is an employment-orientated obligation, whose significance may diminish as norms of good faith and fair dealing become more dominant in contract law as a whole. This need not be a cause of concern for employees. The scope for good faith to act as a

---

[137] *Murphy v Westpac Banking Corporation* [2014] FCA 1104 (14 October 2014), [732]; quoting *Silverbrook Research Pty Ltd v Lindley* [2010] NSWCA 357, [5]–[6].

[138] Earlier cases, such as *Riverwood International Australia Pty Ltd v McCormick* (2000) 177 ALR 193, would appear to remain good law.

[139] *Walker v Citigroup Global Markets Pty Ltd* [2006] FCAFC 101.

force for change is huge, as recent Canadian developments show. In Canada, the Supreme Court in *Bhasin v Hrynew* recognized that good faith constitutes an overarching principle in the general law of contract, which allows more specific developments within the employment contract to be mainstreamed.[140] Thus, the obligation on the employer in Canada (emerging from cases such as *Shah v Xerox Canada*) to treat an employee with civility, decency, respect and dignity can be seen as an instance of good faith and is rendered more secure as a result.[141] The centrality of good faith also entrenches common law restrictions on the exercise of discretion conferred on one party by a contract. The Canadian courts take the view that, as a corollary of the general organizing principle of good faith, a common law duty arises, which requires that discretionary powers granted under a contract be exercised fairly and reasonably and not in a manner that is capricious or arbitrary.[142] Good faith serves as a means of rationalization of the existing law, but also functions as a powerful catalyst:[143]

> The application of the organizing principle of good faith to particular situations should be developed where the existing law is found to be wanting and where the development may occur incrementally in a way that is consistent with the structure of the common law of contract and gives force for change due weight to the importance of private ordering and certainty in commercial affairs.

A law of contract where good faith played a central role would undoubtedly prompt further evolution in the law of the employment contract and lead to the sort of specific changes that materialize through the adoption of mutual trust. For instance, in the United Kingdom, *Scally* modified the law on provision of information, and *Bhasin* might be thought to have taken Canadian law closer to a general requirement of disclosure, but the courts have not yet gone this far.[144] The Canadian case of *Trillium Motor World v General Motors* suggests that disclosure would be more likely to be required where a relationship of employment or franchise is concerned.[145] The scope for a general obligation of good faith to enhance the content of the employment contract is almost without

---

[140] *Bhasin v Hrynew* [2014] 3 SCR 494.

[141] *Evans v Avalon Ford Sales (1996) Ltd* 2015 NLTD(G) 100; *Shah v Xerox Canada Ltd* [2000] OJ No 849 (QL).

[142] *Bell Canada v Unifor* [2014] CanLII 63107.

[143] *Rodd v Alberta Health Services* 2015 ABQB 320, [66].

[144] *2176693 v Cora Franchise* (2015) ONSC 1265.

[145] *Trillium Motor World v General Motors* (2015) ONSC 3824.

limit. An underlying norm of good faith can (like mutual trust) serve as a fundamental canon of interpretation. *Styles v Alberta Investment Management Corporation* addressed the not uncommon situation of the impact of dismissal on ancillary elements of the remuneration package, such as a bonus or income protection scheme.[146] In *Styles*, the claimant had been made an award under an incentive scheme, but was not entitled to payment until a later date. The employer dismissed the claimant before that date arose and sought to argue that the right to payment fell through, as the contract stipulated that the employee must be employed at the date of payment. The court found for the employee on the basis that, although the employer had the right to terminate without cause and thereby determine the composition of its workforce, it could not do so in a manner that unfairly undermined the legitimate contractual interests of the employee. In particular, the court could control the employer's discretion to prevent an unfair expropriation of the employee's compensation, upon which the employment contract was based and for which the employer had already received a benefit:[147]

> It is not fair for the employer to take the benefit of the employee's hard work and then exercise a discretion which has the effect of depriving the employee of the compensation earned for that hard work. When the exercise of the employer's discretionary contractual power to terminate without cause is combined with the exercise of the discretion to deny the employee of any LTIP grants, the resulting deprivation of LTIP benefits previously awarded to and approved for the Plaintiff employee is unfair; and, given the inexplicable or unjustifiable nature of the deprivation outside the framework of discretion, appears to be arbitrary.

In the United Kingdom, mutual trust has become, in practical terms, entrenched relatively quickly, though, given its status as a default rule, there remains a possibility that the employer may seek to contract-out. By way of contrast, the Canadian experience suggests that the centrality of good faith leads much more directly and decisively to a prohibition on contracting-out.[148]

Good faith has the capacity to tackle other fundamental issues, including those going to the duration of the relationship. *Data & Scientific v Oracle* flags the possibility that the scope of fair dealing might extend to regulating the employer's discretion where renewal of a

---

146 *Styles v Alberta Investment Management Corporation* 2015 ABQB 621.

147 ibid [115].

148 *Bhasin* (n 140) 75.

contract is in issue.[149] This is an area of employment relations where employees can be very vulnerable and there is considerable scope for abuse.

It should also be acknowledged that there are limits to the benefits that good faith can bring for employees. In *Malik*, Lord Steyn held that mutual trust was 'apt to cover the great diversity of situations in which a balance has to be struck between an employer's interest in managing his business as he sees fit and the employee's interest in not being unfairly and improperly exploited'.[150] It did not, however, prevent either side from having regard to their own interests. The Canadian jurisprudence since *Bhasin* is of the same view. *Evans v Paradigm Capital* makes clear that the duty of good faith does not prevent parties from making legitimate choices motivated by economic self-interest.[151]

CONCLUSION

In the United Kingdom, the obligation of trust and confidence has continued to receive consistent and cogent judicial endorsement. It seems reasonable to conclude that, at common law, the United Kingdom has signed up to the holistic bargain depicted by Keesing:[152]

> In addition to remuneration, the employee gains marketable skills, experience and reputation, personal and financial security, and a sense of identity, dignity and involvement in the community. While these benefits are difficult to define precisely within the contract, courts have given content to them through the implied term of mutual trust and confidence, which embodies the overarching expectation of parties to an employment contract that each will behave fairly and cooperatively in the exercise and fulfilment of their contractual powers and duties.

In the United Kingdom, mutual trust and confidence is entering a new phase where it is becoming a more mainstream obligation, as norms of fair dealing become more central to the law of contract. This trend is unlikely to have any negative consequences for employees, but will instead render mutual trust more secure, as it will be more congruent

---

149 *Data & Scientific v Oracle* (2015) ONSC 4178. See also *Transco v O'Brien* [2002] ICR 721.

150 *Malik* (n 18) 46.

151 *Evans v Paradigm Capital* (2016) ONSC 4286.

152 Grace Keesing, 'Contractual Rights and Remedies for Dismissed Employees After the "Employment" Revolution' (2012) 36 MULR 104.

with general principles. Australia, by a very different route, may be arriving at a similar position, whereby resorting to good faith may compensate for the rejection of mutual trust. In the limited period of time in which mutual trust has existed, very significant changes have occurred in the general law of contract and, in a number of systems (including Australia), good faith has assumed a much more central role.[153] The position in New Zealand is, perhaps, the most complete. A statutory scheme, influenced by common law developments, embodies a progressive vision of the employment relationship:[154]

> it may be that the most significant development at the general level will be the development of an obligation of fair management practice. The combination of the law on personal grievances and the term of mutual trust and confidence had the effect of limiting the exercise of employer prerogative and this development should be substantially reinforced by the duty of good faith. In practical terms, employers must ensure that they have defensible and robust human resource management practices capable of surviving judicial scrutiny where a challenge arises. It might be argued that such a development represents a statutory formulation of Freedland's hypothesized overarching principle of a requirement of fair management and performance applicable to all employment contracts.

---

[153] The decision of the Canadian Supreme Court in *Bhasin* (n 140) provides a cogent example.

[154] Anderson (n 3) 715.

8. The work/personal interface

INTRODUCTION

Hugh Collins begins his discussion of 'Work and Life' in *Employment Law*[1] with a poignant narrative of the repression of the Luddite rebellion, when a formerly agrarian community of artisans vainly resisted the mechanization and subjugation of their labour in the mills. Collins describes a 'new geography of industrialization',[2] which separated the workplace from the household, and imposed a rigid division between work time and home life. It is, perhaps, ironic that the latest technological revolution – the explosion of the digital age – has blurred those divisions again, but not necessarily to the benefit of workers' autonomy. The 24/7 economy, and advancements in electronic communications and surveillance technology, have eroded any clear separation of work from private life for many contemporary employees.

The employee's claim to a right to maintain an autonomous private life alongside employment has long been contested territory in employment law. Employer intrusion into a worker's private life is nothing new. A well-known example is the Ford's social department, which monitored employee standards of cleanliness in the home, drinking and social habits, religious views, spending practices and the 'evil custom' of taking in boarders.[3] Until 1945, employees of the Royal Bank of Scotland were unable to marry until their income reached a level usually attainable only after 12 years' service.[4] Contract law, unassisted by any mandatory statutory employee entitlements, favours the employer when the demands of work and one's personal life conflict. In *Turner v Mason*,[5] a housemaid who left the house one evening in order to visit her dying mother, against the instructions of a heartless employer, was held to be justifiably

---

[1] Hugh Collins, *Employment Law* (Oxford University Press 2003) 76–7.

[2] ibid 77.

[3] Richard Snow, *I Invented the Modern Age: The Rise of Henry Ford* (Scribner 2014).

[4] Royal Bank of Scotland, 'Object 49: "marriage ban" memo, 1932' (2015) <www.heritagearchives.rbs.com>. Such policies were far from uncommon.

[5] *Turner v Mason* (1845) 14 M & W 112, 117–18.

dismissed from her post. The employer's prerogative to command obedience to duties during working hours was – and, to a great extent, largely remains – absolute under employment contract law. The rights to paid and unpaid leave to attend to illness and emergencies, and to undertake caring responsibilities and recreation, are the fruits of hard won victories from earlier industrial struggles. Where these rights appear in employment contracts, it is generally as a consequence of the influence of mandatory provisions in statutes or statutory instruments. While employees (at least, those in permanent, continuing positions) have become accustomed in recent decades to paid leave for managing the vicissitudes of private life (for example, illness, pregnancy and child care, death of close relatives), the claim that employers must also accommodate the employee's complete freedom of expression has been more contentious.[6] In this chapter, we consider the interplay of common law and statutory influences in establishing contemporary boundaries between work and personal life.

While such boundaries may be partly determined by express terms in the contract of employment (especially where human resources policy manuals are incorporated as contract terms[7]), they are more commonly influenced by terms implied by the common law. These include the employee's implied obligations of fidelity and obedience to all lawful and reasonable orders. Also included, at least in the United Kingdom and New Zealand, is the more recently implied mutual obligation not to destroy trust and confidence in the employment relationship.[8] Generally, the implied duties of loyalty and obedience create the opportunity for employers to impose an open-ended set of strongly asymmetrical obligations upon employees.[9] Even in *Commonwealth Bank of Australia v Barker*, the Australian High Court preserved the employee's duty to maintain the employer's trust and confidence, while denying the existence of any mutual trust obligation.[10] The indeterminacy of these obligations allows the courts to define the boundary between work obligation and personal liberty on a case-by-case basis, generally in the context of a dispute over the validity of a dismissal or other disciplinary

---

6 See Paul Wragg, 'Free Speech Rights at Work: Resolving the Differences between Practice and Liberal Principle' (2015) 44(1) ILJ 1.

7 See Chapter 5.

8 The existence of any implied obligation of mutual trust and confidence was rejected by the Australian High Court in *Commonwealth Bank of Australia v Barker* (2014) 253 CLR 169. See generally Chapter 7.

9 See Chapter 7.

10 *Barker* (n 8) [30].

action, and in the shadow of the common law's inherent values. One of those values tends to be a presumption that, at least in the private sector, employers enjoy a largely unfettered prerogative to manage their own enterprises according to their own economic, social and cultural interests. Another is that the parties to an employment contract are autonomous legal actors who have voluntarily assumed mutually determined obligations. Hence, an employee who objects to the employer's command has a self-help remedy in resignation.[11] Of course, this conception pays little regard to the reality of unequal bargaining power in the market place, and the pressure upon employees to keep their jobs.[12]

In times past, trade unions have attempted to delimit the employer's managerial prerogative to command extensive obedience to all manner of orders, by bargaining for terms in collective bargains or arbitrated awards to prescribe the limits of working time, duties and work practices. The extensive prescription of work practices in many of the old arbitrated awards made under early Australian and New Zealand legislation[13] was a means for worker representatives to assert some restraints on the demands that employers could make upon employees' time and energies. Extensive prescription in awards has been legislated out of existence in New Zealand, since 1991,[14] and Australia, since 1996,[15] in the interests of greater 'flexibility'. Collective enterprise bargaining is the only remaining means for trade unions to directly influence the extent of managerial prerogative, and many contests over allegedly intrusive management practices are mounted by unions in the context of enterprise bargaining disputes. For example, unions have objected to the instigation of intrusive drug testing policies, on the basis that they have the potential to monitor and punish private conduct that is unrelated to the employees' capacity to work.[16]

---

[11] See Hugh Collins, 'The Protection of Civil Liberties in the Workplace' (2006) 69(4) MLR 619, 620, 624.

[12] Lord Wedderburn, *The Worker and the Law* (3rd edn, Penguin 1986) 5.

[13] Conciliation and Arbitration Act 1904 (Cth) to the Industrial Relations Act 1988 (Cth); the Industrial Conciliation and Arbitration Act 1894 (NZ) to the Labour Relations Act 1987 (NZ).

[14] Employment Contracts Act 1991 (NZ).

[15] See Workplace Relations Act 1996 (Cth), s 89A (now repealed), which reduced 'allowable award matters' to only 20 matters.

[16] See e.g. *BHP Iron Ore Pty Ltd v Construction, Mining Energy, Timberyards, Sawmills and Woodworkers Union of Australia, Western Australia Branch* (1998) 82 IR 162, which permitted the implementation of random and targeted drug testing. See also *Shell Refining Australia Pty Ltd v Construction, Forestry,*

Given declining union membership, in many industries and workplaces, it will be the various statutory regimes that seek to protect employee interests in job security and safe, non-discriminatory workplaces that will have the greatest impact on the exercise of managerial prerogative in employment relationships, although often in unexpected ways.

THE LIMITS OF MANAGERIAL PREROGATIVE

An early example of a dispute over the extent of the employer's prerogative to command arose in a case before the President of the Commonwealth Court of Conciliation and Arbitration. Mr Justice Higgins was asked to determine whether an employer should be free to exercise an alleged common law 'right' to ban tramways workers from wearing a union badge. Mr Justice Higgins described the employer's claim of a 'common law right' to dictate matters of dress as a 'quaint theory', and denied its existence. His Honour said:[17]

> A servant has to obey lawful commands, not all commands. The servant does not commit a breach of duty if he refuses to attend a particular church, or to wear a certain maker's singlets. The common law right of an employee is a right to wear what he chooses, to act as he chooses, in matters not affecting his work. Prima facie, a man may wear what he likes so long as he does not offend against decency; and the burden lies upon the employer to show the contrary. Of course an employer may, by due notice, get rid of an employee who does not dress to his liking; but the employee is not guilty of a breach of duty in refusing.

Mr Justice Higgins ultimately settled an award permitting the tramways conductors to wear their brass union badges as pocket watch fobs.

This case continues to have purchase in the twenty-first century, as a statement of the 'common law right of the employee' to personal autonomy in matters not affecting their work. But what matters *will* affect work, in the digitally enabled world of flexible home-work? Much

---

Mining and Energy Union [2009] AIRCFB 428; *Endeavour Energy v Communications Electrical, Electronic, Energy, Information, Postal, Plumbing and Allied Services Union of Australia* [2012] FWAFB 4998; *Raymond Briggs v AWH Pty Ltd* [2013] FWCFB 3316; *Maritime Union of Australia v DP World Brisbane Pty Ltd; DP World (Fremantle) Ltd; DP World Melbourne Ltd; DP World Sydney Ltd* [2014] FWC 1523.

[17] *Australian Tramways Employees' Association v Brisbane Tramways Co Ltd* (1912) 6 CAR 35, 42.

contemporary case law has extended the reach of the employer's influence over personal life, on the basis that employers have been able to sustain arguments that their business interests have been, or are potentially being, affected by employees' private conduct (we discuss this case law below). Perhaps ironically, some of this extension has been warranted by the imposition of increasingly onerous statutory burdens on employers to take responsibility for the work health and safety and freedom from harassment of their staff. The employer's vicarious liability under common law, and particular statutory duties under work health and safety and discrimination laws, has encouraged the human resources management function in contemporary enterprises to promulgate more prescriptive workplace culture policies, and has justified discipline of employees for out-of-hours conduct. So Mr Justice Higgins' 'right of the employee to act as he chooses' is under some threat in contemporary times.

On the other hand, the enactment of unfair dismissal statutes has challenged the accuracy of Mr Justice Higgins' statement of the employer's liberty to 'get rid of' an employee with incompatible personal tastes. Today, in all three jurisdictions under consideration, an employer is likely to be bound by obligations to demonstrate a valid reason for dismissal, and to show observance of fair procedures in pursuing dismissal as a disciplinary measure.[18] Merely objecting to the 'cut of one's jib' is no longer, of itself, an acceptable ground for giving staff notice of termination of employment contracts, at least, not for those staff who enjoy the protection of statutory schemes.[19]

Articulating the limits on managerial prerogative in matters affecting employees' personal autonomy in their private lives has been a controversial matter, especially where the introduction of new diagnostic and surveillance technologies has enhanced employers' capacity (if not their entitlement) to monitor employees. These include (often questionable) psychometric testing tools, medical tests for drug use, genetic testing for susceptibility to congenital conditions, closed circuit cameras, GPS tracking devices and monitoring of computer use. The explosion of social media as a form of communication has demolished any meaningful boundary between the private and the public in many people's lives. Once upon a time, complaining about the boss or sharing some 'blue' humour or distasteful opinions over a few beers at the pub would rarely

---

[18] See Chapter 10.

[19] Unfair dismissal laws do admit of exceptions in respect of certain classes of employee, generally those who are not covered by enterprise bargains and are on salaries exceeding a high income threshold.

reach the boss' ears, at least, not in any way that would create an evidence trail that might be used in subsequent workplace disciplinary proceedings. Now, expressions of workplace disgruntlement on Facebook, or political rants on Twitter, can lead to dismissal, depending on the employer's ability to make the necessary connection between the employee's conduct and the employer's legitimate prerogative to command obedience and loyalty in matters affecting work. The employee's capacity to argue that such conduct is a private and personal matter is complicated by the wide dissemination of communications in the post-Facebook world. Not only will many people hear about it, but many may respond in pitchfork-wielding mode, directing righteous outrage not only at the worker, but at the employing enterprise, who may respond by seeking to distance itself from the worker. An Australian television journalist, Scott McIntyre, learned this when he tweeted controversial opinions about Anzac Day (a matter to be treated with considerable reverence, according to mainstream opinion in Australia) and lost his job as a consequence of a hurricane of abuse from the general public following the incident.[20]

We now interrogate some of these areas of contention – out-of-hours conduct, drug testing, social media use, and surveillance – in light of the relative influence of common law contractual principles and statutory developments in settling new parameters for the employer's prerogative to command, and the employee's liberty to enjoy, a private life.

First, we identify whether and, if so, why, certain otherwise private conduct has been held to fall within the scope of the employer's prerogative to command. When will certain conduct constitute breach of the employment contract, warranting discipline or dismissal? Orthodoxy suggests that the employer can only command the employee to obey 'lawful and reasonable' orders, which means that the employer can expect obedience to matters that fall within the agreed scope of the employment contract.[21] One consequence of the contemporary practice of requiring employees to sign detailed written contracts of employment, with finely calibrated 'position descriptions', is that the scope of any particular employment contract may be considerably narrower now than it might have been, in the days when masters made verbal offers of

---

[20] See *Mr Scott McIntyre v Special Broadcasting Services Corporation t/a SBS Corporation* [2015] FWC 6768.

[21] See *Darling Island Stevedoring and Lighthouse Ltd; Ex parte Halliday and Sullivan* (1938) 60 CLR 601, 621–2. See also Greg McCarry, 'The Employee's Duty to Obey Unreasonable Orders' (1984) 58 ALJ 327.

general employment to servants. Typically, though, many detailed contract documents include a catch-all obligation to undertake any duties required by a supervisor, notwithstanding the careful articulation of a range of particular duties. As we saw in Chapter 5, employers regularly seek to extend the operation of the implied obligations of obedience and loyalty using express workplace conduct rules, and workplace policies and procedures manuals.

Notwithstanding common law principles, we consider whether any statutory constraint on the exercise of forms of workplace discipline (for example, unfair dismissal protection) will restrain the employer from taking action against the employee on the grounds of private conduct. It is one thing to find that the employee owes no positive duty to obey a command that falls outside the scope of employment and infringes private autonomy. It is another to require an employer to continue to employ a person whose private commitments or habits are objectionable to the employer's own values, especially where the employer asserts that the employee's private conduct has inflicted, albeit indirectly, some kind of reputational harm upon the employer. This may explain a perception that unfair dismissal laws (particularly in the United Kingdom) have not been especially effective in protecting employees from dismissal where an employer has taken exception to some aspect of the employee's private conduct.[22] This perception may have been reinforced in the eyes of employees by the Court of Appeal's assessment of the relationship between the controversial band of reasonableness test and Article 8 of the European Convention on Human Rights.[23] It was found that the test was compliant with Article 8, and it was said to be very difficult to 'see how a procedure which could be considered objectively fair if adopted by a reasonable employer could nonetheless be properly described as an unfair procedure within the meaning of Article 8'.[24] Beyond unfair dismissal protection, we need to consider the operation of a range of other protective statutes that prohibit discrimination against employees on the basis of certain characteristics, including their religious and political commitments and their sexual preferences. On the one hand, these statutory protections afford employees some freedom to live as they please without adverse consequences in their employment. On the other

---

[22] See Virginia Mantouvalou, 'Human Rights and Unfair Dismissal: Private Acts in Public Spaces' (2008) 71(6) MLR 912; Astrid Sanders, 'The Law of Unfair Dismissal and Behaviour outside Work' (2014) 34(2) Legal Studies 328; Wragg (n 6).

[23] *Turner v East Midlands Trains* [2012] EWCA Civ 1470, [2013] ICR 525.

[24] ibid [52]. This position is criticized by Mantouvalou (n 22).

hand, to the extent that those statutes expand the employer's vicarious liability for harm inflicted by employees upon others, they may, in fact, justify further incursion into the employee's claim of an autonomous private life.[25] In *Woolworths Ltd v Brown*, for instance, the court took the view that employers should be allowed some latitude in formulating policies to facilitate their own compliance with a 'bewildering array of statutory obligations' in this 'modern era'.[26]

Finally, we must consider the extent to which judicial concern with the maintenance of coherence between statutory regulation and common law rights and duties has extended or constrained the employer's prerogative to control an ever-widening realm of employee life.

OUT-OF-HOURS CONDUCT

We leave, for the time being, consideration of private or outside-of-work conduct that offends an employer only because the employer insists upon protection from competition, or a right to absorb all of an employee's capacity for productive endeavour. These kinds of conflicts are dealt with in Chapter 9, which focuses on employees' human capital. Here, we consider activity of a more intrinsically private nature, which might invoke some kind of moral condemnation from the perspective of the employer. We shall set aside the kinds of criminal activity that may ultimately frustrate an employment contract as a consequence of the incarceration of the employee, and focus on the kind of conduct that, on its face, has not interfered with the employee's attendance at work or performance of duties. Examples include recreational drug use,[27] sexual activity of which the employer disapproves,[28] brawling outside of work,[29]

---

[25] This has been an argument mounted in the United States, but contested in the context of United Kingdom law: see Astrid Sanders, 'The Law of Unfair Dismissal and Behaviour outside Work' (2014) 34(2) Legal Studies 328, 335–6.

[26] *Woolworths Ltd v Brown* (2005) 145 IR 285, [24].

[27] For example, *Mathewson v RB Wilson Dental Laboratory* [1989] IRLR 512 (UK Employment Appeals Tribunal).

[28] For example, *Saunders v Scottish National Camps* [1980] IRLR 174 (UK Employment Appeals Tribunal); *Pay v Lancashire Probation Service* [2004] ICR 187 (UK Employment Appeals Tribunal) (employee involved in bondage and sadomasochist practices); *Streeter v Telstra Corporation* (2008) 170 IR 1 (employee engaged in group sex activities after a staff Christmas function); *Moreton Bay College v Teys* [2008] QCA 422 (college principal engaged in extramarital affair); *Spiller v Wallis Ltd* [1975] IRLR 362.

[29] *Rose v Telstra Corp Ltd* (1998) 45 AILR [3–966].

sexual harassment,[30] drink driving,[31] and social media use (discussed below). In this category might also fall relationships outside of work that, when they break down, impinge negatively on harmony in the workplace.[32]

On common law principles, engagement in these kinds of activities would not constitute a breach of the employment contract warranting summary dismissal, unless the employer could demonstrate some connection with their interests. Nevertheless, the common law (unaided by any statute or collective bargain) would still countenance termination of the employment contract for any reason upon giving proper notice, according to the terms of the contract. It is only when an employee is entitled to the benefit of some statutory protection from dismissal (or some contractual term promising procedural fairness, derived from the employer's commitment to comply with contemporary unfair dismissal statutes[33]) that any real question of the employer's obligation to accommodate employees' private lives arises.

In the United Kingdom, employers' powers of dismissal are constrained by section 94 of the Employment Rights Act 1996 (UK),[34] which subjects an employer's reasons for dismissal to scrutiny, to determine whether those reasons fall within the 'band of reasonable responses' to the employee's conduct.[35] However, a combination of the standard tests and a broad approach to the employer's legitimate interests can leave employees vulnerable. In *Leach v Office of Communication*, the employee was arrested in Cambodia on suspicion of having sexually abused one or more children.[36] He was charged, but acquitted by the Cambodian courts.[37] His employment did not involve him working with children or on issues specifically relating to children. Subsequently, the Metropolitan Police Child Abuse Investigation Command (CAIC) made an unsolicited disclosure to the employer that he posed a risk to children. The CAIC did not regard the employee's acquittal as significant, because

---

30 *McManus v Scott-Charlton* (1996) 140 ALR 625.

31 *Kolodjashnij v J Boag and Son Brewing Pty Ltd* (2010) 195 IR 279.

32 *Smith v Christchurch Press Co Ltd* [2001] 1 NZLR 407 (CA).

33 See *Edwards v Chesterfield Royal Hospital NHS Foundation Trust; Botham (FC) v Ministry of Defence* [2011] UKSC 58.

34 See Chapter 10.

35 *Iceland Frozen Foods v Jones* [1982] IRLR 439, [24], per Browne-Wilkinson J. See discussion in Sanders (n 25), 339–40.

36 *Leach v Office of Communication* [2010] IRLR 844. The decision was later upheld by the Court of Appeal: [2012] EWCA Civ 959, [2012] ICR 1269.

37 Subsequently, after the tribunal proceedings were over, the claimant was arrested and sentenced to imprisonment in Cambodia.

of what they regarded as deficiencies in the Cambodian criminal justice system. The employer went on to dismiss and, given the disclosure, the dismissal was held to be fair on the basis of the risk of damage to the employer's reputation. This outcome is not surprising, given the focus in the law of unfair dismissal on process. Where the employer has complied with the law in that respect, it will be difficult to challenge the substantive outcome. However, as a result, it becomes almost inevitable that greater weight will be placed on protecting the employer's interests rather than the employee's. A perceived risk to the employer's reputation is fully addressed, even though a dismissal 'in the absence of any established misconduct may involve a grave injustice' to the employee. Moreover, the Employment Appeals Tribunal acknowledged that it 'sticks in the throat that an employee may lose his job, and perhaps in practice any chance of obtaining further employment, on the basis of allegations which he has had no opportunity to challenge in any court of law – or may indeed have successfully challenged'.[38]

To the extent that United Kingdom law has introduced constraints on an employer's prerogative to raise reasons for dismissal based upon the employee's conduct in private life, it would appear to be as a result of the courts conceding that the Human Rights Act 1998 (UK), which gives domestic effect to the European Convention on Human Rights, has indirect horizontal effect. In other words, the Human Rights Act does not apply only to direct interactions between the state and its citizens, but also governs the factors that the Employment Appeals Tribunal ought to take into account in adjudicating whether a private sector employer's reasons for dismissal are unfair.[39] Nevertheless, developing case law has disappointed those who would see the Human Rights Act as supporting greater protection for employees' liberty to exercise personal freedoms without risking their jobs.[40] On the whole, the common law values have prevailed: the employer's interest in pursuing its own economic interests, controlling its own reputation, commandeering the use of its own property and resources, and engaging only those who maintain its trust and confidence has outweighed employee claims to substantial autonomy in their personal lives. Employees will look on with envy at other aspects of the common law, such as the law of confidentiality, where the courts

38 *Leach* (n 36) [27].
39 See Collins (n 11) 620.
40 See ibid; Mantouvalou (n 22); Sanders (n 25); Wragg (n 6).

have been much more willing to accommodate the values of the Convention.[41]

Even those scholars who are most jealously protective of employees' rights to a private life concede that the employer has a legitimate interest in private outside conduct if it has some bearing on the performance of duties, the reputation of the employer, or the maintenance of the employer's trust and confidence that the employee is capable of performing the duties with integrity. Mantouvalou (who argues for a strong human rights-based protection of a right to a private life at work) concedes that, where an employee's off duty behaviour has a 'high likelihood' of impact on the employer's business reputation, it will justify dismissal, and gives examples of a supermarket worker with a conviction for shoplifting, and a nursery school worker with a conviction for accessing child pornography.[42]

The willingness of the courts to give considerable weight to the employer's judgments of its business interests was clearly demonstrated in the New Zealand case of *Hallwright v Forsyth Barr*,[43] where customer response and potential loss of clients were central to the dismissal of a senior investment analyst, following his conviction for causing grievous bodily harm after a road rage incident. The incident attracted considerable publicity, to which Forsyth Barr was linked. In her judgment, Judge Inglis reviewed the relevant law in some detail and confirmed that:[44]

> It is not necessary that the conduct itself be directly linked to the employment but rather that it have the potential to impact negatively on it. That is why an employee can be held to account for what might otherwise be regarded as a private activity, carried out away from the workplace and with no ostensible connection to the employment or other employees.

Her Honour went on to hold that the central issue was not the seriousness of the conduct, but the perceived impact on the employer's business,[45] and that there was no obligation on the employer to demonstrate actual loss or damage to its reputation.[46]

In Australia, determinations of whether an employer's reasons for dismissal are 'valid' and whether the decision to dismiss is not 'harsh' are determined by an administrative tribunal, exercising a discretion to

---

41 Sanders (n 25).

42 Mantouvalou (n 22) 921, 931.

43 *Hallwright v Forsyth Barr* [2013] NZEmpC 202.

44 ibid [49], relying on *Smith* (n 32).

45 *Hallwright* (n 43) [50].

46 ibid [59].

impose a 'fair go all round' on the parties.[47] Australian tribunal decisions, perhaps as a consequence of these tribunals' origins as arbitrators of collective industrial disputes, have often shown considerable respect for employees' entitlement to maintain their own moral values. So, in *Appellant v Respondent*,[48] a male flight attendant was reinstated after being dismissed for what amounted to seduction of a female colleague during the time that both employees were off duty, on a stop-over between flights. The decision of a single Commissioner[49] that this was an unfair dismissal was confirmed, on the basis that the employer had no business in regulating private activities during the employees' own time, notwithstanding that the female employee had raised the complaint. In *Streeter v Telstra Corp Ltd*,[50] Ms Streeter was held to be validly dismissed after a co-worker complained that she had engaged in highly promiscuous sexual activity after a work Christmas party, but only on the basis that she had been dishonest when answering the employer's questions about the incident. Although the activities were accepted to be of a 'highly personal nature' that would not normally attract the interest of the employer, the fact that a co-worker had complained of the matter enlivened the employer's obligation to investigate the matter, and gave rise to Ms Streeter's obligation to give honest answers.[51]

Increasingly, employers are able to find the relevant connection between their legitimate interest and the employee's private conduct, in the form of responsibility or concern for the impact of the conduct on other individuals at the workplace. This responsibility may result from relatively new statutory obligations to take all reasonable steps to protect other employees from certain kinds of harm. For example, in *McManus v Scott-Charlton*,[52] the Federal Court was asked to judicially review an administrative decision to discipline a public servant for repeatedly contacting a co-worker out of work hours. The man had developed a romantic interest in his co-worker, and continued to pester her after working hours when instructed by the employer to leave her alone. The court determined that the employer's direction that he must not contact her, even outside of work, was a lawful and reasonable order on a number of grounds. At one level, the employer was able to justify its

---

47 See Chapter 10.

48 *Appellant v Respondent* (1999) 89 IR 407.

49 Drake DP, in AIRC Print P9977 (1 May 1998).

50 *Streeter* (n 28).

51 For a note on the case, see Amanda Kennedy, 'More Sinned Against than Sinning? *Telstra Corporation Ltd v Streeter*' (2008) 21(1) AJLL 59.

52 *McManus* (n 30).

disciplinary measures on the basis that the conduct was having an adverse impact on work performance, because members of staff were 'paying reduced attention to their duties' while worrying about the matter.[53] Perhaps more important to the reasoning in the case, however, was the impact of the employer's own obligations under the vicarious liability provisions of section 106 of the Sex Discrimination Act 1984 (Cth) to take 'all reasonable steps to prevent harassment'.[54] The conduct occurred 'in connection with the employment of the [victim]', according to section 28B of the Sex Discrimination Act, because the parties were co-workers. The statutory imposition of vicarious liability for conduct 'in connection with employment' has been held to be significantly wider than the common law principle that employers will be vicariously liable only for acts committed 'in the course of employment'.[55] This raises the spectre of the problem of 'coherence' in the law. Courts are unlikely to find that employees enjoy a common law right to preservation of a personal life free of the risk of dismissal, in circumstances where the employer bears statutory obligations to monitor and control that conduct to the extent that it impinges on others connected with the workplace.

This kind of argument defeated a school principal who sought to establish that his employer owed him a duty of care in the way that it managed investigation of alleged child abuse at the school. The court refused to find that such a duty could exist, in the face of contradictory statutory obligations under child protection legislation.[56] The Australian High Court has affirmed that common law rights and obligations will not be developed in areas heavily regulated by statute.[57]

DRUG TESTING

The employer's legitimate interest in health and safety matters has also been used to justify the imposition of intrusive drug testing at work,

---

[53] ibid 638–9.

[54] See Therese MacDermott, 'The Duty to Provide a Harassment Free Work Environment' (1995) 37 JIR 495.

[55] See *South Pacific Resort Hotels Pty Ltd v Trainor* (2005) FCAFC 130. Recent Australian High Court authority has determined that an employer may be liable even for the criminal acts of an employee, if the employment created the 'occasion' (but not merely the 'opportunity') for the crime: see *Prince Alfred College Incorporated v ADC* [2016] HCA 37.

[56] See e.g. *State of New South Wales v Paige* (2002) 60 NSWLR 371.

[57] *Barker* (n 8).

usually through a workplace policy which, even if not formally incorporated into employment contracts, enlivens the employee's duty to obey 'lawful and reasonable' orders. An employer clearly has an interest in maintaining a drug-free workplace during business hours and, in more dangerous areas of work (where employees are operating machinery, for instance), on-site drug testing is generally accepted as legitimate. But how intrusive can it be, and to what extent is any form of testing that will detect out-of-hours conduct legitimate? Unions have taken up the cudgels against employers who have sought to impose what the unions consider to be unnecessarily intrusive forms of testing (such as blood and urine sampling, instead of mouth swabs).[58]

The courts recognize that drug testing raises problems. In *Endeavour Energy v Communications Union of Australia*, it was said that:[59]

> the employer has a legitimate right (and indeed obligation) to try and eliminate the risk that employees might come to work impaired by drugs or alcohol such that they could pose a risk to health or safety. Beyond that the employer has no right to dictate what drugs or alcohol its employees take in their own time. Indeed, it would be unjust and unreasonable to do so.

This statement was quoted with approval in New Zealand in *Hayllar v The Goodtime Food Co Ltd*,[60] where the court was critical, among other things, of the failure to justify the testing of the employees in terms of the policy, and the failure to follow the policy in a number of other respects. That being said, however, the courts appear to be generally supportive of drug testing policies,[61] but may be less so inclined to permit testing where elements of procedural unfairness are involved.[62]

One strong argument in the employer's favour, where drug and other health-related issues are concerned, is that the measures the employer

---

58 See e.g. *Maritime Union of Australia* (n 16), where it was held – after a detailed interrogation of the relative efficacy of different testing methods in detecting certain illicit substances, and their levels of impairment on workplace performance – that urine testing ought not to be used.

59 *Endeavour Energy v Communications Union of Australia* [2012] FWA 1809, [36]; noted with approval in *Endeavour Energy* (n 16).

60 *Hayllar v The Goodtime Food Co Ltd* [2012] NZEmpC 153, [2012] ERNZ 333; see also *Hooper v Coca-Cola Amatil (New Zealand) Ltd* [2012] NZ EmpC 11, (2012) NZELR 519; and *Electrical Union 2001 Inc v Mighty River Power Ltd* [2013] NZEmpC 197.

61 *New Zealand Amalgamated Engineering, Printing and Manufacturing Union Inc v Air New Zealand* [2004] 1 ERNZ 614, (2004) 2 NZELR 157 (EmpC).

62 *Hooper* (n 60).

seeks to take are warranted in order to comply with its obligations under health and safety legislation. For example, in *Construction, Forestry, Mining and Energy Union v Glencore Mt Owen Pty Ltd* the employer's duty to 'eliminate risks to health and safety, so far as reasonably practicable' under section 17(a) of the Work Health and Safety Act 2011 (NSW) was found to provide sufficient justification for a ban on smoking in the workplace,[63] although, in that case, the employer had agreed to fund 'quit smoking' programs. Scientific evidence that environmental tobacco smoke is harmful to non-smokers in the workplace was influential in the decision.[64]

The mining and construction industry cases on drug testing indicate a concern to give some weight to the interests of the employee in avoiding scrutiny of recreational habits that do not impair work performance.[65] In *Anderson v Sullivan*,[66] it was held that police officers could also be directed to provide urine samples for drug testing, even where the test was likely to detect out-of-hours drug use, because the 'distinctive nature of policing' justified the employer's concern to maintain public interest in the integrity of the police force (in circumstances where the drugs in question were illicit), and in protecting the public from 'possibly impaired judgment in the use of weapons and vehicles' by police.[67] In this case, arguments based on human dignity and privacy were canvassed, but, on balance, the 'more compelling' public interest in police integrity was found to outweigh those concerns.[68]

Employer requests, or commands, that employees subject themselves to other forms of medical testing have also prompted disputes over the line between the employee's personal autonomy and the employer's interests. In *Bliss v South East Thames Regional Health Authority*, the employer's requirement that a senior doctor submit to psychological testing after he fell into disfavour with colleagues was held to be so offensive as to constitute a breach of the employer's obligation not to destroy mutual trust and confidence.[69] The position may well be different where the employer has reasonable cause. When the requirement to

---

[63] *Construction, Forestry, Mining and Energy Union v Glencore Mt Owen Pty Ltd* [2015] FWC 7752.

[64] ibid [22].

[65] See *Raymond Briggs v AWH Pty Ltd* [2013] FWCFB 3316, [2]; *Maritime Union of Australia* (n 16) [79].

[66] *Anderson v Sullivan* (1997) 78 FCR 380.

[67] ibid 399.

[68] ibid 398.

[69] *Bliss v South East Thames Regional Health Authority* [1985] IRLR 308.

submit to medical tests is directed to ensuring that an employee is fit to return to work after a workplace injury, it may be justifiable, so long as the request is made on 'reasonable terms' with due respect for the employee's privacy, especially where the employer owes duties under workers' compensation legislation to ensure a safe return to work.[70] A blanket requirement that all truck drivers working for a transport company must submit to a Physical Risk Review Program was, however, held to be excessive, even though the employer sought to introduce this program in response to new statutory obligations under the National Heavy Vehicle Accreditation Scheme.[71]

SOCIAL MEDIA

Any claim that employees may once have made to a private life, free of interference from an employer, has been compromised extensively in recent years by the proliferation of forms of social media. As Commissioner Bissett warned in *Sally-Anne Fitzgerald v Dianna Smith t/as Escape Hair Design*:[72]

> What might previously have been a grumble about their employer over a coffee or drinks with friends has turned into a posting on a website that, in some cases, may be seen by an unlimited number of people. Posting comments about an employer on a website (Facebook) that can be seen by an uncontrollable number of people is no longer a private matter, but public comment.

To date, the case law in New Zealand appears to have been confined to issues such as the abuse of the employer or co-employees on social media and, usually, this has been an aggravating factor in the decision.[73] The only considered comment on such issues, at least in the employment realm, is that of *Hook v Stream Group (NZ) Pty Ltd*,[74] in which the court

---

70 See *Blackadder v Ramsey Butchering Pty Ltd* (2002) 113 IR 461, 476, affirmed on this point in *Blackadder v Ramsey Butchering Services Pty Ltd* (2005) 221 CLR 539.

71 See *Transport Workers' Union of Australia v Cement Australia Pty Ltd* [2015] FWC 158.

72 *Sally-Anne Fitzgerald v Dianna Smith t/as Escape Hair Design* [2010] FWA 7358, [50].

73 See e.g. *Dickinson v Chief Executive, Ministry of Social Development* ERA AA508/10, 13 December 2010; *Adams v Wellington Free Ambulance Service Inc* ERA WA81B/10, 23 July 2010.

74 *Hook v Stream Group (NZ) Pty Ltd* [2013] NZEmpC 188, [33].

relied heavily on Australian authority, citing *Linfox Australia Pty Ltd v Stutsel*,[75] where it was noted that:

> Unlike conversations in a pub or cafe, the Facebook conversations leave a permanent written record of statements and comments made by the participants, which can be read at any time into the future until they are taken down by the page owner. Employees should therefore exercise considerable care in using social networking sites in making comments or conducting conversations about their managers and fellow employees.

Judge Inglis commented that: 'The cases generally recognise that Facebook is not a strictly private forum, and that asserted expectations of privacy will likely be tested. Depending on the circumstances, posted comments may substantiate a dismissal/disciplinary action or, by logical extension, vitiate a claim of constructive dismissal'.[76]

In Australia, numerous unfair dismissal applications have turned on whether an employer has been able to assert a valid reason for dismissing a person because of social media postings.[77] The decisions are fact specific, so it is difficult to draw any clear principles from them;[78] however, some mercy has been shown in cases involving postings on sites with privacy settings that ought to have limited circulation, and where the posting is quickly repented and removed.[79] Cases that have been found against the employee often involve some other indication of wrongdoing. For example, staff who have posted social media pictures of themselves enjoying leisure activities at a time when they were supposed to have been on legitimate sick leave have received no mercy at the hands of the tribunals, on the basis that the dismissal was for dishonesty.[80] A complication in these cases can be that the comments are not only critical of the employer, and so raise an argument that trust and confidence in the employment relationship has been destroyed, but may also involve some

---

75 *Linfox Australia Pty Ltd v Stutsel* [2012] FWAFB 7097, [26].

76 *Hook* (n 74) [36].

77 See e.g. *Tamicka Louise Dover-Ray v Real Insurance Pty Ltd* [2010] FWA 8544; *Applicant v Respondent* [2010] FWA 1062; *Escape Hair Design* (n 72); *Stutsel v Linfox Australia Pty Ltd* (2011) 217 IR 28; *O'Keefe v William Muir Pty Ltd t/as the Good Guys* [2011] FWA 5311. For commentary on some cases, see L Thornthwaite, 'Social Media, Unfair Dismissal and the Regulation of Employee's Conduct Outside Work' (2013) 26 AJLL 164. See also *Teggart v Teletech UK* [2004] IRLR 625.

78 In the United Kingdom, the Employment Appeals Tribunal has declined to provide general guidance: *Game Retail v Laws* EAT/0188/14.

79 See *Lukzsewski v Capones Pizzeria Kyneton* [2009] AIRC 280.

80 *Antony Dekort v Johns River Tavern Pty Ltd* [2010] FWA 3389.

kind of bullying or harassing conduct directed at other employers, whether supervisors or co-workers.[81] This engages the employer's responsibility to provide a psychologically safe workplace for all staff. Again, the imposition of responsibilities upon employers by a range of protective statutes has created a justification for more intrusive monitoring of workers' out-of-hours conduct than even the common law would tolerate.

The law in this area is still embryonic and it is difficult to assess how it will evolve. The courts recognize that there is a balance to be drawn between an employer's desire to remove or reduce reputational risk from social media communications by its employees, and the employee's right of freedom of expression.[82] In the United Kingdom, in *Smith v Trafford Housing Trust*, an employee who was a practising Christian posted comments on Facebook that were critical of gay marriage.[83] His Facebook page made reference to his employment and the employer invoked the disciplinary process. As a result, the employee was demoted. Counsel for the employer accepted that the demotion was a breach of contract, unless it could be shown that the Facebook postings amounted to misconduct. This question was decided with reference to the employer's Code of Conduct and Equal Opportunities Policy. It was held that, in the circumstances, no breach of contract had occurred, as the content of the post was not likely to bring the employer into disrepute.

The favourable outcome in *Smith* notwithstanding, employees will be concerned to know how heavily freedom of expression will weigh in the judicial scales. There was a helpful acknowledgement in *Smith* that 'frank but lawful expression of religious or political views may frequently cause a degree of upset, and even offence, to those with deeply held contrary views, even where none is intended by the speaker. This is a necessary price to be paid for freedom of speech'.[84] At the same time, it was also acknowledged that the employer has the capacity to issue instructions to restrict the activities that the employee may pursue. It is a matter for speculation whether a court would ever find a term or instruction so restrictive that it would be unenforceable on grounds of public policy. *Smith* suggests that the courts will not look favourably on poor or ambiguous drafting, given the competing interests at stake: the employee 'must be entitled to ascertain from the codes and policies to

---

81 See *Teggart* (n 77).

82 *Game Retail* (n 78).

83 *Smith v Trafford Housing Trust* [2012] EWHC 3221 (Ch), [2013] IRLR 86.

84 ibid [82].

which he is subjected what he is and is not permitted to do, and to understand the extent to which those obligations extend beyond the workplace into his personal or social life'.[85]

SURVEILLANCE

A new frontier for the development of principles preserving workers' entitlement to a private life, free of employer scrutiny, is the emerging use of surveillance and tracking technology. Two arguments stand in the way of employees establishing any 'right to privacy' while they are at work, in the face of employers' newly acquired capacity to monitor their movements and on-screen activities.[86] One is the common law's resistance to recognizing any right to privacy at work, on the basis that work occurs within the public sphere.[87] Another is that even those statutory protections that citizens may enjoy from covert surveillance of their activities are easily overridden by express contractual terms.

So, while employees have some limited protection from surveillance in the workplace without their consent,[88] it is a simple matter for a well-advised employer to obtain the necessary consent. In *Flanagan v Thales Australia Ltd T/as Thales Australia*,[89] it was held that it is sufficient for the purposes of giving consent under surveillance legislation that the employee ticks a pop-up box on screen that says, 'I understand that my use of these systems may be monitored to the extent permitted by law'.

Legislation controlling the use of covert surveillance may offer some limited protection to employees from scrutiny outside of work. In

---

[85] ibid [53].

[86] See Hazel Oliver, 'Email and Internet Monitoring in the Workplace: Information Privacy and Contracting-Out' (2002) 31(4) ILJ 321, for criticism of the orthodoxy that employment occurs in 'the public', and that employers should be permitted to insist that employees contract out of any remaining rights of privacy.

[87] See *Dye v Commonwealth Securities Ltd* [2010] FCA 720. Even statutory protections tend to treat employment as a matter of public interest: the Privacy Act 1988 (Cth), s 7B(3) exempts employee records.

[88] See Workplace Surveillance Act 2005 (NSW); Workplace Privacy Act 2011 (ACT); Listening and Surveillance Devices Act 1972 (SA); Listening Devices Act 1991 (Tas); Surveillance Devices Act 1999 (Vic); Surveillance Devices Act 1998 (WA); Surveillance Devices Act 2007 (NT).

[89] *Flanagan v Thales Australia Ltd T/as Thales Australia* [2012] FWA 6291.

Chappell v Griffin Coal Mining Company Pty Ltd,[90] a union organizer was able to secure an injunction preventing the employer from using a video of him criticizing the employer in colourful language outside the worksite gates while preparing for industrial action. The injunction was granted on the basis that the video was taken by security guards standing inside the fences, without Mr Chappell's consent, in contravention of the Surveillance Devices Act 1998 (WA). The court was careful to limit the scope of the injunction to use of the video, by stating that, if the security guards were able to give testimony of what they had heard, without refreshing their memories with the aid of the tainted recording, the employer might still be able to establish that Mr Chappell's uncivil outrage was sufficiently in breach of its workplace conduct policies to warrant dismissal.

In the United Kingdom, the European Convention on Human Rights may not offer protection in 'routine' cases. In *McGowan v Scottish Water*, the employer became suspicious that timesheets were being falsified.[91] He then put in place covert surveillance, and private investigators secreted themselves opposite the front door of the employee's house and filmed him coming and going. The employee was dismissed and the sole issue on appeal to the Employment Appeals Tribunal was whether Article 8 of the Convention was engaged and the employee's rights in that respect breached. The view was taken that the employer's action was proportionate and that the action taken was therefore compliant with the Convention, even though it was acknowledged that the employer's actions raised 'at least a strong presumption that the right to have one's private life respected is being invaded'.[92]

ONE FINAL ISSUE

Chappell's case provides a reminder that employers are able to use their prerogative to command obedience in ways that constrain employees' liberty to express their political commitments. A command expressed as an obligation to adhere to certain political or religious beliefs may be ineffective, but if it is expressed as an obligation to observe certain polite standards of conduct at (and in connection with) work, it may fall within the legitimate parameters of employer control. This is well illustrated by

---

[90] *Chappell v Griffin Coal Mining Company Pty Ltd* [2016] FCA 1248.

[91] *McGowan v Scottish Water* [2005] IRLR 167. A breach was established in *Halford v United Kingdom* [1997] IRLR 471.

[92] *McGowan* (n 91) [11].

a recent body of case law from Australia, involving the exercise by trade unionists of what they had imagined were their statutory rights to freedom of association. *Construction, Forestry, Mining and Energy Union v BHP Coal Pty Ltd*[93] concerned an application by a trade union for the reinstatement of one of its members, who had been dismissed at the height of an industrial dispute for holding up a sign suggesting that workers who were crossing picket lines to go to work were 'scabs'. The Fair Work Act 2009 (Cth) protects employees from any 'adverse action' taken against them by an employer, if the employer is motivated by reason of the employee's exercise of a statutory right to take industrial action or participate in any kind of union activity.[94] In this case, the supervisor who took the decision to dismiss the employee asserted that he had been motivated only by the employee's breach of the workplace code of conduct by using deeply insulting language in his picket line sign. The High Court of Australia confirmed that there had been no adverse action for any prohibited reason. The employer's prerogative to impose certain standards of civility on workplace communications ultimately trumped century-old protection for workers' freedom of expression and association.

This case has been followed by other decisions holding that workers who engage in this kind of robust language in the context of industrial disputes are susceptible not only to discipline and potential dismissal, but to fines and compensation orders for breaching those same adverse action provisions themselves. To call a fellow worker a 'scab' is to engage in adverse action against that fellow worker on the basis of that person's exercise of a freedom *not* to associate. In *Maritime Union of Australia v Fair Work Ombudsman*,[95] a full bench of the Federal Court unanimously affirmed the decision of the primary judge[96] that insults of this kind directed at co-workers can constitute 'adverse action' that 'has the effect, directly or indirectly, of prejudicing the person in the person's employment', according to section 342(2)(b) of the Fair Work Act 2009 (Cth). The court affirmed the imposition of penalties at 75 per cent of the

93 *Construction, Forestry, Mining and Energy Union v BHP Coal Pty Ltd* [2014] HCA 41.

94 See Fair Work Act 2009 (Cth), ss 346–7.

95 *Maritime Union of Australia v Fair Work Ombudsman* [2016] FCAFC 102.

96 *Fair Work Ombudsman v Maritime Union of Australia* [2014] FCA 440, (2014) 243 IR 312.

maximum amount of penalties prescribed for adverse action.[97] The majority (Tracey and Buchanan JJ) also affirmed the primary judge's assessment of compensation to each of the victims of the conduct. The employees who had worked during the strike were awarded $A20,000 each, and one employee who had suffered the insult of 'scab' unjustly was awarded $A40,000 (indicating that it is worse to be called a scab if you are not one). The dissenting judge, Bromberg J, would have reduced this compensation substantially, given the lack of any evidence of serious harm to the victims. He provided a comparison with compensatory awards in other kinds of cases involving the victims of crime, and found these awards manifestly excessive.

A subsequent unfair dismissal decision of the Fair Work Commission in *Gary McDermott v BHP Coal Pty Ltd* also considered the seriousness of using the word 'scab' at work.[98] Fortunately for the employee concerned, the Commission decided that he had not used the word in the context of any industrial militancy, nor as a form of aggression towards or personal vilification of any co-worker, so (given his exemplary 13-year-long record of employment) agreed to reinstate him. Nevertheless, in the course of his reasons, Commissioner Spencer opined that it would be 'fair and reasonable' to have a 'zero-tolerance' policy for the use of the word 'scab' at work, so long as the policy was clearly communicated to employees.[99]

The lesson from these cases is that the employer's prerogative to set its own standards of civil communications at work prevails over other rights that we might once have imagined workers would enjoy in the free expression of their political views and freedom of association. One of the most interesting aspects of the decision in *Gary McDermott* is that the supervisor's own description of Mr McDermott, to his face, as a 'useless c**t', was not sanctioned by the employer's code of conduct, but, in testimony, the employer's representative described that expression as merely 'inappropriate' and 'not nearly the same severity as the word "scab"'.[100] If employers can set up their own idiosyncratic and anti-union lexicon of filthy words for sanction at the workplace, they have most certainly wrested control of much of the political freedom of thought and action that Mr Justice Higgins assumed back in 1912.

---

97 Penalties were set at $A80,000 for the union and $A15,000 for the delegate who engaged in the conduct: *Fair Work Ombudsman v Maritime Union of Australia (No 2)* [2015] FCA 814, (2015) 252 IR 101, [37]–[38].

98 *Gary McDermott v BHP Coal Pty Ltd* [2016] FWC 6935.

99 ibid [219].

100 ibid [214].

A similar limited tolerance of the right of unionists to express political views or take a negative stance to one's employer is apparent in New Zealand. In *Game v Northland Co-operative Dairy Co Ltd*,[101] a union delegate became involved in a dispute relating to the entitlement to redundancy payments of members of another union, at a time when the employer was planning to close down and make all employees, including Game, redundant. Game was dismissed for two acts of alleged misconduct. The first, providing an employer email list that was used by the union to bombard the respondent with faxes and emails, may have justified dismissal, but the second was more contentious. Game took part, in his own time, in a demonstration outside a supermarket, where pamphlets urging people not to buy the respondent's goods were distributed. Game's role was confined to collecting signatures for a petition and handing out leaflets printed by the organizers. The employer's view that this constituted an attack on its 'bottom line' and a breach of contract – a somewhat stretched argument – was accepted by the court. In the United Kingdom, the position appears to be more benign, but the Court of Appeal has left open the possibility of denying a trade union member the statutory protection afforded for taking part in trade union activities, should the contents of a speech be 'malicious, untruthful or irrelevant to the task in hand'.[102]

CONCLUSION

In an era of increasingly pervasive and intrusive electronic communications and surveillance technology, the contest between the employer's prerogative to control all manifestations of its business 'persona' and the employee's claim to an autonomous private life will continue to present challenges for the common law interpretation of the scope of the implied obligation to obey. It is also likely to provide 'meat' for many arguments about the 'unfairness' of dismissals in applications under statutory schemes (considered further in Chapter 11). A similar contest arises when the employee's claim concerns economic interests in pursuing profitable activities outside of working hours, or competing with the

101 *Game v Northland Co-operative Dairy Co Ltd* EmpC AC 28/01, 14 March 2000.

102 *Bass Taverns v Burgess* [1995] IRLR 596, 599.

employer following the cessation of the employment relationship. This aspect of the contest between the employer's claims and the employee's liberty is addressed in the following Chapter 9.

9. Employee mobility

THE NEW 'PSYCHOLOGICAL CONTRACT' AND THE 'PORTFOLIO' CAREER

It has been said that, in the new digital economy, where old notions of 'womb to tomb' service to a single employer have been replaced by the 'portfolio'[1] careers of a highly mobile workforce, employees no longer bargain for job security. According to the new 'psychological contract' of employment, they bargain for employability.[2] Post-boomer generations do not expect to stay in a job forever, and neither do post-Thatcher employers expect to retain staff throughout a full career.[3] Fixed-term contracts have come to dominate employment practices in many fields, especially those in the so-called 'knowledge economy', where rapid technological evolution is changing the nature of business enterprise. In past eras, business enterprises were typically built around a significant investment in tangible capital – land, factories, machineries and equipment. In the knowledge economy, the chief investment of many enterprises is in human skill, know-how and relationships. This chapter considers the way in which this phenomenon – the pre-eminence of human intellectual and social capital in business and industry – has influenced the development of employment contract law.

Three aspects of the employment relationship are pertinent to this discussion. The first is the question of ownership of the fruits of human ingenuity when valuable intangible property, such as copyrights, designs,

---

[1] The portfolio career describes the working patterns of those who juggle a number of, often disparate, professional commitments, for example the app designer, travel writer, Uber driver and bartender, who derives income from several part-time and/or freelance working arrangements.

[2] See Katherine Stone, *From Widgets to Digits: Employment Regulation for the Changing Workplace* (Cambridge University Press 2004) 3. See also Katherine Stone, 'The New Psychological Contract: Implications of the Changing Workplace for Labor and Employment Law' (2001) 48 UCLA Law Review 519.

[3] Neoliberalism sacrifices individual job security in the interests of greater overall labour market participation: see Hugh Collins, 'The Meaning of Job Security' (1991) 20(4) ILJ 227, 229.

trademarks and patents, are created by employees. Issues arise when the express terms of an employment contract are silent, and employers seek to rely on the implied term that the employer owns all property created by the employees in the course of their employment. Disputes arise when employees create valuable intangible property in their own time, offsite, and in pursuit of their own independent projects, but in a field of interest to the employer.

A second concern is the scope for employers to seek protection from competition from their employees during the employment relationship. Does an employer have a legitimate claim to a right to absorb all of an employee's productive capacity within the scope of the enterprise's business interests, in a world of fixed-term, part-time, temporary and casual working engagements, and 'portfolio' careers? The old expression, 'moonlighting', surely has questionable relevance when the employer has not even committed to employing workers for all of their daylight working hours. Interrogation of this issue involves a study of the extent of the employee's obligation of loyalty and fidelity during employment, but outside of official working hours. Even beyond a termination of the employment relationship, this duty of loyalty may constrain the employee's liberty to 'usurp' an emerging business opportunity, if that opportunity arose within the context of the employee's duties as an employee.[4]

The third, and potentially more complex, question concerns employer strategies to protect themselves from competition after the termination of the employment relationship, either by garden leave clauses that keep the employment contract, and, hence, the duty of fidelity, alive beyond the cessation of the relationship itself, or by means of post-employment restrictive covenants that purport to protect an employer from competition, even after termination of the contract itself. Garden leave clauses have become common in the employment contracts of high level employees. Restraints on post-employment activity have become common in standard employment contract documentation, and not only in contracts with high level executives and sales personnel.[5] An ancient common law doctrine, making illegal restraints of trade that are against the public interest, purports to protect employees' liberty to continue their careers in competition with a former employer, where such a restraint is

---

[4] See *Coordinated Industries Pty Ltd v Elliott* (1998) 43 NSWLR 238.

[5] See Christopher Arup et al., 'Restraint of Trade: The Legal Practice' (2013) 36(1) University of NSW Law Journal 1, 6.

intended to prohibit competition per se.[6] Incremental modifications to this doctrine over time have allowed room for the enforcement of such restraints, so long as they go no further than is reasonably necessary to protect a legitimate interest of the employer.[7] What constitutes a 'legitimate interest' – once confined to property and property-like rights – has extended in recent times to encompass an employer's claim over marginally 'confidential' forms of business information,[8] relationships with customers and suppliers,[9] and – more recently and arguably most contentiously – relationships with their own staff.[10] The claim of a legitimate interest in a 'stable workforce' has supported the enforceability of restraints preventing departing employees from offering employment to former colleagues. In some jurisdictions – notably New South Wales, where statute has favoured employer interests[11] – there has been a steady weakening of the requirement that restraints be 'reasonable'. The geographic and temporal extent of restraints is stretching, so as to impair employees' pursuit of future employment and self-employment opportunities.[12]

---

6 For a history of this doctrine, see Harlan Blake, 'Employee Agreements Not to Compete' (1960) 73 Harvard Law Review 625. For a thorough study, see John Dyson Heydon, *The Restraint of Trade Doctrine* (3rd edn, LexisNexis 2008).

7 See *Nordenfelt v Maxim Nordenfelt Guns and Ammunition Co* [1894] AC 535. A covenant that simply precludes competition without any basis in a legitimate interest is unenforceable: see *Marlov Pty Ltd v Murat Col* [2009] NSWSC 501.

8 See e.g. *Woolworths Ltd v Olson* [2004] NSWCA 372.

9 See e.g. *Wright v Gasweld Pty Ltd* (1991) 22 NSWLR 317.

10 See e.g. *Office Angels Ltd v Rainer-Thomas* [1991] IRLR 214; *Dawnay, Day & Co Ltd & Wilcourt Ltd v De Braconier D'Alphen* [1998] ICR 1068; *TSC Europe (UK) Ltd v Massey* [1999] IRLR 22; *Alliance Paper Group plc v Prestwich* [1996] IRLR 25; *Aussie Home Loans v X inc Services* [2005] NSWSC 285; *Kearney Australia Pty Ltd v Crepaldi* [2006] NSWSC 23, [58]; and *Cactus Imaging Pty Ltd v Peters* [2006] NSWSC 717.

11 See the Restraints of Trade Act 1976 (NSW), which allows a court to read down an otherwise unreasonable restraint to preserve its operation. For an explanation of this legislation, see Heydon (n 6) 296–301. Similar legislation in New Zealand permits a court to modify an unreasonable restraint of trade to make it reasonable: see Illegal Contracts Act 1970 (NZ), s 8; applied in *H & R Block Ltd v Sanott* [1976] 1 NZLR 213, 218–19.

12 See e.g. *HRX Holdings Pty Ltd v Pearson* [2012] FCA 161, which allowed a restraint of 20 months; and *Miles v Genesys Wealth Advisors Ltd* [2009] NSWCA 25, which permitted a 30-month restraint.

A further development is the readiness of courts to enforce these restraints by injunction, and not only by awarding the usual remedy of damages for breach of a contractual obligation. Injunctive relief, even if granted only on an interlocutory basis,[13] can sterilize the employee's capacity to exploit their own skilled labour, in contradiction to the supposed benefits of the new 'psychological contract', which – if given any legal status at all – ought to eschew such constraints. These legal developments, driven by the courts applying a narrow conception of 'sanctity of contract',[14] work at cross purposes with the ambitions of an agile workforce.

OWNERSHIP OF THE FRUITS OF LABOUR

Contemporary employment contract doctrine holds that, in the absence of any contrary provision in the contract or any statutory mandate,[15] the employer can claim ownership of new property created by employees in the course of their employment. It was not always so. According to US labour historian Catherine Fisk, 'prior to the last quarter of the nineteenth century, courts confronted with disputes about ownership of valuable workplace knowledge generally concluded that the employee owned it'.[16] It may be more accurate to say that, at that point in our history, courts did not recognize such knowledge as property at all, but treated it as part of the personal attributes of individuals.[17] It was only after industrialization that the statutory creation of intellectual property rights (such as copyrights, designs and patents) prompted the judicial development of an

---

[13] The grant of an injunction pending final resolution often determines an issue, because of the inevitable court delays in listing matters for final hearing.

[14] See *Seven Network Operations v Warburton (No 2)* [2011] NSWSC 386.

[15] See e.g. the Patents Act 1977 (UK), ss 40–42, which grant employees inventors' rights to compensation for inventions made in the course of employment. See Jeremias Prassl, 'Intellectual Property and the Contract of Employment' in Mark Freedland et al. (eds), *The Contract of Employment* (Oxford University Press 2016) 592–5.

[16] Catherine Fisk, 'Reflections on the New Psychological Contract and the Ownership of Human Capital' (2002) 34 Connecticut Law Review 765, 771–2. See also Katherine Stone, 'Knowledge at Work: Disputes over the Ownership of Human Capital in the Changing Workplace' (2002) 34 Connecticut Law Review 721.

[17] For another perspective on the importance ascribed in earlier times to free competition, see Harlan Blake, 'Employee Agreements Not to Compete' (1960) 73 Harvard Law Review 625.

implied contractual term enabling employers to assert ownership of this new kind of capital. Perhaps the implication of this term was warranted in an era when employees expected to be engaged by the same firm for the term of their natural lives. One wonders whether such an assumption would have been made had the question arisen during our contemporary era, when the disintegration of large enterprises and the emergence of networks of smaller entrepreneurial businesses have created more precarious forms of work.[18] It is questionable that such a term would pass the current necessity test for the creation of a new implied term.[19] Certainly, someone must be ascribed with ownership of new property (property cannot be ownerless, or it is not 'property' at all); but, in the absence of any express term, why must it necessarily be the employer, and not the creator themselves, especially where the drafting of employment contracts is generally in the hands of employers who must surely be taken to have addressed their minds to the issue? It would be rare for a contemporary written employment contract prepared under legal advice to neglect inclusion of an intellectual property clause. The inclusion in the Patents Act 1977 (UK) of statutory rights for employees to claim some compensation when employers have acquired ownership of their inventions indicates that the potential unfairness of the operation of an implied term ascribing ownership to an employer has not escaped the notice of legislators.[20]

Redrock Holdings v Hinkley[21] provides an example of the odd consequences that can arise from the operation of the implied term. Adam Hinkley was a 'boy genius' who, while still in high school, began developing what proved to be a valuable library of programming tools,

---

[18] See Hugh Collins, 'Independent Contractors and the Challenge of Vertical Disintegration to Employment Protection Laws' (1990) 10 Oxford Journal of Legal Studies 35. See also Alain Supiot, *Beyond Employment: Changes in Work and Future of Labour Law in Europe, A report prepared for the European Commission* (Oxford University Press 2000).

[19] See *Commonwealth Bank of Australia v Barker* (2014) 253 CLR 169; [2014] HCA 32.

[20] The Patents Act 1977 (UK), s 39(1) provides that inventions belong to the employer if created in the course of the normal duties of an employee, but s 40 provides that an employee whose invention has brought 'outstanding benefit' to the employer may bring a claim for some compensation. Note, however, that the Copyright Designs and Patents Act 1988 (UK), s 11(2) preserves the common law assumption that ownership of copyright works vests in the author's employer when the work is created in the course of employment. See Michael Spence, *Intellectual Property* (Oxford University Press 2007) 102–3, 194–8.

[21] *Redrock Holdings v Hinkley* [2001] VSC 91, (2001) 50 IPR 565.

which he used to create and develop other computer programs. He continued to develop this library of tools after securing employment with Redrock, and he used the same tools to produce some programs for a private business he ran with his father. After a couple of years, Adam left Redrock with the intention of joining others in a new dot-com venture. After he transferred his intellectual property rights in the programming tools to the newly incorporated company (Hotline), the venture collapsed because the other investors failed to inject sufficient capital to support the start-up. In bitter disappointment, Hinkley left the company, but only after deleting or encrypting all copies of his software tools so that no one less talented than him could use them. In the ensuing three-way dispute over ownership of these tools, Redrock asserted ownership of the programming tools.

The court applied the test from *Triplex Safety Glass Co v Scorah*[22] to find that copyright in the library was owned by the former employer, because about 90 per cent of the work in developing the programs had been done during working hours, and – most importantly – the library of tools was held to have been essential for the operation of Redrock's programs and, hence, its business. Hinkley and his father lost their claim, not only to exclusive ownership of the tools, but to any entitlement to use the programs at all. Given that reproduction of a 'substantial part' of a literary work constitutes breach of copyright,[23] and 'substantial part' has been interpreted as any recognizable part of the work,[24] this decision meant that Hinkley could not continue to work with and develop his own creations. One wonders whether Hinkley would have agreed to that arrangement when he first accepted employment with Redrock, had Redrock's claim of ownership over his creations been expressed in clear contractual terms.

A decision that might reflect different perspectives of a specialized employment court and the ordinary courts is *Empress Abalone Ltd v Langdon*.[25] In that case, the defendant had been employed for a specific, publicly funded project to help the employer develop spherical pearls. Mabe (half round) pearl implants were used for control purposes. The employee, an expert in the field, had his own abalone tanks at home and, outside of working hours, developed a bead enabling him to grow mabe

---

22 *Triplex Safety Glass Co v Scorah* (1937) 55 RPC 21, 28. See also *Sterling Engineering v Patchett* [1955] AC 534, 544.

23 See Copyright Act 1968 (Cth), s 14.

24 See *Hawkes & Son (London) Ltd v Paramount Films Service Ltd* [1934] 1 Ch 593.

25 *Empress Abalone Ltd v Langdon* [2000] 2 ERNZ 147 (EmpC).

pearls. The Employment Court held that the invention had been developed in the employee's own time, outside the scope of the duties he was employed for and without using the employer's facilities. The employer was held not to have established a right to any interest in the patent. On appeal,[26] the Employment Court was held to have correctly determined that the true issue was whether the invention was within the scope of what the defendant was employed to do, but held that the judge failed to have regard to other evidence that bore on the scope of the defendant's employment. The matter was remitted to the Employment Court for reconsideration, although, after examining the full scope of the employment, the Employment Court upheld its original decision.[27] It seems unlikely that this result would have been reached by a common law court.

EMPLOYER CONTROLS ON OUT-OF-HOURS PRODUCTIVE LABOUR

One of the pitfalls for Hinkley was that he continued to work on his library of computer tools during working time, and embedded them in products specifically made for Redrock. When an employee works on projects in their own time, away from the work premises, there is a greater likelihood that they will succeed in asserting ownership over inventions. In *Spencer Industries v Collins*,[28] a marketing manager for a tyre retreading enterprise was able to assert ownership over a patent in a new process he had developed in his own time, notwithstanding that the process was designed to strip treads off old tyres and was, therefore, of direct interest to the employer's business. His success was largely due to an argument that he had offered his invention to the employer in exchange for greater job security and seniority in the family firm, but his offer was rebutted, with the direction that he should stick to his job of selling the product and give up his hobby of invention. The employer's own words established that invention was not within the scope of his employment duties, so the *Triplex Glass* test was determined in Collins' favour.

---

[26] *Empress Abalone Ltd v Langdon* [2000] 2 ERNZ 53 (CA).

[27] *Empress Abalone Ltd v Langdon* [2000] 2 ERNZ 441 (EmpC). The Court of Appeal could not impose its own construction of the contract due to restrictions on the scope of appeals from the Employment Court: see Employment Relations Act 2000 (NZ), s 214(1).

[28] *Spencer Industries v Collins* [2003] FCA 542.

Appeals to arguments based on the scope of the contract will not always resolve a dispute over ownership of new inventions where the employee is held to be a senior member of staff who owes fiduciary obligations beyond the contractual duty of fidelity.[29] This was the case in *Victoria University of Technology v Wilson*,[30] where a senior professor who ran a research centre for a university was required to render an account of profits to the university in respect of an inventive computer resource that he created with a colleague, largely in his own consulting time and outside the scope of his teaching and research duties to the university. The university was held to have no right under contract to claim the invention, but Wilson was nevertheless found liable to account as a fiduciary, because he had chosen to exploit for himself an opportunity that came to his notice in his capacity as a senior university leader. However, holding a senior position will not necessarily disadvantage an employee where the claimed invention is sufficiently removed from their contractual duties.[31]

Another equitable doctrine that tends to favour the former employer's interests is the duty not to breach confidence. Unlike the contractual duty of fidelity, the equitable duty to preserve confidences is capable of survival beyond the term of an employment contract[32] so long as the information is truly confidential[33] and is not merely accumulated know-how.[34]

---

[29] See Chapter 7 on fiduciary obligations.

[30] *Victoria University of Technology v Wilson* [2004] VSC 33, (2004) 60 IPR 392.

[31] *Helmet Integrated Systems Ltd v Tunnard* [2006] EWCA Civ 1735, [2007] IRLR 126 (CA); *University of Western Australia v Gray* (2009) 259 ALR 224.

[32] See *Campbell v Frisbee* [2002] EWCA Civ 1374.

[33] An explanation of what is genuinely 'confidential' information in a workplace context, and therefore able to be protected by such a covenant, can be found in *Wright v Gasweld Pty Ltd* (1991) 39 IR 256, 271, per Kirby J. See also *Saltman Engineering Co Ltd v Campbell Engineering Co Ltd* (1948) 65 RPC 203, 215, per Lord Greene; and *Coco v AN Clark (Engineers) Ltd* [1969] RPC 41, 47, per Megarry J. For a critique of the application of this law in a workplace context, see Andrew Stewart, 'Confidentiality and the Employment Relationship' (1988) 1 AJLL 1, 5–12; and Andrew Stewart, 'Ownership of Property in the Context of Employment' (1992) 5 AJLL 1, 1–10.

[34] *Faccenda Chicken Ltd v Fowler* [1987] Ch 117.

GARDEN LEAVE

'Garden leave' describes an increasingly common practice whereby an employer who does not wish to permit a departing employee to take up duties in a rival firm holds the employee to an obligation to remain under contract until the expiry of their notice period, but without performing any duties. The employee is required to stay at home and attend to the garden.[35] (If this practice had developed in Australia, it would more likely have been termed 'surfing leave'.) Some cases have challenged an employer's entitlement to put an employee on garden leave on the basis of a claimed duty to provide work, although not always successfully.[36]

In response to this risk, it is now common for standard employment contracts to include express garden leave clauses and long notice periods.[37] Courts have, however, begun to limit the length of time during which an employee can be placed on garden leave, by assessing these clauses against the doctrine that makes illegal restraints of trade that go further than reasonably necessary to protect a legitimate interest.[38] (This doctrine is discussed in the next section.) In retaliation to this incursion on the employer's claim to a prerogative to keep former employees from competing, some contracts now include onerous 'liquidated damages' clauses to punish an employee for breaking a notice period. The courts are likely to be sympathetic to such clauses given the difficulties involved in assessing damages. This is illustrated by *Tullett Prebon (Australia) Pty Ltd v Purcell*, where an investment broker, Purcell, purported to give notice under an employment contract that was determined to be for a fixed term. The employer refused to accept his notice and sought an injunction to enforce a period of garden leave coextensive with the remainder of the fixed term, being a period of some 15 months. This was held to be excessive under the restraint of trade doctrine, so an injunction was awarded for six months.[39] When that period came to an end, the employer issued Purcell with a direction to return to work for the nine

---

35 See *Delaney v Staples* [1992] 1 All ER 944, 947.

36 See *Bearingpoint Australia Pty Ltd v Hillard* [2008] VSC 115.

37 The decision in *JM Finn & Co Ltd v Holliday* [2013] EWHC 3450 (QB), [2014] IRLR 102, provides a recent example.

38 See *Credit Suisse v Armstrong* [1996] ICR 882, 892; *Peters (WA) Ltd v Petersville Ltd* (2001) 205 CLR 126; *Tullett Prebon (Australia) Pty Ltd v Purcell* [2008] NSWSC 852, (2008) 175 IR 414; *Tullett Prebon plc v BGC Brokers* [2010] EWHC 484 (QB), [222]–[225]; *Jardin v Metcash Ltd* (2011) 285 ALR 677, [84]–[86]; *Holliday* (n 37).

39 *Purcell* (n 38).

months remaining of his initial fixed-term contract. Purcell refused, so the employer successfully sued him for $A503,100 in damages, assessed according to a formula in the contract.[40] Purcell's case illustrates the way that the tug of war for talent in competitive industries has prompted the inclusion in employment contracts of the kinds of clauses that would once have been seen only in commercial contracts.

In *Air New Zealand Ltd v Kerr*, the Employment Court considered that 'the correct approach to be adopted is that a garden leave provision should be taken into account by the Court when considering the reasonableness of the duration of any post-employment restraint covenant'.[41] In *Kerr*, the employee, a senior manager with Air New Zealand, had been immediately placed on six months' garden leave when he informed Air New Zealand that he intended to take up a position with a rival airline. The court held that a six-month restraint was more than adequate to protect the confidential information of concern, and that this protection had been achieved by the requirement that garden leave be taken for that period.

POST-EMPLOYMENT RESTRAINTS

Many employers seek to extend their protection from competition from former staff, even beyond the termination of the employment contract after a proper notice period, by including restrictive covenants in employment contracts that purport to run for many months, or possibly years, and over an extensive geographical area.[42] The employer must have a legitimate interest to protect, but the clause remains enforceable even if that interest does not continue to exist.[43] However, the absence of an ongoing interest would go against the employer in relation to the granting of remedies.[44] Typically, employers will include standard form

---

[40] *Tullett Prebon (Australia) Pty Ltd v Purcell* [2009] NSWSC 1079 (Ward J); affirmed unanimously by the New South Wales Court of Appeal: [2010] NSWCA 150.

[41] *Air New Zealand Ltd v Kerr* [2013] NZEmpC 153, [71].

[42] In *Printers and Finishers Ltd v Holloway and others* [1964] 3 All ER 731, 736, Cross J held that information which was not confidential at law could be protected only by express covenant.

[43] *Towry EJ v Bennett* [2012] EWHC 224 (QB).

[44] *TFS Derivatives v Morgan* [2006] IRLR 246.

clauses designed to prevent employees from competing with them in any future engagement. The elaborate structure of the typical set of restraint clauses is generally designed to preserve their enforceability, in the face of the common law doctrine making restraints of trade that offend the public interest in a freely competitive labour market illegal.[45] Over time, and depending upon the jurisdiction, this common law doctrine has suffered some erosion. In the United Kingdom, it would appear that the duty not to destroy mutual trust in the employment relationship has had some work to do in restraining employers from imposing unreasonable post-employment restraints.[46] This should not be overstated, and the law remains very much protective of the employer's interests. In Australia, the practice of enforcing increasingly oppressive restrictive covenants has grown, free of any such restraint.

While the general principles of restraint of trade are accepted in New Zealand law, the courts have tended to apply those principles in a conservative manner. In *Gallagher*, in 1998, the Court of Appeal accepted an analysis of decided cases by the Employment Court that revealed that it is exceptional for a restraint of even one year's duration, let alone longer, to have been found to be reasonable.[47] In that case, the Court of Appeal, stressing that restraints were determined as a matter of law, reduced a four-year restriction to one year.[48] The employee in question was a senior executive at a company in a highly competitive international business. Twelve months has been described as being 'at the upper end of periods which are likely to be upheld by the Court'; longer

---

45 'Cascading' or 'blue pencil' clauses are designed to permit severance of any clause found to be excessive, while leaving others operational. See Heydon (n 6) 284–96.

46 See also David Cabrelli, 'The Effect of Termination upon Post-Employment Obligations' in Mark Freedland et al. (eds), *The Contract of Employment* (Oxford University Press 2016) 579.

47 *Walley v Gallagher Group Ltd* [1998] 3 ERNZ 1153 (EmpC) was undisturbed in this respect on appeal (*Gallagher Group Ltd v Walley* [1999] 1 ERNZ 490 (CA)). See also the survey in *University of Auckland Primary Health Care Trust v Sewell* [2000] 1 ERNZ 781 (EmpC), in which a three-year restraint was held to be unreasonable in the absence of 'compelling evidence' as to its necessity. See also the figures in the Appendix to Phillip Skelton and Rob Towner, 'Fidelity and Restraints – Should the Court Exercise More Restraint?' (Employment Law Conference 5, 2010) 27.

48 *Gallagher* (n 47).

periods require strong justification.[49] The more usual pattern appears to be between three and six months.[50]

The rationale of the common law prohibition on restraints doctrine, as expressed by Lord Atkinson in *Herbert Morris Ltd v Saxelby*,[51] is essentially that the sterilization of productive labour is so antithetical to the public interest that the courts of law will not enforce any private bargain to restrain trade.[52] Under the common law, such a private bargain is void for illegality. The doctrine does not depend upon any inequality of bargaining power or vulnerability of a party to the contract (although that may be a distinct or additional ground for avoiding a restrictive covenant[53]). It applies even when the contracting parties are well-advised commercial players.[54] Too often trial judges forget this, and imply that the fact of the parties' own agreement, usually a boilerplate clause, stating that the parties agree that all restraints are reasonable and may be enforced by injunction, is sufficient to justify the enforcement of a restraint.[55] In *John Fairfax Publications Pty Ltd v Birt*,[56] Brereton J

---

49 *Grey Advertising (New Zealand) Ltd v Marinkovich* [1999] 2 ERNZ 844, 857 (EmpC). In that case, the court held that there was an 'arguable case' that the 12-month period was not unreasonable. A one-year restraint was upheld in *Sulkem Co Ltd v Adams* NZEmpC AEC41/97; *Space Industries (1979) Ltd v McKavanagh* [2000] 1 ERNZ 490 (EmpC); and *Hally Labels Ltd v Powell* [2011] NZEmpC 63, [2011] ERNZ 233.

50 See *Cain v Turners and Growers Fresh Ltd* [1998] 3 ERNZ 314 (EmpC). Three months was also suggested as being appropriate for a hairstylist whose employer focused on customer satisfaction and retention: *Servilles Ltd v Whiting* EmpC AC47/00, 2 June 2000.

51 *Herbert Morris Ltd v Saxelby* [1916] 1 AC 688, 699.

52 Surprisingly, Australia's statutory competition law (which supports the same free market philosophy) exempts restrictive covenants in services and employment contracts from the controls on abuse of market power: see Competition and Consumer Act 2010 (Cth), s 51(2).

53 See *Schroeder Music Publishing Co v Macaulay* [1974] 1 WLR 1308. It should be said that *Macaulay* has not been as influential as it might have been. David Cabrelli posits an alternative view that addressing unconscionable conduct is the core rationale for the restraints doctrine, and that the sterilization of productive labour argument is a later gloss from nineteenth-century laissez faire economics. See Cabrelli (n 46) 578.

54 *Maggbury Pty Ltd v Hafele Australia Pty Ltd* [2001] HCA 70; *Gallagher Group Ltd v Walley* [1999] 1 ERNZ 490 (CA).

55 The parties' own agreement, especially if it followed legal advice, may be a factor in determining whether a restraint protecting a legitimate interest is 'reasonable': see *Metcash Ltd v Jardin (No 3)* [2010] NSWSC 1096, [48].

56 *John Fairfax Publications Pty Ltd v Birt* [2006] NSWSC 995, [95].

upheld a restraint keeping a young man with a dependent wife and children out of work for three months on the basis that the young man was the 'author of his own misfortune'.[57] In that case, the employee also pleaded hardship, which is a defence to the enforcement of an otherwise reasonable restraint.

The sanctity of contract argument was taken a step further in *Seven Network Operations Ltd v Warburton (No 2)*, where Pembroke J said that a restrictive covenant should even be enforced in circumstances where an employee was not aware of the boilerplate clause in the contract.[58] Nineteenth-century 'sanctity of contract' appears to have trumped the more ancient wisdom of the common law in these recent Australian cases.[59]

Legitimate Interests

Confidential information

One of the legitimate interests that will justify a reasonable post-employment restraint is genuinely confidential information belonging to the employer. In *Wright v Gasweld Pty Ltd*,[60] Kirby P set out strict criteria for identifying genuinely confidential information. It needed to be the fruit of considerable skill and effort; it had to be jealously guarded by the employer; employees needed to be informed that the information was confidential; it needed to be the kind of information that the industry concerned customarily treated as confidential; and it needed to be disclosed only to high level employees on a 'need to know' basis. Once information became known to the public, it could not be confidential,[61] and any information that was part of the employee's own stock of knowledge and skill could also not be confidential to the employer.[62]

---

[57] ibid [49]. See also *Bulldogs Rugby League Club Ltd v Williams* [2008] NSWSC 822 (8 August 2008), [66], and other 'author of their own misery' cases discussed further below.

[58] *Seven Network Operations Ltd v Warburton (No 2)* [2011] NSWSC 386 (12 May 2011), [3], citing *Toll (FGHCT) Pty Ltd v Alphapharm Pty Ltd* (2004) 219 CLR 165, [43]–[44], which held that the 'enforcement of a commercial contract does not depend on a party's knowledge of its terms'.

[59] A recent exception is *Wallis Nominees (Computing) Pty Ltd v Pickett* [2012] VSC 82 (14 March 2012), where Sifris J refused to enforce an unreasonable restraint.

[60] *Wright v Gasweld Pty Ltd* (1991) 22 NSWLR 317, 334.

[61] See *Maggbury* (n 54). See also *Del Casale v Artedomus (Aust) Pty Ltd* (2007) 73 IPR 326.

[62] *Faccenda Chicken* (n 34).

In more recent times, however, mundane forms of business information have been accepted as sufficiently confidential to justify a restraint, such as the means of laying out a supermarket to maximize stock turnover[63] and strategies for selling real estate advertising space.[64] Arguably, this kind of 'information' is nothing more than industry know-how, which cannot be separated from the employee's own skill and talent. Rather than shielding employees' entitlement to take their own skill and know-how into future careers, the courts have been willing to accept the argument articulated in *Littlewoods Organisation Ltd v Harris*[65] that an injunction preventing the employee from taking up new employment should be granted for the very reason that it is practically difficult to segregate the employer's confidential information from the employee's own know-how, and the protection of the employer's confidential information must prevail. The ready adoption of the *Littlewoods* argument demonstrates how far contemporary contract law has strayed from the ancient wisdom. One is reminded of Shakespeare's *Merchant of Venice*, and Shylock's contract for a 'pound of flesh' as payment for a breach of contract. The court in the play forbade him his remedy, because extracting his pound of flesh would also rob his victim of vital blood that had not been part of the bargain. The contemporary tendency of courts hearing restraint cases is to require employees who have made these ill-considered bargains to surrender up their liberty to exploit their own know-how, skills and talents to the full – their very lifeblood – in order to render to the employer a mere pound of dubiously confidential information.

The New Zealand courts have tended to be sceptical of claims of possible damage from information received by a former employee. In *Air New Zealand Ltd v Kerr*, the volume of information was such that the court considered that, at best, the defendant would 'only [be] likely to have been able to recall some things and, even then, probably generally'.[66]

Customer relationships

A second category of legitimate interest, protectable by a reasonable restraint, is the employer's interest in maintaining its client relationships.

---

63 *Woolworths* (n 8).

64 *John Fairfax Publications Pty Ltd v Birt* [2006] NSWSC 995.

65 *Littlewoods Organisation Ltd v Harris* [1977] 1 WLR 1472, 1479.

66 *Kerr* (n 41) [54]. In that case, it also appeared that the competing airline was already in possession of much more information than the defendant might have been able to recall.

Former employers have been held to be entitled to enforce covenants whereby departing employees agree not to solicit customers or clients, on the basis that the employer has a legitimate interest in the personal bond that customers may develop with the employer's staff.[67] The employer can lay claim to that 'customer connection' because the employer has provided the resources to enable a 'front-line' employee to establish, develop and maintain a productive relationship with the customer. If the employee decamps to a rival enterprise, the employer may be vulnerable to losing that connection with the customer. This interest is protectable by a restraint of limited duration, preventing the employee from soliciting business from the customer. How long the restraint should last will depend upon the nature of the business and the relationship. In industries where client relationships are relatively ephemeral and customer loyalty is low, only very short restraints are warranted. In businesses where customers develop long-term attachments to trusted advisors, long restraints have been held to be justifiable. For example, in *Miles v Genesys Wealth Advisers Ltd*, a 30-month injunction was granted to restrain a personal investment advisor from servicing former clients, because those kinds of clients tended to remain with an advisor for the long term.[68] (Missing from the judgment was any consideration of the inconvenience that enforcement of this injunction would have on the clients themselves, none of whom had any contractual obligation to continue to do business with the former employer firm.)

Strictly speaking, the customer connection is not a proprietary interest at all, although it has been described as such in some case law.[69] The use of proprietary language is unfortunate because it clouds a proper understanding of the limits of the employer's legitimate interest. Because it is a personal obligation owed by the former employee not to exploit personal connections, it should only apply to customers with whom the employee developed a personal connection, not to all clients of the business.

A further questionable extension to the legitimacy of such restraints has come from cases widening the meaning of 'solicitation' to include occasions when the client makes the first overture to the departing

---

67 *Lindner v Murdoch's Garage* (1950) 83 CLR 628, 633–4.

68 *Miles v Genesys Wealth Advisers Ltd* [2009] NSWCA 25, [38].

69 See e.g. *Koops Martin v Dean Reeves* [2006] NSWSC 449, [29], per Brereton J: 'Goodwill, of which customer connection is the essence, is akin to a proprietary interest'. In *Hartleys Ltd v Martin* [2002] VSC 301, [116], the court said that employees had taken 'part of the plaintiff's assets with them in the form of clients'.

employee.[70] When extended thus, a restraint potentially restricts the freedoms of people who never signed up to any limitation of their own choices of business contacts. A particularly worrying development has been the willingness to restrain former employees from accepting an engagement with a prospective client of the former employer, who had never agreed to do business with the former employer in the first place.[71]

Stable workforce?

A third, and highly contentious, 'legitimate interest' supporting a restraint is the employer's interest in maintaining a stable workforce by stopping departing employees from offering employment to their former colleagues. Restraint clauses of this type are colloquially named 'anti-poaching' clauses, invoking an invidious analogy with the conduct of hungry peasants in past times who trespassed on a lord's land to steal his game. The cases that have accepted this premise assume that connection with employees is analogous to 'customer connection', or that a stable workforce constitutes part of business 'goodwill'. This rationale is well illustrated by the reasoning in *Cactus Imaging Pty Ltd v Peters*:[72]

> employees are not property, but, all else being equal, a business with a stable trained workforce will be more attractive to a purchaser and command a higher price than one with a workforce which is unstable, disruptive or poorly trained, just as a loyal and satisfied clientele makes a business more attractive and valuable. In my opinion, staff connection constitutes part of the intangible benefits which may give a business value over and above the value of the assets employed in it, and thus comprises part of its goodwill. It is amenable to protection by a covenant in a manner similar to customer connection, even in the absence of protectable confidences.

From an accounting stance, this is no doubt true, but it is questionable whether an employer's interest in maintaining a contented and productive workforce should constitute a sufficiently legitimate interest to justify the imposition of constraints on employees who wish to leave. As Jenkins LJ said in *Kores Manufacturing Co Ltd v Kolok Manufacturing Co Ltd*, the

---

[70] See *Barrett v Ecco Personnel Pty Ltd* [1998] NSWCA 30, [20], [35]; upholding *Ecco Personnel Pty Ltd v Barrett* [1996] NSWSC 475; *Ecolab Pty Ltd v Klen International Pty Ltd* [2007] FCA 1376, [54]; *Wright v Ryan* [2005] NSWCA 368; *Smith Martis Cork & Rajan Pty Ltd v Benjamin Corporation Pty Ltd* (2004) 207 ALR 136; *Michael Wilson and Partners Ltd v Nicholls* [2008] NSWSC 501.

[71] See *IceTV v Duncan Ross and others* [2007] NSWSC 635.

[72] *Cactus Imaging Pty Ltd v Peters* [2006] NSWSC 717, [55].

value of a stable workforce is 'an interest which employers are entitled to protect by all legitimate means, as by paying good wages and making their employment attractive', but not by recognition of any legal right to prevent those staff from exercising an unfettered choice of where they will work.[73] If an employer cannot prevent staff from leaving and taking with them to a competitor the 'skill, experience, know-how and general knowledge inevitably gained'[74] during employment, it is difficult to see how an employer could claim a legitimate interest in restraining others from inviting them to leave.

English authority on the legitimacy of these kinds of restraints has been divided. In *Office Angels Ltd v Rainer-Thomas*,[75] the court upheld a covenant preventing a person from recruiting temporary staff on the books of a temporary employment agency in London. *Office Angels* has been relied upon as authority supporting enforceability of such clauses, despite a later decision of the English Court of Appeal in *Hanover Insurance v Schapiro*, which found such a covenant to be unenforceable because 'an employer does not have any sort of proprietary interest in a stable team of staff entitling the employer to impose restrictions on the solicitation of staff'.[76] Subsequently, *Dawnay Day & Co Ltd v De Braconier D'Alphen* held that investment bankers could be prevented from 'poaching' the staff on the teams of the bond broking desks with whom they had worked.[77] Influential facts in this case were that the broking business was conducted by established and experienced 'desks' or teams, and there was a strong culture of 'following the leader' in the industry. The special kind of loyalty built up between the leader and the team was treated as analogous to 'customer connection'. The analogy is tenuous. While a customer's loyalty may be due to overall good service funded from the resources of the firm, the loyalty of staff to a leader is the fruit of personal charisma.

Office Angels and *Dawnay Day* have been influential authorities.[78] In *TSC Europe (UK) Ltd v Massey*,[79] it was held (ignoring the *Hanover*

---

73 *Kores Manufacturing Co Ltd v Kolok Manufacturing Co Ltd* [1958] 2 All ER 65, 74.

74 *FSS Travel & Leisure Systems Ltd v Johnson* [1997] EWCA Civ 2759, per Mummery LJ. Woolf MR and Millett LJ agreed with this statement.

75 *Office Angels Ltd v Rainer-Thomas* [1991] IRLR 214.

76 *Hanover Insurance v Schapiro* [1994] IRLR 82, 84.

77 *Dawnay Day & Co Ltd v De Braconier D'Alphen* [1997] IRLR 442, [44] (CA).

78 See also *Alliance Paper Group plc v Prestwich* [1996] IRLR 25.

79 *TSC Europe (UK) Ltd v Massey* [1999] IRLR 22.

Insurance case) that an employer did enjoy a legitimate interest in maintaining a stable, trained workforce. The restraint in question was found to be excessive because it purported to prevent recruitment of any personnel who had worked for the employer, not only those with whom the former employee had a close working relationship or senior personnel who might hold confidential information of the firm, suggesting that such restraints are really an extension of the employer's entitlement to prevent leakage of confidential information. Some of these cases are also complicated by the fact that the departing employee was once a business owner in the employing business, so the restraint may be justified by a past business sale transaction.[80] In the United Kingdom, it appears that clauses of this sort will be enforceable unless they are unreasonably wide.[81]

Australian case law has tended to follow *Dawnay Day*.[82] For example, in *Hartleys Ltd v Martin*[83] two stockbrokers were injuncted from employing their personal assistant, Ms Briggs, when they left the employer's firm. Ms Briggs had already given notice to her employer, but was effectively prevented from taking up new employment by the enforcement of a contract to which she was a complete stranger. The injustice of such a result escaped any comment in the judgment.

Reasonableness

Once it has been established that the employer has a legitimate interest to protect, there will also be an enquiry into whether the restraint goes no further than is reasonably necessary to protect that interest. This will

---

80 See Adrian Brooks, 'The Limits of Competition: Restraint of Trade in the Context of Employment Contracts' (2001) University of NSW Law Journal 27, para 48.

81 In *CEF Holdings v Mundey* [2012] IRLR 912, [49], [52], the employer's attempt to enforce the clause failed. The view was taken that the authorities showed that 'Employee Recruitment Restriction Clauses will be upheld where they apply to identifiable employees, who formed part of the team which included the employee, who was being enjoined'. Moreover, 'the critical differences between, on the one hand, the cases in which similar provisions were upheld, and, on the other hand, the present case is that the restriction in this case relates to all the fellow employees of the ... Defendants, a very large proportion of whom were not known to them and this category included people with whom they have had no contact, and who they could not identify'.

82 *Aussie Home Loans v X Inc Services* [2005] NSWSC 285; *Kearney Australia Pty Ltd v Crepaldi* [2006] NSWSC 23, [58]; *Cactus Imaging* (n 72).

83 *Hartleys Ltd v Martin* [2002] VSC 301.

involve interrogation of the scope, geographical and temporal extent of the restraint, and the circumstances in which the restraint was agreed. The scope of a restraint should not seek to capture duties or activities wider than those the employee performed for the former employer. Geographical reach should not exceed the former employer's market, and the time should not exceed the length of time that is needed to protect the interest concerned. Commercially valuable confidential information, for example, should not be protected for any longer than it would normally take for the information to become stale, or widely known in the public arena. Over time, at least in Australia, the duration of enforceable restraints appears to be extending[84] – somewhat antithetically to the proposition that our labour laws should support workforce mobility in the interests of greater economic productivity. Some of this extension appears to have been justified on the basis that employers are agreeing to pay for the period of restraint.[85] While this takes away any hardship argument (that the employee may starve without the liberty to pursue gainful employment), it does not accommodate the rationale of enabling freely competitive labour markets. Such agreements remain objectionable upon that rationale, even where parties, at an earlier stage in their relationship, have made a private bargain to accept restriction.

Enforcement by Injunction

The result in *Hartleys v Martin* (discussed above) might not have been so oppressive had the court simply enforced the restraint by an award of damages. If the stockbrokers had been required to pay Hartleys for the inconvenience of the loss of a staff member, the remedy would not have burdened a person who was not party to the contract. Injunctive relief confers a property-like right.[86] Injunctions are significantly more coercive than damages awards and, for that reason, have generally been eschewed in favour of a proper assessment of damages, especially in the context of any kind of commercial transaction.

---

[84] Where once a three- or six-month restraint may have been permitted, restraints of 12 months and longer are becoming more common: see *Metcash* (n 55); *Pearson v HRX Holdings Pty Ltd* [2012] FCAFC 111, (2012) IR 369 (20 months).

[85] See *Woolworths* (n 8); *Pearson* (n 84).

[86] For a thorough analysis of this argument, see Guido Calabresi and A Douglas Melamed, 'Property Rules, Liability Rules and Inalienability: One View of the Cathedral' (1972) 85(6) Harvard Law Review 1089.

The readiness of courts to grant injunctions to enforce restrictive covenants in employment contracts is arguably a perverse development in the law, owing its genesis to the undeservedly influential case of *Lumley v Wagner*,[87] in which Lord St Leonards made an exceptional decision to grant an injunction to enforce a promise in a personal services contract.[88] Like a mutant gene, that decision has evolved over time to create a monstrous distortion in contemporary Australian employment law.[89] On the authority of that old case, which involved a restraint upon an entertainer for a few short weeks remaining in her performance contract, it is now possible for corporate employers in twenty-first century Australia to prevent staff from taking up positions with competitors after the proper termination of their employment contract in any part of the globe for one year (or possibly longer), without meeting the usual threshold for justifying injunctive relief in place of an order for damages.[90]

There have been some extreme examples. In *Bulldogs Rugby League Club Ltd v Williams*,[91] a rugby league player (Sonny Bill Williams) who changed his mind after signing a five-year contract to play rugby league for a Sydney-based club was ordered not to play rugby union in France for the remainder of that five-year term. In the business of vigorous contact sports, a five-year restraint is potentially career destroying. It is difficult to see why an injunction was warranted on the basis of analogy

---

[87] *Lumley v Wagner* (1852) 1 De GM & G 604.

[88] Meagher, Heydon and Leeming describe *Lumley* as the '*fons et origo* and prototype' of the enforcement by injunction of negative covenants in contracts for 'special services': see RP Meagher, JD Heydon and MJ Leeming, *Meagher Gummow & Lehane's Equity: Doctrines and Remedies* (4th edn, LexisNexis 2002) 755, para [21-220]. The pedigree and status of the doctrine of *Lumley* is fully expounded in ICF Spry, *The Principles of Equitable Remedies: Specific Performance, Injunctions, Rectification and Equitable Damages* (4th edn, Lawbook 1990) 561–92. Recent Australian cases often cite *Curro v Beyond Productions Pty Ltd* (1993) 30 NSWLR 337, 346–8, which approved and followed *Lumley*.

[89] For an extended argument on the unwarranted influence of *Lumley*, see Joellen Riley, 'Sterilising Talent: A Critical Assessment of Injunctions Enforcing Negative Covenants' (2012) 34(4) Sydney Law Review 617. *Lumley* has also been criticized in the United States: see Lea S VanderVelde, 'The Gendered Origins of the *Lumley* Doctrine: Binding Men's Consciences and Women's Fidelity' (1992) 101 Yale Law Journal 775, 776, 792–9.

[90] See e.g. *HRX Holdings* (n 12), where an injunction was granted prohibiting a recruitment specialist from taking up employment in Australia or New Zealand until the expiry of a two-year restraint.

[91] *Bulldogs Rugby League Club Ltd v Williams* [2008] NSWSC 822.

with *Lumley*. Sonny Bill was very unlikely to rob Canterbury Bankstown of its audiences by playing another code of rugby in France. The football fields of Toulon are by no means as proximate to Belmore Oval as Her Majesty's Theatre was to Covent Garden in 1852.

Sonny Bill's case involved enforcement of a contract during its term. Others involving enforcement of post-employment include *Seven Network (Operations) Limited v Warburton (No 2)*, in which Pembroke J granted an eight-month injunction to delay Mr Warburton (who had been second in charge at Seven) from taking up the role of chief executive officer at Network Ten. No detailed assessment of the usual discretionary factors for grant of equitable relief was made before granting the injunction.[92]

High levels of remuneration may be influential in judicial determinations of these issues. In the United Kingdom, the courts have regarded it as appropriate to hold highly paid employees to contracts they entered into:[93]

> The court will also have in mind the strong public interest in employees being held to contracts which they have freely entered into for substantial remuneration. That interest pulls in the opposite direction to the public interest in employees being freely able to exercise their skills in work by transferring from one employer to another.

In *HRX Holdings Pty Ltd v Pearson*[94] (an Australian decision), Buchanan J restrained a recruitment specialist from changing jobs for a period of 20 months. Pearson was a talented recruiter, with an extensive network of valuable contacts, before he joined a boutique firm, HRX, in 2005. In 2011, he decided that he wanted to return to a large organization. Buchanan J enforced Mr Pearson's two-year non-compete clause on the basis that Mr Pearson was a uniquely talented person (a person of 'quirky brilliance'[95]) who had become the face of HRX, and was the person with whom all clients had dealt. Once upon a time, an employee's own personal charisma and talents would not qualify as the kind of property-like interest over which a former employer could legitimately claim ownership.[96] Again, the injunction was granted without any consideration

---

[92] *Seven Network (Operations) Ltd v Warburton (No 2)* [2011] NSWSC 386 (12 May 2011) [94].

[93] *BGC Brokers* (n 38).

[94] *HRX Holdings* (n 12); affirmed on appeal: *Pearson v HRX Holdings Pty Ltd* [2012] FCAFC 111, (2012) IR 369.

[95] *HRX Holdings* (n 12) [53].

[96] See Heydon (n 6) 117–21.

of the usual discretionary factors. The fact that HRX agreed to pay Pearson for all but three months of the two-year restraint appears to have been decisive. How that payment compared with expected remuneration in the new firm was not considered. Payment ought not to legitimize an otherwise unreasonable restraint. In *Tullett Prebon (Australia) Pty Ltd v Purcell*,[97] it was held that '[c]ompensation for remaining out of the market, however generous, does not create a legitimate protectable interest where none otherwise exists'.

The power of an injunction to sterilize talent, to the disadvantage of both the individual and the marketplace more generally, is reason enough to warrant greater discernment when granting injunctions. It is disturbing that the approach now being developed by the Australian courts is to ignore or discount the usual discretionary factors, such as whether the injunction will cause hardship to the person subject to it, and whether the person seeking it will suffer any damage should it not be granted.

For example, in *Otis Elevator Co Pty Ltd v Nolan*,[98] Brereton J said that 'I am of the view that the mere fact that the injury to the plaintiff is slight or non-existent is insufficient to justify declining an injunction on discretionary grounds; so also is the mere fact that enforcement of the injunction would occasion considerable hardship to the defendant'. The New South Wales approach might be contrasted with that of the Supreme Court of New York in *Jacobi Tool & Die Manufacturing Inc and Jacobi v Mondi and others*:[99]

> A party seeking the drastic remedy that a preliminary injunction confers must establish a clear legal right to that relief under the law and upon undisputed facts set forth in the record [citations omitted]. To prevail on a motion for preliminary injunction relief, the movant must clearly demonstrate a likelihood of success on the merits, the prospect of irreparable harm or injury if the relief is withheld and that a balance of the equities favours the movant's position.

Effect of the Employer's Breach

Another factor in play when considering the legitimacy and enforceability of post-employment restraints is the reason for the termination of the employment in the first place. It seems particularly harsh if employees

---

97 *Purcell* (n 38) [87].

98 *Otis Elevator Co Pty Ltd v Nolan* [2007] NSWSC 593, [30].

99 *Jacobi Tool & Die Manufacturing Inc and Jacobi v Mondi and others* 2007 WL 3325854 (NY Supp), 3.

are bound to a promise not to compete with the employer in circumstances where the employer decided to terminate the employment contract. In *IceTV v Duncan Ross and others*,[100] for example, an inventor and a business manager were prevented from taking up employment offers in the media technology industry, notwithstanding that the former employer had, itself, dismissed the two innovators because its business was failing and it could not afford their services any longer. The injustice of enforcing a restraint when the former employer has no use for the employee's labour is breathtaking. A year after the decision, and after a failed appeal of the decision, the two men remained unemployed.

On the other hand, in *Ecolab Pty Ltd v Stephen Garland*,[101] no injunction was granted to prevent an employee from taking up employment with an industry competitor after he had taken an involuntary redundancy, although he was required to observe a restraint upon soliciting former customers.

What if the employment contract is terminated not by the giving of proper notice, but by the employer's breach? Older English authority[102] held that an employer who wrongfully dismissed an employee could not enforce any obligations under the employment contract, including any covenant restraining post-employment competition.[103]

It is not entirely clear that the more recent decision of *Rock Refrigeration Ltd v Jones*[104] is sound authority for this proposition.[105] Lord Wilson observed in *Societe Generale, London Branch v Geys* that 'The enforceability of … a restrictive covenant by the repudiator against the innocent

---

[100] *IceTV* (n 71).

[101] *Ecolab Pty Ltd v Stephen Garland* [2011] NSWSC 1095.

[102] Beginning with *General Billposting Co v Atkinson* [1909] AC 118, and culminating in *Rock Refrigeration Ltd v Jones* [1996] IRLR 675 (CA).

[103] See Robert Dean, *The Law of Trade Secrets and Personal Secrets* (2nd edn, Lawbook Co 2002) 428, para [11.170]. See Breen Creighton and Andrew Stewart, *Labour Law: An Introduction* (3rd edn, Federation Press 2000) 255. See also Breen Creighton and Andrew Stewart, *Labour Law: An Introduction* (4th edn, Federation Press 2005) 365, n 267.

[104] *Rock Refrigeration* (n 102). For a note on this case, see Michael Jefferson, 'Restraint of Trade: Dismissal and Drafting' (1997) 26 ILJ 62.

[105] Cabrelli criticizes *Pearson v HRX Holdings Pty Ltd* [2012] FCAFC 111, (2012) IR 369 as doctrinally incongruous with the proposition (confirmed in *Faccenda Chicken* (n 34)) that the employee's duty to maintain the employer's confidences survives the end of the employment contract: see Cabrelli (n 46) 566–9.

party is now the subject of some debate'.[106] *Rock* concerned a post-employment restraint clause, which was stated to take effect on termination of employment 'howsoever caused'. The employee argued that the restraint was invalid because it purported to apply even upon termination for the employer's breach of contract, and such a result would be offensive according to *General Billposting Co v Atkinson*.[107] Only one of the three judges deciding the matter (Morritt LJ) defended the proposition in *General Billposting*, that is 'if the contract is terminated because the employer's repudiation has been accepted by the employee then the covenant will no longer bind the employee'.[108]

Phillips LJ rejected this proposition on the basis that the post-employment restraint should be regarded as a secondary obligation of the contract, which would (on the authority of *Heyman v Darwins Ltd*[109]) survive the termination of the contract, notwithstanding that the parties would no longer be bound by its primary obligations. Phillips LJ did not consider that a rejection of *General Billposting* would be unfair to dismissed employees because they had a remedy in statutory compensation for unfair dismissal: 'It does not seem to me necessarily fair or reasonable that an employer who is held liable to pay such compensation should also be at risk of losing the protection that is reasonably necessary to safeguard his confidential information or goodwill'.[110]

This argument is, of course, based on the availability of compensation under UK statute law. In Australia, unfair dismissal protection rarely covers the kinds of high income employees who are subject to restraints of trade and, even where available, provides no more than six months' compensation in the most egregious of cases.[111]

It is possible that the fact that an employer has dismissed an employee in breach of contract will be a matter that goes to the reasonableness of the restraint. A court exercising an equitable discretion to grant an injunction to enforce a covenant in a contract ought to have regard to the usual maxims of equity: 'who seeks equity must do equity'[112] and 'who

---

106 *Societe Generale, London Branch v Geys* [2012] UKSC 63, [2013] 1 AC 523, [68].

107 *General Billposting* (n 102).

108 *Rock Refrigeration* (n 102) 12.

109 *Heyman v Darwins Ltd* [1942] AC 356.

110 *Rock Refrigeration* (n 102) 20. Note that Simon Brown LJ did not decide this issue.

111 As at 1 July 2017, the income limit for unfair dismissal protection was $A142,000.

112 Meagher, Heydon and Leeming (n 88) paras [3-055] ff.

comes into equity must come with clean hands'.[113] The court in *Cantor Fitzgerald International v Bird*[114] appears to have taken this approach (implicitly if not explicitly). In that case, the employer sought to hold three employees to a long notice period and post-employment restraints to stop them from taking up employment with a rival firm. No injunction was granted in respect of two of them, on the basis that the employer had constructively dismissed them when it purported to unilaterally change their remuneration terms, threatened to withdraw their entitlements to bonuses and used abusive language. This palpable breach of the implied term of mutual trust warranted refusal of the injunction. The court was prepared to grant an injunction in respect of the third employee, who had been treated more respectfully. The only explanation for the differential treatment of the employees in this case is that the court's decision whether to grant an injunction in these cases is discretionary.

CONCLUSION

Why have the Australian decisions, in particular, strayed so far from the ancient wisdom? It would appear that contemporary courts are so focused on the interests of the corporate employer that they neglect to weigh in the balance the interests of the human citizens in these cases. In *Informax International Pty Ltd v Clarius Group Ltd*,[115] for example, the court was considering a restraint based on the employer's supposed interest in a stable workforce. Counsel for the defendant employee argued that the line of authority supporting such an interest came dangerously close to treating workers as chattels. Perram J was dismissive of this concern:[116]

> Without wishing to become embroiled in that debate unnecessarily it may be useful to observe that just as there is difference between ownership of the copyright in a book and ownership of copyright in individual words, so too there may be a real conceptual distinction between the notion that an employer might have interests in the arrangement of its staff as a whole and the notion that it has an interest in any particular employee.

With respect, this analogy is misconceived. Human beings are not like words. A word may be used in a million different literary works, and still

113 ibid paras [3-110] ff.
114 *Cantor Fitzgerald International v Bird* [2002] IRLR 867, [140]–[145].
115 *Informax International Pty Ltd v Clarius Group Ltd* [2011] FCA 183.
116 ibid [50].

be available for use in a million more. A person who is part of the 'stable workforce' that a colleague has refused to impair by 'poaching' will suffer considerable limitation of their own opportunities to escape to more attractive employment if a court enforces another's covenant not to offer them employment. People are not property. In old property terms, they are not like 'apples and pears'.[117] Neither are they like the newer form of intellectual property. Never has it been truer that there is nothing in the law so dangerous as a metaphor.

The law in the United Kingdom has been consistent in its protection of employers' interests, but does not appear to be exhibiting the tendencies that are currently being seen in Australia. At the same time, the cautious incrementalism of the common law serves to ensure that the law is updated in line with the needs of the employer. The cases on clauses restricting employee 'poaching' provide a good example. However, increasing concern over the levels of senior executive remuneration may prompt the courts in the United Kingdom to move more in line with the Australian courts. In *UBS Wealth Management v Vestra Wealth*, it was said that, in the context of the implied term of fidelity: 'Every business is entitled to expect loyalty, fidelity and diligence from its staff. That is part of the bargain for which they are paid … The more senior the staff, the greater the remuneration and the greater the degree of loyalty, fidelity and diligence is required'.[118]

---

[117] *Hanover Insurance Brokers Ltd v Shapiro* [1994] IRLR 82, [16].

[118] *UBS Wealth Management v Vestra Wealth* [2008] EWHC 1974 (QB), [2008] IRLR 965, [10].

10. Security in employment

In this chapter, we consider the extent to which employees in the United Kingdom, Australia and New Zealand enjoy security in their employment[1] and, in particular, protection against unjustified dismissal. The advent of statutory protection against unfair dismissal can justifiably be seen as the most important change in the legal character of the individual employment relationship since the repeal of the master and servant acts. Prior to unfair dismissal legislation, employees could have no legal expectation of continuity in their employment and were subject to arbitrary dismissal at any time. The common law rules governing dismissal are simple: as late as 1971, Lord Reid stated: 'At common law a master is not bound to hear his servant before he dismisses him. He can act unreasonably or capriciously if he so chooses but the dismissal is valid'.[2] The year of Lord Reid's statement, however, also saw the first statutory protection against unfair dismissal introduced in the United Kingdom,[3] followed closely by Australia in 1972[4] and New Zealand in 1973.[5]

The introduction of unfair dismissal legislation was an important turning point in the balance between the common law and statute, and between employers and employees. While legislative intervention in the

---

[1] Security in employment is an imprecise term, but, for the purposes of this chapter, it may be taken to mean that an employee should not be dismissed other than for a justifiable reason and that, even if a dismissal is justifiable on economic grounds, the employee should be entitled to some form of transitional financial protection.

[2] *Malloch v Aberdeen Corporation* [1971] 1 WLR 1578, 1581 (HL).

[3] Industrial Relations Act 1971 (UK), s 22.

[4] The first state statutory scheme allowing individuals to challenge a 'harsh, unjust or unreasonable' dismissal was introduced in South Australia in 1972: see Anna Chapman, 'The Decline and Restoration of Unfair Dismissal Rights' in Anthony Forsyth and Andrew Stewart (eds), *Fair Work: The New Workplace Laws and the Work Choices Legacy* (The Federation Press 2009). We will not discuss the complex Australian system prior to the comprehensive federal legislation in 1993. On the pre-1993 period, see Andrew Stewart, 'Employment Protection in Australia' (1989) 11 Comp Lab LJ 1.

[5] Industrial Relations Act 1973 (NZ), s 117.

employment relationship was not unusual, it had previously been concerned with either facilitating the collective settlement of conditions of employment or laying down statutory minimum conditions. Unfair dismissal legislation went considerably further in allowing the courts to intervene in an employer's day-to-day management of its business, its 'right to manage'. This was not only a controversial but also a revolutionary step; it had an important impact on the development of the common law of employment and was to have major consequences for the internal processes and management of employing entities. Unfair dismissal legislation was the first major challenge at an individual level to 'the very function of the common law to preserve subordination inherently within employment'.[6]

However, in spite of the revolutionary nature of the reforms of the 1970s, they enjoyed broad political support and were supported by both unions and employers. As we will see, this can, in part, be accounted for by the perceived injustice of the common law position, but was also attributable to the industrial relations environment of the period. Nevertheless, almost half a century later, statutory protection against unfair dismissal remains in place in all three jurisdictions, in spite of the much changed, more hostile and less consensual industrial relations environment. As labour market regulation has come to be increasingly influenced by neoliberal economic and political theories, and as union power has eroded, the justification for employment protection has become increasingly contested.

In this chapter, we do not attempt to cover the details of the common law or the legislative scheme of each jurisdiction in any detail, a task well performed elsewhere.[7] Instead, we focus first on identifying the key legislative characteristics of unfair dismissal protection in each jurisdiction and, second, on evaluating the extent to which the common law approach to dismissal influences the statutory regimes. We first summarize the common law's approach to dismissal and then consider the differing legislative responses to employment security in our three jurisdictions, how these responses have varied over time and the current degree of protection. The final part of the chapter will discuss how the

---

6 Lord Wedderburn, 'Labour Law: From Here to Autonomy?' (1987) 16 ILJ 1, 9.

7 See Simon Deakin and Gillian S Morris, *Labour Law* (6th edn, Hart 2012) Ch 5; Andrew Stewart et al., *Creighton and Stewart's Labour Law* (6th edn, Federation Press 2016) Pt 5; Gordon Anderson and John Hughes, *Employment Law in New Zealand* (LexisNexis 2014) Ch 9.

common law rules have influenced statutory schemes, and the current relationship between the common law and the statutory schemes.

DISMISSAL AT COMMON LAW

The common law approach to dismissal is simple: an employer may dismiss its employee 'at any time and for any reason or for none'[8] and, as long as that action is carried out in accordance with the terms of the contract, the employee will have no remedy. In the absence of express terms governing the manner of dismissal, the only requirement is that the contractual period of notice or, if no period is specified, reasonable notice, be provided. If proper notice is not given, the dismissal will be 'wrongful' and the employer will be liable for damages equivalent to wages or salary lost from the date of dismissal to the earliest date on which proper notice would have expired. The common law assumes that the employer would have terminated the contract on terms most favourable to itself. The quantum of damages is, therefore, tightly constrained and, other than in very limited circumstances, does not extend to financial loss beyond the notice period. As a result of the much criticized *Addis* rule,[9] consequential loss, such as loss of reputation inhibiting future employment or emotional harm, is not recoverable.[10] In the great majority of cases, where contractual notice periods may be only a few days to a few weeks, legal action will almost certainly be uneconomic.[11]

---

8 *Ridge v Baldwin* [1964] AC 40, 65, per Lord Reid.

9 *Addis v Gramophone Co Ltd* [1909] AC 488 (HL). While the *Addis* rule has been subject to considerable judicial and academic criticism, the courts, with the exception of New Zealand, have proved unwilling to deviate from it. In New Zealand, see *Whelan v Waitaki Meats Ltd* [1991] 2 NZLR 74 (HC); *Ogilvy and Mather v Turner* [1993] 2 ERNZ 799 (CA); and *Andrews v Parceline Express Ltd* [1994] 2 ERNZ 385 (CA); and compare *Baltic Shipping Co v Dillon* (1993) 176 CLR 344 (HCA), which affirmed the application of *Addis* in employment cases.

10 In the United Kingdom, the acceptance of a duty not to destroy mutual trust and confidence has opened up limited avenues for claiming damages related to the stigmatizing effect on future employment of an employer's breach of contract during employment: see *Malik v Bank of Credit & Commerce International SA (in liq)* [1998] AC 20. See also *Spring v Guardian Assurance plc* [1995] 2 AC 296, and see the discussion in Chapter 11.

11 The high-income earner cases, where employees are able to claim the loss of a chance of earning bonuses or other performance-related remuneration component, are an exception. See e.g. *Horkulak v Cantor Fitzgerald International* [2003] IRLR 756; *Silverbrook Research Pty Ltd v Lindley* [2010] NSWCA 357; *Ma v Expeditors International Pty Ltd* [2014] NSWSC 859.

Moreover, if an employee is guilty of serious misconduct, dismissal may be summary and, if the misconduct is subsequently discovered, the right to damages is negated. Damages may be further reduced if the employee fails to mitigate their loss by not seeking, or refusing, suitable alternative employment. Employment is close to being at the will of the employer and, even if the contract stipulates a notice period, employment may be terminated immediately by payment in lieu of notice, effectively the payment of liquidated damages.[12]

For the purposes of this chapter the important point for our purposes is that, in 1971, this position was essentially the same in all three jurisdictions. Textbooks of the time relied on the same, usually English, authorities on the substantive principles of the law, together with a sprinkling of local examples illustrative of matters such as reasonable notice or disobedience. Statutory reform therefore started from a common foundation but, as we shall see, statutory schemes were strongly responsive to domestic influences.

Evaluating the Common Law Position

The merits or otherwise of the common law's approach to dismissal need only be summarized. From an employer's perspective, the power to dismiss without reasons and, in practice, on terms dictated by the employer, is extremely valuable, both economically and for disciplinary reasons. Economically, it allows a substantial component of the commercial risk associated with employment to be shifted to employees. In the absence of good reasons to the contrary, employers typically insist on short notice periods so that if there is an economic or business downturn, or employment requirements change, employees can be dismissed, or dismissed and re-hired on less favourable terms, to protect profitability. From a disciplinary perspective, poor performance need not be managed in line with good practice, as the employee can be dismissed. The same applies to 'troublemakers'; indeed, any form of resistance to employer discipline is easily punished. Moreover, capricious dismissal can be used to send a strong warning to other employees of the legal insecurity of their employment.

---

[12] The entitlement to pay in lieu of notice needs to be expressly agreed, but generally is in most employment contracts, and indeed in statutory notice provisions. See e.g. Fair Work Act 2009 (Cth), s 117(2)(b). See *Sanders v Snell* (1998) 196 CLR 329, [16], for the proposition that an entitlement to pay in lieu will not be implied where parties have stipulated a notice period without expressing a right to pay in lieu.

More generally, economists have advanced a number of arguments to justify employment at will on grounds such as economic efficiency and that employment protection hinders movement within labour markets, including movement into employment.[13]

The common law right of employers to dismiss naturally came at a significant economic and legal cost to employees, given that the economic security of both the employee and their dependants is heavily reliant on employment. The employers' power to dismiss may undermine or negate protective legislation and even contractually agreed conditions. The possibility of dismissal has a seriously chilling effect on any employee considering raising such matters, including health and safety issues, underpayment of wages or employee abuse generally. Economically, employees, and often the state, carry both the short- and long-term transitional cost of finding new employment. For many employees, the immediate financial consequences are likely to be significant and, in some cases, disastrous. Dismissal is also likely to seriously undermine the employee's reputational and professional or occupational capital, jeopardize their economic investment in education and training and, in some cases, may have serious psychological implications. Dismissal, even for long-serving employees, could come at any time, without reasons and with no right to be heard, let alone to appeal.

At this point, we can leave the common law in suspended animation and return to it in the final part of the chapter, where we will discuss the extent to which, if at all, the above approach has evolved in each of the three countries.

Legislative Intervention

While the common law approach to dismissal described above may have been sustainable in a master and servant regime and when a significant proportion of the working population were both disenfranchised politically and industrially, it was less sustainable in the long term. By the 1970s, the lack of legislative regulation became untenable in the face of strong drivers for legal reform. Employees were never accepting of an employer's unilateral power to dismiss and were acutely aware of the consequences of its abuse. It was therefore unsurprising that, where possible, workers resorted to alternative remedies, including non-legal remedies. The most important of these was seeking collective support

---

[13] Most famously, Richard Epstein, 'In Defense of the Contract at Will' (1984) 51 U Chi L Rev 947.

from co-workers up to and including strike action, an important consideration given the high levels of union density in the 1960s and 1970s. The level of industrial stoppages attributable to dismissal disputes was a major driver of reform.[14]

By the 1970s, the notion of legislative employment protection was far from novel. Employment protection for some public sector employees had been long established in New Zealand[15] and Australia,[16] although this was not the case in the United Kingdom until the 1990s.[17] More generally, well before the 1970s, precursors to statutory reform can be found in the disputes procedures of collective agreements or awards and in the ability to create industrial disputes in the Australasian arbitration systems.[18] However, such processes were limited in their coverage with no guaranteed individual right of recourse to a process to challenge a dismissal. They were collective in character, with their effectiveness often dictated by union strength, the strength of union delegate structures and the willingness of unions to support a dismissed employee.

A further driver of reform was a greater international recognition that there should be constraints on an employer's power to dismiss. This recognition was manifested in the International Labour Organization's (ILO's) adoption of Recommendation 119 Concerning Termination of

---

[14] See Paul Davies and Mark Freedland, *Labour Legislation and Public Policy* (Clarendon Press 1993) 200; Gordon Anderson, 'The Origins and Development of the Personal Grievance Procedure in New Zealand' (1988) 13 NZJIR 257, 261. Australia was possibly the outlier here. It was some time before the Australian High Court accepted that a dispute over the termination of employment of a single worker could constitute an 'interstate industrial dispute' sufficient to bring the complaint within the dispute resolution powers of the federal industrial tribunal. Once this occurred, and 'termination change and redundancy clauses' had become standard award clauses, pressure mounted to enact a standard scheme applicable to all eligible workers. See Anna Chapman, 'The Declining Influence of ILO Standards in Shaping Australian Provisions on Unfair Dismissal' (2003) 29 Mon LR 104.

[15] An employee's rights to a hearing and to an appeal, if accused of disciplinary offences, were established in 1912, when the first standardized public service structure was established: Public Service Act 1912 (NZ), s 56.

[16] At the federal level, some level of statutory protections has been in place since 1922: Phillipa Weeks, 'Reconstituting the Employment Relationship in the Australian Public Service' in Stephen Deery and Richard Mitchell (eds), *Employment Relations: Individualisation and Union Exclusion, An International Study* (The Federation Press 1999) 71.

[17] Deakin and Morris (n 7) 193.

[18] Public servants also often enjoyed appeal rights from a decision to dismiss, although the influence of this is unclear.

Employment at the Initiative of the Employer (1963), a recommendation that reflected increased regulation of dismissal within a number of European countries. The core principles of Recommendation 119, and later Convention 158,[19] were twofold: a worker's employment should not be terminated 'unless there is a valid reason for such termination connected with the capacity or conduct of the worker or based on the operational requirements of the undertaking, establishment or service', and a worker who considers their employment to have been unjustifiably terminated should have the right of appeal to a neutral body.

While the drivers for reform in the three jurisdictions seem to have been primarily domestic, the adoption of Recommendation 119 was supported by all three governments. Although it appears to have played a limited role in reforms in both the United Kingdom and New Zealand, it did highlight the lack of legal protection against dismissals, set clear standards for such protection and is likely to have had some impact on policy.[20] When, later, Australia adopted federal employment protection in 1993, Convention 158 was seen 'as a useful, although dispensable, source of ideas and constitutional power for legislation in this area'.[21]

By the 1970s, policymakers were effectively left with two choices: to accept the common law position, which in practice meant employment at the employer's will for the majority of the workforce (subject only to a requirement to provide notice of termination); or to attempt to achieve some degree of balance between the employer's right to dismiss and the employee's expectation of continued employment in the absence of a justifiable reason for its termination. Given that the former had largely ceased to be a political option, and that, in both the United Kingdom and New Zealand, a clear consensus for reform had developed,[22] the most important issue became the extent to which there should be protection against dismissal beyond that contractually agreed by the parties or, more

---

19 ILO Convention 158 on Termination of Employment at the Initiative of the Employer 1982.

20 Davies and Freedland (n 14) 195; R Green, 'Procedures to Settle Disputes Over Alleged Wrongful Dismissal' (Industrial Relations Centre, Victoria University of Wellington 1966). The latter paper, which was influential in New Zealand's reforms, stressed Recommendation 119 Concerning Termination of Employment at the Initiative of the Employer 1963.

21 See Anna Chapman, 'The Declining Influence of ILO Standards in Shaping Australian Statutory Provisions on Unfair Dismissal' (2003) 29 Mon LR 104, 106. The constitutional reference is to the use of the external relations power to implement legislation at a federal level.

22 As discussed below, the political position in Australia was more complex because of its federal structure.

accurately, as dictated by the employer and the courts. At heart, the core of the debate was the appropriate balance between economic and social justice factors and, legally, the extent to which an employer's common law 'rights' should be constrained by statute. All statutory interventions reflect elements of these arguments, but the balance in each jurisdiction varied with its economic circumstances, its system of industrial relations and the political strength of any particular strand of argument. We now turn to these responses.

LEGISLATIVE REGULATION OF DISMISSAL

As noted above, while there were precursors to legislative intervention, the statutory initiatives of the 1970s saw the development of employment protection move to a more comprehensive model with wider coverage, and one based on the individual employee's right to challenge a dismissal. Although the legislative structures adopted in each jurisdiction differed markedly, a number of common characteristics are noticeable.

In the United Kingdom, a clear consensus for reform seems to have emerged by the early 1960s, but there was still debate over whether reforms should be by way of further developing existing voluntary procedures or through more comprehensive reform. That debate had been resolved in favour of wider reforms by the end of the 1960s and the provisions enacted in 1971 can be viewed as representing a cross-party consensus, having been introduced by a Labour government and enacted by the following Conservative government in largely the same form.[23] By 1963 the United Kingdom had already introduced transitional protection for dismissed employees in the form of minimum notice periods.[24] The Industrial Relations Act 1971 (UK) took the further step of providing a comprehensive and detailed scheme of protection against unfair dismissals, including detailed provisions relating to matters such as the circumstances that might constitute a dismissal and the test of fairness. With limited exceptions and subject to a qualification period, the Act covered all employees and provided a detailed formal structure through which complaints of unfair dismissal might be pursued. Whilst there have been countless reforms, the original scheme remains recognizable to this day.

[23] The development of this consensus is described by Davies and Freedland (n 14) 196.

[24] Contracts of Employment Act 1963 (UK). This form of protection was enhanced by the Redundancy Payments Act 1965 (UK).

New Zealand's reforms were also based on a consensus that had developed prior to 1970, when legislation to provide protection against 'wrongful' dismissal was enacted. However, the use of the word 'wrongful' made this reform ineffective.[25] Effective reform was enacted three years later as part of the broader reforms of the Industrial Relations Act 1973 (NZ), an Act based almost entirely on the joint recommendations of the peak employer and union organizations.[26] In contrast to the United Kingdom, New Zealand's reforms reflected its goal of establishing a procedure that would reduce industrial conflict and which was firmly embedded in the arbitration system. Access to its new personal grievance process was restricted to union members covered by an award and the settlement process reflected existing dispute settlement processes.[27] The legislative provisions consisted of one substantive subsection that defined a 'personal grievance' to include a claim of 'unjustifiable dismissal', but which extended to unjustified actions affecting an employee's employment to their disadvantage.[28] The remainder of the section set out the requirements for a standard personal grievance procedure to be included in all awards, together with a continuity of work requirement. A generally applicable model based on the individual employment relationship was not put in place until 1991.

While legislative intervention in the United Kingdom and New Zealand was straightforward, the system in Australia was considerably more complex. Although it seems clear that there was a broad consensus that employees should be protected against unfair dismissal, a national approach to regulating dismissal did not emerge until 1993. Prior to 1993, protection consisted of a potpourri of federal and state measures falling into two broad models: the industrial disputes model that had developed within the arbitration system and the individual rights model that was more typical of state systems.[29] At the federal level, the first protection from capricious dismissal was negotiated by trade unions seeking the inclusion of a standard 'termination, change and redundancy'

---

25 Anderson (n 14) 260.

26 Joel Seidman, 'New Zealand's Industrial Relations Act, 1973' (1974) 110 Int'l Lab Rev 515, 515. In contrast to the United Kingdom, the original Bill was introduced by a National government, but passed under a Labour administration.

27 Anderson (n 14) 262: as union membership was compulsory, all employees bound by an award were covered, but there were significant gaps, especially in relation to clerical workers whose award coverage was limited by a salary cap.

28 Industrial Relations Act 1973 (NZ), s 117(1).

29 For a detailed account, see Stewart (n 4).

(TCR) clause in federal industrial awards.[30] Some states had already enacted legislation to give effect to the ILO's Recommendation 119, and the subsequent Convention 158.[31] Together, these various elements provided some level of employment protection, but inevitably there were significant gaps, jurisdictional challenges, and different approaches and processes depending on jurisdiction. Even as late as 1989, Andrew Stewart was able to write that: 'In essence Australia is still in the process of coming to grips with the issue of unfair dismissal'.[32] It was not until the Industrial Relations Reform Act 1993 (Cth) that Australia enacted a coherent national system of protection against unjustified dismissal.[33] Moreover, unlike both the United Kingdom and New Zealand, the nature of the protection was immediately contentious and was introduced at a time when neoliberal deregulatory agenda had gained considerable traction. Indeed, the Australian federal scheme was arguably enacted to curtail the operation of the TCR clauses, which produced claims for significant contract damages for breach. A line of authority (ultimately overturned by *Byrne v Australian Airlines*[34]) conferred substantial damages awards on unfairly dismissed workers, far in excess of the ultimate cap (of six months' wages) imposed by the new statute. So, on one view, enactment of the statute operated to appease the employers, not to satisfy the unions.

Stability of Legislation

In the 1970s, it was still possible to agree with Kahn-Freund that the main object of labour law was 'to counteract the inequality of bargaining power' inherent in the employment relationship.[35] Two decades later, this

---

30 See *Termination Change and Redundancy Case* (1984) 8 IR 34; 9 IR 115.

31 See Industrial Relations Act 1972 (SA), s 15(1)(e); Industrial Relations Act 1979 (WA), s 23A; Industrial Relations Act 1984 (Tas), s 30.

32 Stewart (n 4) 41.

33 This Act initially covered all employees of 'constitutional corporations', federal public servants and some specific occupations covered by federal awards. In 2006, a major revision of the federal legislation extended coverage of federal law to all incorporated private sector employers, thus excluding access to state laws for much of the private sector. Subsequently, the individual states, except Western Australia, have gradually referred their industrial relations law-making powers to the Commonwealth, thus extending the coverage of the federal system. See Rosemary Owens, 'Unfinished Constitutional Business: Building a National System to Regulate Work' (2009) 22 AJLL 258.

34 *Byrne v Australian Airlines* (1995) 185 CLR 411.

35 Otto Kahn-Freund, *Labour and the Law* (Hamlyn Trust 1972) 8.

was no longer true, and the priorities of labour regulation had changed to 'regulating for competitiveness', a central component of which was the evocative, if loosely defined, notion of 'flexibility'.[36] Proponents of neoliberal deregulation, who were particularly influential in all three jurisdictions, regarded employment protection as undermining both competitiveness and flexibility, as well as the efficient operation of labour markets generally. At the same time, employee counter-voice had become increasingly muted, as union influence declined with decreasing union density. Unsurprisingly, therefore, there has been considerable pressure in all three jurisdictions to reduce employment protection. Perhaps surprisingly, in the light of these pressures, the statutory framework in both the United Kingdom and New Zealand has remained relatively stable, in contrast to much greater volatility in Australia; but 'relatively stable' is relative, and in all three jurisdictions there have been changes detrimental to employees. Broadly, such changes have three features: first, a reduction in the coverage of statutory protection; second, a move to more employer-focused criteria and discretions for assessing the fairness of a dismissal; and finally changes to the adjudication processes intended to achieve more speedy resolution but, in some cases, to deter applications by allowing remedies to become uneconomic.[37] As discussed below, the courts have reinforced this trend by rejecting common law developments that might provide alternative remedies, effectively freezing the common law in the 1970s.[38]

The principal indicator of changing attitudes in the United Kingdom has been periodic changes to the employment qualification for bringing an unfair dismissal action. This has fluctuated in time, from the original six months up to as much as two years (as at present), but, at some stages, has also excluded particular classes of employees, notably those on fixed-term contracts and those of small employers. The statutory test for unfairness was tightened in 1980, but, otherwise, the law has remained largely intact, other than for procedural changes that have been used to deter at least some claims.[39]

---

[36] See generally the discussion in Hugh Collins, 'Regulating the Employment Relation for Competitiveness' (2001) 30 ILJ 17.

[37] This is particularly so in the United Kingdom, where the level of fees has had a dramatic impact on the number of applications. See the recent report of the House of Commons Justice Committee, *Court and Tribunal Fees* (2016–17).

[38] There have been a limited number of exceptions, which are discussed in Chapter 11.

[39] These changes are summarized in Deakin and Morris (n 7) 422.

New Zealand's personal grievance procedure, by contrast, has been remarkably stable given the general instability of labour law between 1973 and 2000 and, in particular, the enactment of a neoliberal inspired deregulatory programme in the Employment Contracts Act 1991 (NZ). Not only did that Act leave the personal grievance protections intact, it also extended coverage to all 'employees', roughly doubling the numbers covered. New Zealand has never required a qualifying period of employment before a dismissal can be challenged.[40] The more important destabilizing influence has been not legislative but judicial. In the 1990s the Court of Appeal adopted a highly restrictive approach to the interpretation of the provisions, in particular the test of justification. The introduction of a less conservative statutory test for 'justification' in 2004 was a reaction to this development.[41] As with the United Kingdom, there have been a number of procedural changes designed to facilitate the disposal of grievances.

While the UK legislation has been more stable than Australia's, there were nevertheless significant changes in coverage as qualification periods changed in the United Kingdom, even if the remainder of the legislation remained stable. From a labour market perspective, these changes, taken together with the weak statutory protection for economic dismissals and the mutuality requirement limiting access by precarious workers, may be seen as a significant deregulatory reform. More generally, however, it may be that the substantive nature of the protection, as opposed to its coverage, had become strongly entrenched well before the neoliberal revolution, to the extent that any drastic reduction in protection was politically unfeasible. This seems particularly true in the case of New Zealand, during the radical deregulation of labour law in the Employment Contracts Act 1991. As noted, this Act substantially extended the coverage of protection in the face of extremely well-organized and vocal pressure from advocates for deregulation, who regarded anything other than at-will employment as undermining the Act.[42] A more accurate

---

[40] Since 2008, New Zealand has permitted the parties to a contract of employment to agree to a 90-day 'trial period', during which a claim of unjustified dismissal may not be raised: see Employment Contracts Act 1991 (NZ), ss 67A, 67B.

[41] This provision was modified slightly in 2008, but not so as to detract from this general point.

[42] These advocates mounted a continuing and sustained attack on both the personal grievance provisions and the Employment Court for several years after 1991. See Gordon Anderson, *Reconstructing New Zealand's Labour Law: Consensus or Divergence?* (Victoria University Press 2011) 114. It appears that

impression of the acceptance of protections is probably drawn from submissions to the review of industrial relations five years earlier, where it was clear that, not only was protection supported, but there was also support for it being strengthened.[43]

By contrast, federal protection in Australia was not introduced until the neoliberal reforms were already underway. By this time federal governments were dramatically revising their approach to labour law generally, with the objective of creating a comprehensive federal approach that involved the displacement of a considerable amount of state legislation. Additionally, cross-party support for the reforms was weak at the time and the Keating government came under pressure to amend its legislation within the year to exclude non-award high-income earners and to cap remedies.[44] It has since been constantly amended, most notably under the Liberal government's Workplace Relations and Work Choices revisions (in 1996 and 2006 respectively) and, subsequently, Labor's Fair Work reforms.[45] Under Work Choices, three reforms in particular were notable: an exclusion for employers with 100 or fewer employees; an exclusion of dismissals for genuine operational reasons, even if only a minor part of the overall reason; and an extension of the qualifying period of employment from three to six months. Decisions under Work Choices also had the effect of narrowing protection in some situations, including constructive dismissal where high barriers were erected.[46] A number of these reforms were reversed or modified under the Fair Work legislation, which has not yet (at the time of writing) been amended by the current Liberal government.

CURRENT LEGISLATIVE STRUCTURES

We will now consider the overall strength of legislative protection against unfair dismissal by comparing five key features of unfair dismissal legislation: coverage, the criteria for 'dismissal', the test of fairness,

the government partly saw such a change as politically a bridge too far but also believed that retention of protection would aid acceptance of the macro-reforms: see Susan Robson, 'Policy Operations and Outcomes in the New Zealand Employment Jurisdiction 1990–2008' (PhD, University of Otago 2016).

[43] Anderson (n 14) 271.

[44] See Industrial Relations Amendment Act (No 2) 1994.

[45] Both sets of reforms are described in detail in Chapman (n 4).

[46] ibid 219. These decisions required 'duress or pressure' or 'oppressive' conduct by the employer.

remedies, and the process for resolving claims of unfair dismissal. In doing so, we pay particular attention to the extent that the common law has influenced the legislative framework and its interpretation and, in particular, we raise the question of whether legislative schemes have had any substantive impact on the values underlying the common law's approach to the employment relationship.

Coverage

Any worker seeking to challenge a dismissal must first cross the initial barrier to employment protection in all three jurisdictions, that is, they must be able to demonstrate that they were an 'employee'. Standard principles of 'freedom of contract' provide considerable latitude for employers to manipulate the nature of contracts for the personal performance of work.[47] Common examples include categorizing the worker's status as that of a contractor or franchisee, the use of contractual models that break continuity of employment such as casual or short-term contracts, and tactics to avoid direct liability such as triangular employment arrangements. Such practices provide an important tool for the avoidance of protective legislation and, while governments have attempted to control some forms of avoidance, for example through statutory extensions to the definition of an employee, this form of intervention tends to have been minimal at best.

Even once it is established that a person is an employee, there remain considerable barriers to overcome before protection can be accessed. These fall into three main categories, the most common of which is a minimum qualifying period of employment, a restriction that regards protection against an employer's abuse of power as something that must be 'earned'. Additionally, access may be denied or limited to particular groups or classes of employee, usually employees of small employers, or those on some form of limited-term contract or who are earning above an income threshold. All jurisdictions other than New Zealand stipulate a qualifying period of employment before a dismissal can be challenged.[48] However, in all cases, there are exceptions if a dismissal is for a prohibited reason, typically that it was based on general discriminatory grounds such as colour, gender, age, national or racial origins, sexual orientation, disability or the like, or on union membership or activities.[49]

[47] See Chapter 4.

[48] But see n 40 above on trial periods.

[49] The exact grounds vary between the three countries.

Both the United Kingdom and Australia[50] require qualifying periods of employment – two years in the case of the United Kingdom and six months in Australia, except for small employers, where the period is one year. An income threshold, however, is unique to Australia, where its enactment seems to have been due to very strong employer pressure to restrict the rights of senior managers to challenge dismissals and ratchet up agreed severance payments. However, the maximum income level is not high ($A142,000 from 1 July 2017), although its wider impact is ameliorated as it does not apply to employees covered by a modern award or enterprise agreement. Hence, it has only limited application for some highly paid professional employees in the public sector and for those in highly unionized industries such as mining. The most affected groups would appear to be higher middle and senior management in the private sector.

Restrictions on access to protection against unfair dismissal are substantial and affect a substantial proportion of the workforce, even after discounting for workers who do not come within the definition of 'employee'.[51] To a varying extent, both temporally and by jurisdiction, protection from unjustified dismissal seems to be regarded as a privilege to be earned by satisfactory service, rather than a right. Outside New Zealand, the right to challenge a dismissal is largely confined to long-term employees on indefinite contracts; employees who may have worked for the same employer for considerable periods of time but not continuously may be excluded from coverage.

Dismissal

Once coverage is established, an employee faces a second barrier – demonstrating that they have been dismissed. An employment relationship can be terminated in a number of ways, not all of which will constitute a dismissal, which is normally defined as a termination of employment at the initiative of the employer. However, given the variety of circumstances in which dismissal can occur, there is considerable room for either an expansive or narrow definition and, with the exception of New Zealand, where a personal grievance can be raised in relation to

---

[50] For the purposes of this discussion, exclusions because of the overall coverage of the Workplace Relations Act 1996 (Cth) will be ignored.

[51] For a discussion of the extent of excluded employees, see Linda Dickens et al., *Dismissed: A Study of Unfair Dismissal and the Industrial Tribunal System* (Basil Blackwell 1985) Ch 2.

a number of claims that occur during employment,[52] the statutory processes only cover dismissals. Difficulties normally revolve around constructive dismissal and the position of those on non-standard contracts.

Non-standard Contracts

In Australia, 'casual' employment is a well-accepted form of labour engagement and is accommodated in most modern awards and enterprise bargains by the application of a loading (generally of 25 per cent) on hourly rates of pay. As a consequence of a widespread acceptance of the notion of the 'permanent casual' – an employee who is paid on a casual basis but who works regular shifts over a considerable period of time – Australian unfair dismissal protections do extend to casual employees who have been employed on a 'regular and systematic basis' for a period of at least 12 months, and who have enjoyed a 'reasonable expectation of continuing employment'.[53] The position is very different in the United Kingdom, where casual workers will often find it difficult to establish continuity of employment. The employee's difficulties are accentuated by the common law concept of mutuality of obligation.[54]

Constructive Dismissal

The concept of a constructive dismissal – that of resignation attributable to some initiative of the employer – is well established in labour law; the issue that arises is what level of conduct by the employer is sufficient to justify an employee's resignation. The courts have tended to approach this question in traditional contractual terms, that is, whether the employer's breach of contract was sufficiently serious to constitute a repudiation of the contract, which the employee is entitled to accept by resigning.

Both the United Kingdom and Australia have statutory definitions of constructive dismissal, although these vary. In the United Kingdom, there will be a dismissal if the employee terminates the contract 'in circumstances in which he is entitled to terminate it without notice by reason of

---

[52] This provision may, for example, allow a remedy where there is a resignation based on the employer's conduct, but which falls short of constructive dismissal: see *Business Distributors Ltd v Patel* [2001] 1 ERNZ 124 (CA).

[53] See Fair Work Act 2009 (Cth), s 384(2)(a). See *Cori Ponce v DJT Staff Management Services (t/as Daly's Traffic)* [2010] FWA 2078, for an illustration of what is meant by 'regular and systematic work'.

[54] See Chapter 4.

the employers' conduct',[55] whereas Australia provides that the employee must have been 'forced [to resign] because of conduct or a course of conduct engaged in by his or her employer'.[56] In both cases, the statutory test has been regarded as incorporating the common law notion of repudiation. In the United Kingdom, the test is whether 'looking at all the circumstances objectively, that is from the perspective of a reasonable person in the position of the innocent party, the contract breaker has clearly shown an intention to abandon and altogether to refuse to perform the contract'.[57] The position in Australia is complicated by the term 'forced'.[58] When the wording of the statute referred only to termination 'by the employer',[59] it was accepted that the common law concept of constructive dismissal (that is including a resignation that accepted the employer's repudiation of the employment contract) was applicable to statutory unfair dismissals. The change of wording to 'forced' dismissal suggests that an employee who has resigned as a consequence of employer conduct must demonstrate that they had no other option but to resign.[60] Cases are decided by a tribunal making administrative decisions, not by the courts, so it will take an application for judicial review of an administrative decision before it is entirely clear whether 'forced' adds a stronger element of compulsion or overcoming of the employee's 'personal autonomy'[61] to the contractual concept of repudiation.[62] The test that the effect of the employer's conduct is to be 'judged objectively by reference to the effect on a reasonable person'[63] is a similar phrasing to that used in the UK test.

The New Zealand courts, however, have adopted a more restrictive test. While the courts have long approached the issue on the basis of a

---

[55] Employment Rights Act 1996 (UK), s 95(1)(b).

[56] Fair Work Act 2009 (Cth), s 386(1)(b).

[57] *Eminence Property Developments Ltd v Heaney* [2010] EWCA 420, [20]. For a detailed analysis, see Deakin and Morris (n 7) para [5.74].

[58] Fair Work Act 2009 (Cth), s 386(1)(b).

[59] See Workplace Relations Act 1996 (Cth), s 170CE(1).

[60] *Dawes v Presbyterian Care Tasmania* [2014] FWC 4067, [4].

[61] *State of New South Wales v Paige* (2002) 60 NSWLR 371, [286].

[62] In *Rind v Australian Institute of Superannuation Trustees* [2013] FWC 3144, (2013) 231 IR 143, Lewin C held that a woman had been forced to resign when the employer unreasonably refused a request for part-time working hours after a return from maternity leave.

[63] *Elgammal v BlackRange Wealth Management Pty Ltd* [2011] FWAFB 4038, [13].

repudiation of the contract by the employer,[64] an objective neutral or employee-focused test has been disregarded in favour of a test of employer foreseeability. A decade after the *Auckland Shop Employees Union* decision,[65] the Court of Appeal added a new twist to constructive dismissal, holding that the correct approach involved a two-stage process: first, it must be established that the resignation was caused by a breach of duty on the part of the employer; and, second, that breach of duty must be 'of sufficient seriousness to make it reasonably foreseeable by the employer that the employee would not be prepared to work under the conditions prevailing'.[66] While the addition of the foreseeability test has rightly been criticized as having no basis in contract law, or indeed any other basis,[67] the court has reaffirmed its position on several occasions.[68] The restrictive approach of the Court of Appeal to constructive dismissal in the 1990s formed an interesting counterpoint to narrowing the test of justification to ensure that it was more employer friendly.

Prohibited Reasons

Unsurprisingly, all three jurisdictions provide a range of prohibited reasons for dismissal, which are largely unrelated to the employee's conduct and tend to cover conduct that is seen as requiring legal protection. Such reasons typically cover discriminatory dismissals.

In Australia, the Fair Work Act 2009 (Cth) separates 'unfair' dismissal (which is harsh, unjust or unreasonable) from discriminatory dismissal. 'General Protections' in Part 3-1 of the Fair Work Act protects employees against discriminatory dismissal (and discriminatory disciplinary or

---

64 The acceptance of constructive dismissal pre-dated the personal grievance procedure: see *Wellington Clerical Workers Union v Barraud and Abraham* (1970) 70 BA 347 (CA). It was affirmed again by the Court of Appeal in *Auckland Shop Employees Union v Woolworths (New Zealand) Ltd* [1985] 2 NZLR 372, 374, (CA).

65 *Auckland Shop Employees Union* (n 64).

66 *Auckland Electric Power Board v Auckland Provincial District Local Authorities Officers IUOW Inc* [1994] 2 NZLR 415, 419 (CA).

67 Including by the Employment Court in *Matheson (executrix) v Transmissions and Diesels Ltd* [2001] 1 ERNZ 1, 20 (EmpC); and *Taranaki Healthcare Ltd v Lloyd* [2001] 1 ERNZ 546, [59] (EmpC).

68 See *Business Distributors Ltd v Patel* [2001] 1 ERNZ 124 (CA), and *Transmissions and Diesels Ltd v Matheson (executrix)* [2002] 1 ERNZ 22 (CA), thus creating a classic example of the Bellman's rule of three: 'What I say three times is true'. See Lewis Carroll, *The Hunting of the Snark* (Macmillan Publishers 1876).

'adverse' action falling short of dismissal). These protections are framed as providing support for employees exercising certain workplace rights (including the right to exercise freedom of association and engage in industrial activity) and to discourage exclusion on the grounds of race, colour, sex, sexual orientation, age, physical or mental disability, marital status, family or carer's responsibilities, pregnancy, religion, political opinion, national extraction or social origin. There are defences for discrimination on the grounds of 'inherent requirements of the particular position', and for religious organizations that act in 'good faith' to protect the doctrines, tenets, beliefs or teachings of a religion.

Whereas unfair dismissal applications made under the Fair Work Act are determined by a relatively quick, inexpensive and informal process by the Fair Work Commission, contested general protections cases are matters for judicial determination in the federal court system. Also, the reversed onus of proof that requires an employer to bear the onus of showing that they had a legitimate reason for taking adverse action, unaffected by any prohibited reason, has had an unusual, and arguably unfortunate, consequence for employees' claims. The High Court has determined that the reversed onus implies that the employer's subjective reasons for taking action are the only relevant reasons in determining whether the general protections have been breached. An employer who can make a credible claim to have been motivated only by permissible motives will escape liability. So, in one notorious decision, a worker was held to have been legitimately dismissed for carrying a sign bearing the insult 'Scabs' on a picket line. The union's argument, that this was a clear case of adverse action on the grounds of industrial activity, was defeated by the employer's assertion that the only reason for dismissal was the employee's flagrant breach of a workplace civility policy.[69] Similarly, an employee who was disciplined for taking emergency leave to look after sick children, in accordance with his rights under an enterprise agreement, was unsuccessful in his adverse action claim. The employer was able to convince the court that it punished him for unpredictable absences from work, not for exercising his right to take leave to deal with family emergencies.[70] Unfair dismissal protections, which permit a tribunal to determine an application on the basis of providing a 'fair go all round', have proven to be more beneficial than these apparent protections, largely

---

[69] See *Construction, Forestry, Mining and Energy Union v BHP Coal Pty Ltd* (2014) 253 CLR 243.

[70] *Construction, Forestry, Mining and Energy Union v Endeavour Coal Pty Ltd* [2015] FCAFC 76, [34].

because the courts have developed an interpretation of the protections such that they guard only against deliberate and intentional victimization.

PROCESS

The central focus of the unfair dismissal regimes in all three jurisdictions is primarily on natural justice and the right not to be dismissed unless a fair process has been followed. Broadly speaking, the courts have shown that, while they are comfortable with the need for procedural fairness, once a fair process has been demonstrated they are reluctant to inquire more than necessary into an employer's substantive decision, which is seen as a commercial matter. Moreover, as we shall see below, even in the absence of a statutory direction, the courts have allowed employers a wide discretion to exercise their own judgment in making a decision as to whether a dismissal is warranted. The focus of the adjudicative process is, therefore, less on the substantive reason for a dismissal than on whether the employer's process has sufficient integrity to satisfy a court that a finding of misconduct or lack of competence was based on reasonable grounds.

All three jurisdictions have devised procedures that focus on the speedy disposal of claims. First, the time within which a claim must be filed is relatively short. In Australia, an application for an unfair dismissal remedy must be filed with the Fair Work Commission within 21 days, unless there are 'exceptional circumstances'[71] – a remarkably short time when compared to the United Kingdom,[72] where the employee has three months to present a complaint to an employment tribunal. New Zealand is considerably more generous than Australia, in that the employee has 90 days within which to raise an alleged grievance with their employer.[73] However, a grievance need only be formally filed with the Authority within three years.[74]

Second, the processes for resolving claims focus on the speedy disposal of claims through relatively informal processes, where the emphasis is on either the 'substantial merits of the case',[75] a 'fair go all

---

[71] Fair Work Act 2009 (Cth), s 394.

[72] ibid s 111(c).

[73] ibid s 114. This period may be extended if there are 'exceptional circumstances'.

[74] ibid s 114(6).

[75] Employment Rights Act 1996 (UK), s 98(4)(b).

round'[76] or 'according to the substantial merits of the case',[77] and which discourage appeals. In Australia, the Fair Work Commission operates a two-stage process: first, conciliation to encourage an agreed settlement; and second, if that fails, a formal hearing. In recent times, the conciliation proceedings have been conducted by employed mediators via telephone conferencing, instead of in person by commissioners, all in the interests of quicker and cheaper resolution of complaints.[78] New Zealand follows a similar process, but the functions are divided between two bodies: the mediation service and the Employment Relations Authority. Mediation is normally attempted as a matter of course[79] and, in most circumstances, the Authority must direct a matter to mediation before it can investigate the matter and must also prioritize matters that have gone to mediation. An Authority 'inquiry' is also just that – the Authority controls the scope and conduct of the inquiry, including witnesses to be called and claims to be investigated. The UK process is more formal, with hearings being conducted by a three-person employment tribunal and, unlike New Zealand, there is no prior requirement for mediation/conciliation, although the Advisory, Conciliation and Arbitration Service (ACAS) must be notified of the claim.

While New Zealand allows an appeal by right to the Employment Court, Australia restricts appeals to a full bench of the Fair Work Commission unless it is in the 'public interest', and the United Kingdom only allows appeals to the Employment Appeals Tribunal on points of law. Further appeals to the ordinary courts in all jurisdictions require leave and are restricted to matters of law. In Australia, recourse to a court from a decision of the Fair Work Commission is a matter of making an application for judicial review of an administrative decision.

Test of Fairness

In evaluating the strength of employment protection, perhaps the critical factor, other than access to the adjudicative process, is the standard against which an evaluation of the relevant rationale and process is made. All three jurisdictions have adopted a statutory test against which to test

---

[76] Fair Work Act 2009 (Cth), s 382(2).

[77] Employment Relations Act 2000 (NZ), s 157(1).

[78] Therese MacDermott and Joellen Riley, 'ADR and Industrial Tribunals: Innovations and Challenges in Resolving Individual Workplace Grievances' (2012) 38(2) Monash ULRev 82.

[79] In New Zealand mediation resolves around 80 per cent of personal grievances.

the fairness of a dismissal, but these tests have all been subject to considerable overlay of judicial interpretation. This reflects the reluctance of the common law judiciary to erode managerial prerogatives, largely founded on the common law implied terms, and their well-established reluctance to intrude unduly into the rights of owners to manage their business.

Statutory Tests

The UK test is twofold.[80] First, the employer must show that the dismissal is for a reason specified in the Act. These reasons are broad and reflect those in Convention 158: conduct, capability, redundancy; although the additional catch-all 'some other substantial reason' means that these categories are, in the round, fairly open-ended.[81] Once a sufficient reason is established, the determination of whether the dismissal was fair or unfair 'depends on whether in all the circumstances … the employer acted reasonably or unreasonably in treating [that reason] as a sufficient reason for dismissing the employee'.[82] The circumstances include the size and administrative resources of the employer, and the decision is to be determined 'in accordance with equity and the substantial merits of the case'.[83]

Prior to 2004, New Zealand had no statutory test of 'justification', the meaning of this term being left to be developed by the courts. The current statutory test requires an objective assessment of 'whether the employer's actions, and how the employer acted, were what a fair and reasonable employer could have done in all the circumstances at the time the dismissal or action occurred'.[84] In applying the test, a range of factors, related primarily to procedural fairness, must be taken into account. As in the other jurisdictions, the circumstances of the employer, particularly its size and resources, is specifically mentioned. The general requirement to make decisions that 'support successful employment relationships' 'as in equity and good conscience' applies to this as to all decisions of the Authority and the court.[85]

---

80 Employment Rights Act 1996 (UK), s 98.

81 In addition, it is potentially fair where the employee is dismissed after they have breached a duty or statutory provision.

82 Employment Rights Act 1996 (UK), s 98(4).

83 ibid.

84 Employment Relations Act 2000 (NZ), s 103A(2).

85 ibid ss 157 and 189.

Both these tests are applied similarly, the antecedents of the New Zealand test relying heavily on the formulation of the UK test in *Iceland Frozen Foods Ltd v Jones*.[86] Both tests emphasize that a court's inquiry centres on whether the employer reached its decision by following a fairly conducted process and inquiry into the allegations, not on whether or not the alleged conduct actually occurred. Also, both tests allow a considerable band of discretion to the employer when making a decision whether to dismiss – the 'range of reasonable responses'. The major difference between the two jurisdictions is that the UK's approach was built on a statutory test, whereas the New Zealand test was developed by the Court of Appeal in the 1990s to displace a wider, bilaterally focused approach that had been developed after 1973. The current test is largely a statutory formulation of the Court of Appeal's approach.

The Australian test, which is intended to be applied to 'ensure a fair go all around',[87] is simply that a dismissal is unfair if it was 'harsh, unjust or unreasonable'.[88] The test is supported by a range of criteria to be taken into account when deciding whether the test is satisfied.[89] These criteria are not dissimilar to the UK's approach, and include there being a valid reason for the dismissal in terms of conduct or capacity, as well as the size of the employer and the human resource management specialists available to it. They also include the core requirements of procedural fairness. Small businesses with 15 or fewer employees need only comply with the simpler requirements of a special Small Business Fair Dismissal Code, which is an instrument made by the Minister under the Fair Work Act 2009 (Cth), section 388(1).

Economic Dismissals and Redundancy

Dismissal for economic reasons is, perhaps, the key area where employers are most opposed to employment protection. Such protection, it is argued, inhibits economic efficiency and competitiveness by imposing unacceptable costs on employers. Governments of all hues tend to be sympathetic to such arguments. Less vocalized are arguments that the more minimal the protection against such dismissals, the greater the

---

[86] *Iceland Frozen Foods Ltd v Jones* [1983] ICR 17, 24; see *WH Newspapers Ltd v Oram* [2000] 2 ERNZ 448, [24] (CA). The approach in *Iceland Frozen Foods* remains good law in the United Kingdom: *Post Office v Foley* [2000] ICR 1283.

[87] Fair Work Act 2009 (Cth), s 381(2).

[88] ibid s 385.

[89] ibid s 387.

incentive to dismiss employees, and that limiting protection shifts a disproportionate share of the cost of business restructuring onto employees and, potentially, the state. It is also a type of dismissal that is largely independent of the employee's conduct or performance. There is, moreover, a broad spectrum of reasons for economic dismissals. Reasons range from insolvency or attempts to avoid insolvency, through business restructuring involving the abandonment of particular jobs, to the more controversial workforce restructuring where the genuineness of a redundancy may be questionable. Even where the job remains economic, dismissals may be justified because of restructuring or cutting costs by reducing pay and conditions. Resistance to accepting such conditions may also be held to justify a dismissal.

However, not all economic dismissals are redundancies. That term tends to be used only where a position or type of work is no longer required, and any remedies, or the scope of protection, are applied only to this more limited situation.

Thus, the United Kingdom defines redundancy[90] on the basis that the dismissal is wholly or mainly attributable to:[91]

> the fact that his employer has ceased or intends to cease –
>
> (i) to carry on the business for the purposes of which the employee was employed by him, or
> (ii) to carry on that business in the place where the employee was so employed, or
>
> the fact that the requirements of that business –
>
> (i) for employees to carry out work of a particular kind, or
> (ii) for employees to carry out work of a particular kind in the place where the employee was employed by the employer,
>
> have ceased or diminished or are expected to cease or diminish.

The Australian definition of a 'genuine redundancy' is similar in that it requires in part that 'the person's employer no longer required the person's job to be performed by anyone because of changes in the

[90] While a dismissal that comes within these definitions is likely to be substantively fair in both the United Kingdom and Australia, the definition of redundancy is also important as it governs, and limits, entitlement to redundancy compensation.

[91] Employment Rights Act 1996 (UK), s 139.

operational requirements of the employer's enterprise'.[92] Such terminations fall outside the definition of an unfair dismissal.

While New Zealand does not have a statutory definition, it is generally accepted that redundancy is a termination of employment 'being attributable, wholly or mainly, to the fact that the position filled by that worker is, or will become, superfluous to the needs of the employer'.[93]

Genuine redundancy dismissals are always likely to be fair unless aspects can be challenged, such as the selection process or the manner in which the decision was implemented. The employer is subject to merely procedural constraints. As a general rule, courts in all jurisdictions are reluctant to inquire into the merits of a redundancy dismissal as long as it appears genuine. It seems likely that the current situation in New Zealand, where the combination of the employer's good faith obligation to consult and the statutory direction to inquire into 'all the circumstances' of a dismissal allow the court to test the logic of the employer's commercial decision, is the outer limits of any inquiry.[94]

Dismissals on grounds of redundancy may nevertheless prove to be unfair if the criteria for selecting candidates for redundancy can be shown to be directly or indirectly discriminatory. For example, in *Sapevski v Katies Fashions (Australia) Pty Ltd*,[95] a decision to make redundant a certain classification of worker in a garment packing factory was held to be indirectly discriminatory because it targeted only the female workers. All of the workers in that classification were women, even though they regularly undertook the same duties as men employed in the classification of workers who maintained their jobs.

Application of the Tests

Remedies

There are two potential remedies if an employee is found to have been unfairly dismissed: reinstatement in their employment or compensation

---

[92] Fair Work Act 2009 (Cth), s 389(1).

[93] This was derived from s 185 of the Labour Relations Act 1987 (NZ). In *GN Hale & Son Ltd v Wellington Caretakers etc IUOW* [1991] 1 NZLR 151 [15] (CA), the court regarded this definition as corresponding to the ordinary usage of the word. An individual or collective employment agreement may contain a more restrictive definition of redundancy: see *Nee Nee v TLNZ Auckland Ltd* [2006] 1 ERNZ 95 (EmpC).

[94] *Grace Team Accounting Ltd v Brake* [2014] NZCA 541.

[95] *Sapevski v Katies Fashions (Australia) Pty Ltd* [1997] IRCA 219.

for the loss of their employment. Depending on the jurisdiction, compensation potentially may include lost remuneration, other financial loss and compensation for non-financial intangible factors, such as humiliation or loss of reputation. Experience in all three jurisdictions suggests that reinstatement is unusual, and that the other remedies tend to be subject to statutory or judicial restrictions. In particular, compensation for non-pecuniary loss such as humiliation or injury to feelings is not available, other than in New Zealand.[96] Furthermore, in both the United Kingdom and Australia, compensation in most cases is subject to statutory caps. This is not the case in New Zealand, but a similar effect has been achieved from the manner in which the legislative remedies have been interpreted and applied by the Court of Appeal.[97]

Reinstatement

While reinstatement is provided for in all three jurisdictions, and, in some, regarded as the primary remedy, in practice it is rarely granted even if sought. For example, in Australia, in 2014–2015, 14,624 unfair dismissal applications were filed with the Fair Work Commission. Of these, 11,125 were settled at conciliation, but only 71 settlements included any order for reinstatement. Only 349 cases went on to arbitration and, of those, only 17 resulted in a reinstatement.[98] In New Zealand, in 2011, reinstatement was sought in five cases and ordered in only two.[99]

Financial loss

In the United Kingdom, compensation for financial loss is comprised of two elements: the basic award, which is akin to a redundancy payment, and the compensatory award. The latter is an amount that the tribunal considers just and equitable, having regard to the loss sustained by the employee as a result of the dismissal.[100] There is a statutory cap that

---

[96] Employment Relations Act 2000 (NZ), s 123(1)(c); compare Fair Work Act 2009 (Cth), s 392(4) and, in the United Kingdom, see *Dunnachie v Kingston-upon-Hull City Council* [2004] ICR 1052 (HL). See also Douglas Brodie, 'Protecting Dignity in the Workplace: The Vitality of Mutual Trust and Confidence' (2004) 33 ILJ 349.

[97] *Sam's Fukuyama Food Services Ltd v Zhang* [2011] NZCA 608.

[98] See Fair Work Commission, *Annual Report 2014–15* 70–75.

[99] The Employers and Manufacturers Association (EMA) has produced reports on the outcome of dismissal cases: see <www.ema.co.nz/Pages/Home.aspx>.

[100] Employment Rights Act 1996 (UK), s 123(1).

currently stands at £80,000, or the employee's annual pay, whichever is the lower.[101] In Australia, compensation is capped at the lesser of six months' pay or the equivalent of exactly half the current unfair dismissal high income threshold, which, as of 1 July 2017, is $A142,000. This means that the maximum amount of compensation that can be awarded is $A71,000. In New Zealand, there is no financial cap, rather a standard award of three months' lost wages (or the actual loss, if less than three months), although lost income for a longer period may be awarded. Figures compiled by a major employer group show that the average award for lost wages are in the order of NZ$7,000.[102]

Non-financial loss

Of the three jurisdictions, New Zealand seems to be alone in offering compensation for non-financial loss such as humiliation or reputational damage, although such awards are not high. In the second six months of 2015, the great majority were under NZ$10,000 and most were substantially lower.[103] In the United Kingdom, it is not competent to bring a claim for injury to feelings, even where the manner of dismissal has been utterly humiliating.[104] The same is true in Australia.

THE INFLUENCE OF THE COMMON LAW ON STATUTORY DISMISSAL SCHEMES

Statutory employment protection regimes were introduced to limit one aspect of the common law rules governing employment – the employer's legal power of arbitrary dismissal. The question is: to what extent has this objective been achieved? In general, the courts have often failed to adopt a purposive approach to construction and have been unduly influenced by common law reasoning.[105] Some more specific points seem obvious. First, in both the United Kingdom and Australia, significant groups, primarily employees with limited periods of employment, have been deliberately excluded from protection and, in all jurisdictions, contractual

---

[101] There are a limited number of exceptions where the cap does not apply.

[102] EMA (n 99) 2011 report.

[103] Employment New Zealand, 'Compensation Awards 2015' (2015) <www.employment.govt.nz>. The average non-financial award calculated by the EMA for 2011 was just under NZ$6,000.

[104] *Dunnachie* (n 96).

[105] See S Anderman, 'The Interpretation of Protective Employment Statutes and Contracts of Employment' (2000) 29 ILJ 223.

freedom and the bilateral nature of contractual obligations allows employers considerable scope to avoid statutory regimes. This can be achieved either by categorizing workers as contractors or similar non-employee relationships, or by creating triangular employment relationships so that the entity utilizing the employee's labour is legally separated from the employing entity.

Second, in none of the three jurisdictions does the law provide job security or employment protection. At best, it incentivizes employers to ensure that decisions to dismiss are properly informed and involve a fair inquiry and, if not, provides a limited severance payment as compensation. Whether employer inquiries are genuine, in the sense that there is a serious likelihood of continued employment, or whether they are essentially processes for form's sake may be influenced by a range of factors including the degree of union involvement in such processes.

Finally, and perhaps most importantly, the law of unfair dismissal has been assiduously developed in a manner that is highly protective of the employer's right to manage its business. This includes the right to determine what conduct or standards can justify a dismissal, which reinforces the subordinate status of the employee. The critical element in the test for judging an employer's actions is that of the employer; be it that of the reasonable employer, or by asking whether the employer acted reasonably. Such a test, as opposed to a more neutral objective test or one reflecting bipartite values, provides a significant advantage to the employer and makes it clear that employees are expected to meet employer-determined standards. The respective position of the parties is further reinforced by the employer, or employers generally, being able to dictate the terms of what is reasonable. Again, at the level of the employing entity, the common law conception of freedom of contract allows employers to deploy and give contractual effect to a wide range of policies dictating employee conduct both within and outside work. The courts are generally reluctant to override such policies other than in specific circumstances. However, beyond that, the decline in union strength and employee voice has opened up a space in which human resource management practitioners have come to dictate acceptable employee behaviour, primarily through a tendency for 'template' employment policies to expand and converge to set industry or general expectations of employee conduct and capacity. Employers need not rely only on their own policies, but can point to them as recognized employment practice.

DRAWING BOUNDARIES BETWEEN STATUTORY SCHEMES AND THE COMMON LAW

With the exception of New Zealand, where the action for wrongful dismissal has effectively been abolished,[106] employees are still entitled to bring an action for wrongful dismissal, although, in most cases, this would be pointless in the absence of special circumstances. The most likely situation in which a wrongful dismissal action might be considered is either where an employee is excluded from statutory coverage, or where the common law might provide an alternative (or better) source of damages.

The latter of these two possibilities was at the centre of *Johnson v Unisys Ltd*.[107] Johnson had already succeeded in an action for unfair dismissal, but his compensation had been restricted by the statutory cap to just over £25,000. Johnson, who had suffered major psychiatric problems following his dismissal and was unlikely to work again, sought significant damages, primarily based on a breach of the implied term of mutual trust and confidence. While the House of Lords indicated that *Addis*[108] may not prove an insurmountable obstacle to such a claim,[109] their Lordships held that Johnson's claim failed for two principal reasons. The first was an unwillingness to extend the obligation of mutual trust and confidence beyond the ordinary operation of the employment relationship and, in particular, to allow it to constrain an express contractual power to dismiss on notice.[110] However, also central to their Lordships' decision was the appropriate boundary between the courts and Parliament. The House's reasoning was succinctly stated by Lord Hoffmann:[111]

> The second reason is that judges, in developing the law, must have regard to the policies expressed by Parliament in legislation. Employment law requires a balancing of the interests of employers and employees, with proper regard not only to the individual dignity and worth of the employees but also to the general economic interest. Subject to observance of fundamental human

---

[106] Employment Relations Act 2000 (NZ), s 113, remembering that New Zealand's personal grievance procedure is accessible to all employees.

[107] *Johnson v Unisys Ltd* [2001] UKHL 13.

[108] *Addis* (n 9).

[109] *Johnson* (n 107) [15], per Lord Steyn; [44], per Lord Hoffmann; [70], per Lord Millett.

[110] ibid [37], per Lord Hoffmann; [78], per Lord Millett. Similar reasoning was used by the New Zealand Court of Appeal in *Air New Zealand Ltd v Raddock* [1999] 2 NZLR 641 (NZCA).

[111] *Johnson* (n 107) [37].

> rights, the point at which this balance should be struck is a matter for democratic decision. The development of the common law by the judges plays a subsidiary role. Their traditional function is to adapt and modernise the common law. But such developments must be consistent with legislative policy as expressed in statutes. The courts may proceed in harmony with Parliament but there should be no discord.

Not only could mutual trust and confidence not be used to establish a common law action for compensation independent of statute, but neither, it was suggested, could the inclusion of disciplinary rules in the required statutory written statement of particulars of employment. Lord Hoffmann stated the position (obiter) as follows:[112]

> It is I suppose possible that they may have contractual effect in determining whether the employer can dismiss summarily in the sense of not having to give four weeks' notice or payment in lieu. But I do not think that they can have been intended to qualify the employer's common law power to dismiss without cause on giving such notice, or to create contractual duties which are independently actionable.

Although subject to academic criticism,[113] the so-called '*Johnson* exclusion zone' was reinforced in *Eastwood v Magnox Electric plc*,[114] which drew a 'comparatively straightforward' line between the dismissal and claims that arise prior to the dismissal. The problem facing an employee, however, is that:[115]

> In the ordinary course, suspension apart, an employer's failure to act fairly in the steps leading to dismissal does not of itself cause the employee financial

112 ibid [66].

113 Lord Steyn's own critique in *Eastwood v Magnox Electric plc* [2004] UKHL 35, [2005] 1 AC 503 refers to Deakin and Morris (n 7) 410–11, 418–19; Mark Freedland, *The Personal Employment Contract* (Oxford University Press 2003) 162–7, 303–5, 342–5, 362–4; Hugh Collins, 'Claim for Unfair Dismissal' (2001) 30 ILJ 305; and supplementary reflections by Mark Freedland at 30 ILJ 309–11; Bob Hepple and Gillian Morris, 'The Employment Act 2002 and the Crisis of Individual Employment Rights' (2002) 31 ILJ 245, 253; Douglas Brodie, 'Legal Coherence and the Employment Revolution' (2001) 117 LQR 604, 624–5; Lizzie Barmes, 'The Continuing Conceptual Crisis in the Common Law of the Contract of Employment' (2004) 67(3) MLR 435. Making due allowance for differences in emphasis between the writers on the subject, there is apparently no support for the analysis adopted in *Johnson* (n 107).

114 *Eastwood* (n 113).

115 ibid [28], per Lord Nicolls. In the unusual facts of this case, psychological problems relating to a suspension raised an independent cause of action.

> loss. The loss arises when the employee is dismissed and it arises by reason of his dismissal. Then the resultant claim for loss falls squarely within the *Johnson* exclusion area.

Demonstrating that any act of the employer's that occurred prior to dismissal was causative will prove challenging. The exclusion zone has been further extended in *Edwards v Chesterfield Royal Hospital NHS Foundation Trust & Botham v Ministry of Defence*[116] to apply to cases in which there was a breach of an express contractual disciplinary procedure. The consequences of these breaches were significant losses associated with the 'stigma' that attached to the respondents, both of whom were professionals accused of sexual misconduct.[117] In essence, the Supreme Court held that any action that has the effect of circumventing the statutory limitations on dismissal compensation falls within the *Johnson* zone:[118]

> The unfair dismissal legislation precludes a claim for damages for breach of contract in relation to the manner of a dismissal, whether the claim is formulated as a claim for breach of an implied term or as a claim for breach of an express term which regulates disciplinary procedures leading to a dismissal. Parliament has made certain policy choices as to the circumstances in which and the conditions subject to which an employee may be compensated for unfair dismissal. A dismissal may be unfair because it is substantively unfair to dismiss the employee in the circumstances of the case and/or because the manner in which the dismissal was effected was unfair. The manner may be unfair because it was done in a humiliating manner or because the procedure adopted was unfair inter alia because the agreed disciplinary procedure which led to the dismissal was not followed. It may be unfair because defamatory findings were made which damage the employee's reputation and which, following a dismissal, make it difficult for the employee to find further employment. Any such complaint was intended by Parliament to be adjudicated on by the specialist employment tribunal subject to the various constraints to which I have referred. Parliament did not intend that an employee could choose to pursue his complaint of unfair dismissal in the ordinary courts, free from the limitations carefully crafted by Parliament for the exercise of this statutory jurisdiction.

Johnson served to restrict the natural evolution of the common law, by denying that otherwise generally applicable common law controls should

---

[116] *Edwards v Chesterfield Royal Hospital NHS Foundation Trust & Botham v Ministry of Defence* [2011] UKSC 58.

[117] The allegations in question had later not been proven in proceedings of the relevant professional bodies.

[118] *Edwards* (n 116) [40], per Lord Nicolls.

operate in the case of dismissal. This has meant that other groups of workers, such as franchisees, may be better protected.[119] *Edwards* has taken matters a step further by restricting the heads of loss claimable, even though, by the adoption of express contractual terms, the parties appear to have contracted-in to the full range of common law remedies. The approach taken by the UK Supreme Court has been taken a step further by the High Court of Australia in *Commonwealth Bank of Australia v Barker*,[120] where the court declined to imply a mutual obligation of trust and confidence into contracts of employment in Australia, on the basis that: 'The complex policy considerations ... mark it, in the Australian context, as a matter more appropriate for the legislature than for the courts to determine'.[121] In this case, the complaint related to the failure to properly offer relocation options as required by the bank's redeployment policy. While *Barker* may have wider implications, its effect is most likely to be felt in dismissal claims. In this case, the dismissal itself was not unfair, being a genuine redundancy; rather, the action related to damages for a lost employment opportunity that should have been available if the bank's redeployment policy had been properly followed.

THE INFLUENCE OF STATUTE ON THE COMMON LAW

Statute can exercise a positive and stimulating effect on the common law – the emergence of mutual trust and confidence being a prime example. However, where the decision to dismiss is concerned, which may be regarded as being at the very core of the employer's prerogative, statute has exercised a constraining influence. It may also be said that statute has not been regarded by the judiciary as a tool to modernize and strengthen the remedies available where employment contracts are breached. The existence of a statutory remedy of reinstatement has not prompted a reappraisal of the denial of specific performance; nor has the availability of damages for injury to feelings for breach of some statutory rights led to parallel developments at common law. The analogical influence of statute is weak at the point of dismissal.

---

[119] See Douglas Brodie, 'Fair Dealing and the World of Work' (2014) 43(1) ILJ 29.

[120] *Commonwealth Bank of Australia v Barker* (2014) 253 CLR 169, [2014] HCA 32.

[121] ibid [40].

Standing back from dismissal does, however, allow us to conclude that the common law is more concerned with natural justice than would have traditionally been the case. The key case of *Gogay v Hertfordshire County Council* held that the punitive exercise of prerogative powers may be a breach of mutual trust in the absence of due process; the employer would not have lost in *Gogay* had they taken the trouble to establish that there was reasonable cause to suspend.[122] It seems likely that the emphasis in legislative schemes on procedural fairness has helped to bring this about. Nevertheless, even where the impact of statute can be viewed as benign, challenges remain in ensuring that common law development is coherent. For example, in *Yapp v Foreign and Commonwealth Office*, it was found that the process adopted by the employer breached his contractual obligations, but only because it fell outside the range of reasonable responses.[123] Counsel for the employer in *Yapp* thought it appropriate to advocate the band of reasonableness test, given that it applies to the law of unfair dismissal, but its correctness in the context of a common law claim may be questioned. Viewed from the perspective of the law of contract, *Yapp* would seem to be inconsistent with *Bournemouth University v Buckland*, which denies that the band of reasonableness test has a role to play in determining whether a breach of mutual trust and confidence has arisen.[124] *Buckland* endorses 'the unvarnished *Mahmud* test' and indicates that to do otherwise would be contrary to the stance taken in *Western Excavations v Sharp*.[125] In the employment context, the unvarnished *Mahmud* test is a means of providing natural justice in the workplace and ensuring that the worker is treated with dignity. *Yapp* represents a departure from precedent. This is to be regretted, as empowering the employer with an extensive degree of discretion constitutes a partial contracting-out of mutual trust and confidence.

CONCLUSION

The employer's power to control its labour force is centred in the power to dismiss. Employees who are at daily risk of dismissal, and possibly

---

[122] *Gogay v Hertfordshire County Council* [2000] IRLR 703.

[123] *Yapp v Foreign and Commonwealth Office* [2014] EWCA Civ 1512, [2015] IRLR 112.

[124] *Bournemouth University v Buckland* [2010] EWCA Civ 121, [2011] QB 323.

[125] *Western Excavations v Sharp* [1978] QB 761.

economic disaster, are likely to constitute a compliant labour force that is unwilling to raise even mild resistance to employer authority, including conduct that is unlawful. When, as remains the case at common law, this power can be exercised in an untrammelled and totally arbitrary manner, employees are left completely at the mercy of the employer unless they are in a position to exercise collective strength to challenge dismissals perceived as unfair. Modern statutory controls are, at least, as much a response to such action as they were to any notion of workplace justice. Statutory controls on dismissal have gone some way to alleviate the lack of natural justice inherent in the common law, but they have also had the effect of undermining any bipartite approach to employment protection. As collective strength has weakened, governments have tended to reduce access to statutory protections and the courts have proved reluctant to significantly modify their traditional hostility to limitations on the rights of property owners or to limit managerial prerogatives. The courts have accepted the need for fair process and adequate justification but the approach remains highly unitary. The tests of fairness remain employer focused and tend to maximize employer discretions. Legal developments that might have aided an employee, such as the term of mutual trust and confidence and the concept of constructive dismissal, have, in the main, been interpreted conservatively. Unfair dismissal laws have not enhanced employment security. At best, they have provided some level of compensation for the loss of employment – compensation that generally falls far short of any actual loss to the employee.

These developments partly reflect a reluctance by legislators to place what they see as an excessive burden on employers, but also the strong and continuing influence of the common law. As Wedderburn put it: 'The "living thing" of the common law is the judiciary; the principles are changed in application; but the underlying philosophy is not'.[126]

126 Wedderburn (n 6) 9.

11. Common law remedies

INTRODUCTION

In all three jurisdictions, the law provides that, where a party sustains a loss by reason of a breach of contract, they are (so far as money can do it) to be placed in the same situation, with respect to damages, as if the contract had been performed. Pitched at this level of generality, the employee, faced by the employer's breach of the employment contract, may feel reassured by the legal framework. However, the employee's position in terms of damages is grossly unsatisfactory. This is demonstrated by two features of the current law in particular: the heads of loss that may be claimed; and the measure of damages in cases of wrongful dismissal. With regard to heads of loss, the old case of *Addis v Gramophone* continues to loom large and can be seen as constituting a barrier to contract fulfilling its normal compensatory function.[1] This is despite the fact that the case 'was decided in the heyday of a judicial philosophy of market individualism in respect of what was then called the law of master and servant'.[2] Moreover, the measure of damages in wrongful dismissal cases fails to recognize the full extent of the employee's interest in the employment relationship.

The position in respect of equitable orders also leaves a great deal to be desired. This is despite the fact that the courts now recognize that the employee's interest in employment relations should not be seen as purely pecuniary:[3]

> There is now a greater recognition than ever that employment is important to an employee not simply because it provides economic sustenance. Workplaces are a hub of important human exchanges which are vital to the wellbeing of individual workers. Work provides employees with purpose, dignity, pride, enjoyment, social acceptance and many social connections. As well, the performance of work allows for skill enhancement and advances career

1 *Addis v Gramophone Co Ltd* [1909] AC 488.

2 *Johnson v Gore Wood* [2000] UKHL 65, [2002] 2 AC 1, 50.

3 *Quinn v Overland* [2010] FCA 799, [101]; and see *Blackadder v Ramsey Butchering Services Pty Ltd* (2005) 221 CLR 539.

> opportunities. These non pecuniary attributes of work are important and their denial can be devastating to the legitimate interests of any worker, either skilled or unskilled.

Dictums such as the foregoing notwithstanding, the law of remedies remains rooted in the past. The position in respect of specific performance provides a very good example here. It is not clear why this should be so, given the judicial 'discovery' of the true nature of employment relations.

WRONGFUL DISMISSAL: MEASURE OF DAMAGES

In a wrongful dismissal action, the normal measure of damages is the amount that would have been earned during the notice period.[4] In England, this stance is seen as an application of the rule that damages against a contract breaker are assessed on the basis that they would have performed the contract in a manner most favourable to themselves.[5] In *Gunton v Richmond-upon-Thames London Borough Council*, Buckley LJ explained the position as follows:[6]

> Where a servant is wrongfully dismissed, he is entitled, subject to mitigation, to damages equivalent to the wages he would have earned under the contract from the date of dismissal to the end of the contract. The date when the contract would have come to an end, however, must be ascertained on the assumption that the employer would have exercised any power he may have had to bring the contract to an end in the way most beneficial to himself, that is to say, that he would have determined the contract at the earliest date at which he could properly do so.

At one time, the Australian courts were at one with their UK counterparts (both in terms of the approach adopted and the underpinning justification) but, as we shall see, that is changing.[7]

One might question whether the approach in *Gunton* serves to promote the fundamental principle that an award of damages should put the claimant in the position in which they would have been had the contract been performed. Ogus has argued that: 'The plaintiff should be entitled to what benefits he might reasonably have acquired if the contract had been

---

4 *British Guiana Credit v Da Silva* [1965] 1 WLR 248.

5 Anthony Ogus, *The Law of Damages* (Butterworths 1973) 312.

6 *Gunton v Richmond-upon-Thames London Borough Council* [1980] ICR 755, 772.

7 *Bostik (Australia) Pty Ltd v Gorgevski (No 1)* [1992] FCA 209.

performed'.[8] Applying that principle to a case of wrongful dismissal, it is arguable that the loss that flows naturally from the breach can only be determined by asking how long the employment would otherwise have been likely to endure. The dissent of Lord Denning in *Lavarack v Woods*[9] is relevant here. There, the plaintiff had raised a wrongful dismissal action and questions arose as to the appropriate measure of damages. The majority took the view that, since the payment of a bonus was expressed as being at the discretion of the employer, damages should not be awarded in respect of the loss of bonus. However, Lord Denning would have found for the plaintiff on this point. He said that 'the compensation is to be based on the probabilities of the case – on the remuneration which the plaintiff might reasonably be expected to receive – and not on the bare minimum necessary to satisfy the legal right'.[10]

The current position may be defended on the basis that it reflects general principles in the law of contract. The principle may work well in certain contractual contexts and, indeed, it would be open to the parties to bargain on a different basis. Where the employment contract is concerned, matters are different, given the inequality of bargaining power. The terms of the contract are already set by the employer, who can, as a result, terminate the contract lawfully by giving a short period of notice. The question then arises as to whether the employer should be in an equally favourable position when they behave unlawfully. It is difficult to see why the courts should modify the general rules on damages to incentivize bad behaviour. In a different context, in *Societe Generale, London Branch v Geys*, Lord Hope favoured the elective theory of termination, as he believed that the party who is in the wrong should not be permitted to benefit from his own wrong.[11] It is disappointing that that stance has not been adopted in terms of the measure of damages. It is also the case that, when the 'least burdensome' principle is applied to powers of termination, it facilitates ease of exit from a relationship. This is difficult to reconcile with contemporary thinking that regards the employment contract as relational. Freedland has concluded that the courts have adopted 'a firmly free-market transactional approach to the termination of contracts of employment', which does not accept

---

8 Ogus (n 5) 314.

9 *Lavarack v Woods* [1967] 1 QB 278.

10 ibid 288.

11 *Societe Generale, London Branch v Geys* [2012] UKSC 63, [2013] 1 AC 523.

'relational obligations upon the employing entity which would vindicate the dignity and autonomy of the individual employee'.[12]

The principle is not applicable where there is an implied constraint on the exercise of the power that is in dispute. *Clark v BET* involved the assessment of damages in a wrongful dismissal case.[13] The view was taken that a capricious or bad faith exercise of discretion by the employer would have been a breach of contract, and that an award of damages in respect of a bonus payment should allow for this. Walker J went on to conclude that it should not be assumed that any discretion would have been exercised so as to give the least possible benefit to the plaintiff if such an assumption would on the facts be unrealistic.[14] It has been held that implied restraints do not apply to the employer's prerogative to terminate the employment contract.[15]

The position of the employee was improved in one respect by the decision in *Gunton*.[16] It was held that the plaintiff could not lawfully be dismissed until a disciplinary procedure, prescribed by the contract, had been followed. The corollary, in terms of damages, was that any award should allow for the period of time that would have been necessary for the employer to have complied with the procedure. It has since been held, in *Janciuk v Winerite*, that a court will not assess the chances of the employee not being dismissed had the procedure been followed.[17] It is said that the assumption that must be made is that the employer would have dismissed the employee at the first available moment open to him; namely, after the procedure had been exhausted:[18]

> The Court is not concerned to inquire whether the employee would have been dismissed had the contract been performed, but rather for how long would the employee have been employed before the employer was contractually entitled to give notice. This is on the assumption that the employer has not been accused of acting in bad faith where other principles might apply.

---

[12] Mark R Freedland, *The Personal Employment Contract* (Oxford University Press 2003) 360.

[13] *Clark v BET* [1997] IRLR 348.

[14] ibid 349.

[15] See Chapter 7.

[16] It remains to be seen whether *Gunton* (n 6) will survive, given the doubts expressed in *Edwards v Chesterfield Royal Hospital NHS Foundation Trust* [2011] UKSC 58, [2012] 2 AC 22.

[17] *Janciuk v Winerite* [1998] IRLR 63.

[18] ibid 64.

Does the approach in *Janciuk* comply with the 'least burdensome' principle? Only if we assume that it is permissible for the employer to act in any way he sees fit and even to be arbitrary or capricious. The employer has chosen to fetter his discretion by adopting a procedure of this type, and it surely cannot have been intended that the process would be meaningless.

The Australian courts have adopted a more progressive approach in recent years, the pivotal decision being that of the High Court in *Commonwealth v Amann Aviation Pty Ltd.*[19] The approach adopted was to assess what was likely to have happened had the breach of contract not occurred:[20]

> Where compensation is sought in respect of the deprivation of a possible benefit which is dependent upon the unrestricted volition of another it may be impossible to say that any assessable loss results from the breach. However, this statement must be understood in the light of the principle that the mere existence of a contractual right in a party to terminate does not operate automatically to restrict the damages that can be awarded … The court must have regard to the facts and evaluate the possible exercise of the right in all the relevant circumstances of the case.

A valuable illustration of the impact of *Amann Aviation* in the employment context is provided by *Walker v Citigroup Global Markets Australia Pty Ltd.*[21] There, damages were assessed as they would have been in a tort action. The court found that the employer would not have exercised his right to bring the contract to an end on one month's notice without cause. A conclusion that the employer 'would have sacked a skilled and competent employee holding a high profile position within the company without cause is not a natural inference to be drawn without direct evidence. To act in that fashion would deprive it of the services of a valuable employee and risk damage to its reputation in the financial community'.[22]

Ramsey v Annesley College provides another example.[23] There, it was argued that, due to the wrongful termination of employment, the employee lost the opportunity to continue to work and receive salary for a period that exceeded the length of the notice period. It was held that, in

---

[19] *Commonwealth v Amann Aviation Pty Ltd* (1991) 174 CLR 64.

[20] ibid [56], per Mason CJ and Dawson J.

[21] *Walker v Citigroup Global Markets Australia Pty Ltd* [2006] FCAFC 101.

[22] ibid [83]. The court approached the matter on the basis that there was no implied restraint on the employer's power.

[23] *Ramsey v Annesley College* [2013] SASC 72.

principle, that head of damages was available, provided that the employee, on the evidence, had a valuable opportunity to continue in employment that was lost due to the wrongful breach of contract.[24]

ALLOWABLE HEADS OF LOSS

The emergence of the obligation of mutual trust and confidence can be seen as evidencing a judicial conception of employment relations involving non-pecuniary dimensions.[25] This contemporary view might be expected to be reflected in the law of remedies; developments in the primary obligations of the parties should sound in effective secondary obligations if they are to be meaningful. However, both the United Kingdom and Australian courts have been reticent to take a holistic view and further the modernizing agenda. It is striking that Australian cases decided prior to *Commonwealth Bank of Australia v Barker*, which favoured the adoption of mutual trust, also tended to favour a narrow approach to remedies.[26]

As we have seen in Chapter 7, the Australian decision in *Burazin v Blacktown City* restricted the remedies available for breach of mutual trust and confidence, by denying that an action for damages would arise.[27] This is highly anomalous. In any particular case, damages may not be owed because the breach has not caused loss, but it is unusual to encounter a term where the secondary obligation to pay damages can never arise. *Burazin* was influenced by the context in which mutual trust

---

[24] In *Gregory v Philip Morris Ltd* (1988) 80 ALR 455, 483, a dismissal had taken place in breach of a term that had been incorporated from an award issued by the Australian Industrial Relations Commission. The assessment of damages was not limited to the wages that would have been paid during the notice period. Instead, assessment 'involves a comparison of Gregory's position as it was after his dismissal, with the position in which he would have been placed if he had not been wrongfully dismissed. An award of damages should be assessed on the basis of loss of the opportunity to continue the employment, discounted for foreseeable events which might have brought the employment to an end'. More recently, in *Quinn v Gray* [2009] VSC 136, the court took the view that, if further or other loss (other than the wages that would have arisen during the notice period) is demonstrated to flow from the breach, there is no reason why it should not be recoverable.

[25] See also Grace Keesing, 'Contractual Rights and Remedies for Dismissed Employees after the Employment Revolution' (2012) Melb U Law Rw 3.

[26] *Commonwealth Bank of Australia v Barker* [2014] HCA 32, (2014) 253 CLR 169.

[27] *Burazin v Blacktown City* (1996) 142 ALR 144.

and confidence emerged in the United Kingdom, where the term allowed the employee's resignation to constitute constructive dismissal. The creation of mutual trust facilitated access to the statutory remedy of unfair dismissal; the focus was not on common law damages. However, there was nothing to suggest that the term was confined to statutory claims, and subsequent UK cases have made clear that damages may be awarded.

Burazin seems to have regarded mutual trust as inextricably linked to, and limited by, the statutory scheme. A difference in approach, in cases where psychiatric harm has occurred, may also have been relevant. It is worthy of note that, in cases of this sort, the courts in Australia are more protective of the interests of the employee than their British counterparts. The UK courts, on policy grounds, impose restrictions on recovery where psychiatric harm is incurred in the course of employment.[28] By way of contrast, in Australia, the law of employer's liability functions in the same way as it does where physical harm is in issue, although it can be difficult to demonstrate that foreseeability of harm arises.[29] The court in *Burazin* may have formed the view that, as cases where the harm was more serious were taken care of, there was less need to allow access to common law damages. Certainly, the court in *Heptonstall v Gaskin (No 2)* was of the view that part of the explanation for the emergence of mutual trust lay in the rules on recovery in claims for psychiatric harm against the employer in the United Kingdom.[30] More specifically, the restrictions imposed by *White v Chief Constable* were seen as significant.[31] There, the House of Lords established a significant limitation on the scope of the employer's duty. It was held that the law does not recognize a duty to guard employees against psychiatric harm suffered as a result of witnessing injury to others. The result is that, in a case such as *White*, where the employee is not in physical danger, they will only be able to recover should the rules applicable to secondary victims be satisfied. The law of negligence in Australia takes a different view,[32] and Hoeben J in *Heptonstall* took the view that mutual trust was brought in to bridge the gap: 'In Australia the same result has been brought about by

---

[28] *Hatton v Sutherland* [2002] EWCA Civ 76, [2002] 2 All ER 1; *Yapp v Foreign and Commonwealth Office* [2014] EWCA Civ 1512.

[29] Douglas Brodie, *Enterprise Liability and the Common Law* (Cambridge University Press 2010) Ch 9. See also *Koehler v Cerebos (Aust) Ltd* (2005) 222 CLR 44.

[30] *Heptonstall v Gaskin (No 2)* [2005] NSWSC 30.

[31] *White v Chief Constable* [1999] 2 AC 455.

[32] *State of NSW v Seedsman* [2000] NSWCA 119.

the tort of negligence'.[33] This is unconvincing, as mutual trust was not devised to circumvent restrictive rules imposed by the law of tort, nor does it function in that way. The claim in *White* would no more have succeeded in contract than it did in tort.

The restrictive approach in *Burazin* might be thought to be symptomatic of Australian hesitancy over the wisdom of accepting mutual trust, which, of course, culminated in absolute rejection. It also reflects a position held in common with the United Kingdom, where there is a reluctance to improve the remedies available to the employee should there be a breach of contract. *Addis* continues to loom large in discussion in both jurisdictions.[34] This is surprising, given the age of the decision and the fact that it very clearly represents the thinking of a bygone era. The nature of mutual trust and confidence might have suggested that change would be at hand. However, reform in the law of primary obligations has not been paralleled where the law of remedies is concerned. In the Australian case of *McDonald v Parnell Laboratories*, the claimant sought damages arising from the circumstances of her dismissal.[35] This fell on stony ground: 'The argument is contrary to the analysis in *Burazin*. For so long as *Addis* remains good law in Australia, any such argument cannot lead to the grant of relief'.[36] The Australian courts continue to follow *Addis* in the employment context, a position confirmed by the New South Wales Court of Appeal in *Russell v The Trustees of the Roman Catholic Church*.[37] Nevertheless, in *Nikolich v Goldman Sachs*, the Federal Court of Australia held, obiter, that it was strongly arguable that the claim for injury to feelings fell within one of the exceptions to *Addis*.[38] In the United Kingdom, the case law has, for some time, contained a considerable number of exceptions.[39] Indeed, that list continues to lengthen; the most notable instance being the decision of the House of Lords in *Farley v Skinner*, which allowed recovery where a major or important part of the contract, rather than the sole object, was to provide pleasure, relaxation or peace of mind.[40] Against that backdrop, several judges, in contract of employment cases, have sought, without

---

33 *Heptonstall* (n 30) 5.

34 *Addis* (n 1).

35 *McDonald v Parnell Laboratories* [2007] FCA 1903.

36 ibid [92].

37 *Russell v The Trustees of the Roman Catholic Church* [2008] NSWCA 217.

38 *Nikolich v Goldman Sachs* [2006] FCA 784.

39 *Jarvis v Swan Tours* [1973] 1 QB 233.

40 *Farley v Skinner* [2001] UKHL 49, [2002] 2 AC 732.

success, to distinguish *Addis* and extend the list of exceptions. *Addis* remains formidably resilient, however.

The seminal decision in *Malik and Mahmud v Bank of Credit and Commerce*[41] allowed for the possibility of reputation damages, which, hitherto, had been thought to be prohibited by *Addis*. *Malik* accepted that damage to reputation arising due to breach of contract during the course of employment could sound in damages. The position has since been found to be different where dismissal is concerned.[42] In *Shaw v State of New South Wales*, damages were claimed for economic loss due to loss of reputation. The claim was rejected by the Court of Appeal of the New South Wales Supreme Court, which held that damages for loss of future employment prospects caused by a wrongful dismissal are irrecoverable.[43] Even where an action is possible in principle, the chances of recovery are slim.[44]

The position with regard to remedies is different in New Zealand, where the courts have been pioneers in liberating the law in this area from outmoded and artificial restrictions.[45] Thus, in *Whelan v Waitaki Meats Ltd*, Gallen J in the High Court awarded damages for the mental distress suffered by a long-term employee who was peremptorily dismissed from his employment.[46] The judge did so on the basis that the plaintiff 'was entitled to assume that he would be treated by his employer in such a manner as to enable him to retain his dignity within the community and not to have his status affected by a precipitate act open to misinterpretation'.[47] The breach found was related to the manner of dismissal, the very feature that was specifically held in *Addis* not to support damages for distress. The question boils down to what was in the reasonable contemplation of the parties; that is, what general principles command.[48] The New Zealand Court of Appeal has also pleaded for moderation in awards.[49] The position taken by the court in *Whelan* may,

---

41 *Malik and Mahmud v Bank of Credit and Commerce International SA* [1997] UKHL 23.

42 *Edwards* (n 16).

43 *Shaw v State of New South Wales* [2012] NSWCA 102.

44 *BCCI SA v Ali* [2002] ICR 1258.

45 See also the report from the New Zealand Law Commission, *Aspects of Damages: Employment Contracts and the Rule in Addis v Gramophone Co* (R18, 1991).

46 *Whelan v Waitaki Meats Ltd* [1991] 2 NZLR 74; *Stuart v Armourguard Security* [1996] 1 NZLR 484.

47 *Whelan* (n 46) 89.

48 *Mouat v Clark Boyce* [1992] NZLR 559.

49 ibid.

however, be influenced by the fact that, since 1973, employees entitled to raise a personal grievance were able to claim 'compensation' as a remedy for a personal grievance. In 1987, that right had been clarified by statute as being: 'the payment to the employee of compensation by the employee's employer, including compensation for … humiliation, loss of dignity, and injury to the feelings of the employee'.[50] At the time of the *Whelan* decision, only union members had access to the personal grievance process. After coverage was extended to all employees by the Employment Contracts Act 1991 (NZ), actions for wrongful dismissal came within the jurisdiction of the Employment Court and became increasingly less common, and were abolished in 2000.[51]

EQUITABLE ORDERS

Faced with the prospect of unlawful termination on the part of the employer, the employee may wish to keep the contract alive. After all, the employee's interest in employment need not be simply pecuniary and, as we have seen, this is now recognized by the courts. In any event, an award of damages may not be adequate. It seems reasonable to conclude that awards are highly problematic in the employment context, given the limitations that have already been discussed. Traditionally, however, an employee would have found it almost impossible to obtain an order of specific performance. In *Societe Generale, London Branch v Geys*, it was explained that: 'Equity took the view that the remedy of specific performance, or analogous injunction, should not be available so as to require an employee who had wrongfully resigned to go back to work or to require an employer who had wrongfully dismissed the employee to take him back'.[52] In the United Kingdom, up until recently, it was unclear whether judicial practice was reinforced by a theory of automatic termination, whereby a repudiatory breach led to the unilateral termination of the contract. However, in *Geys*, the Supreme Court made clear that general contractual principles were applicable and that rescission was at the election of the innocent party,[53] a position long adopted by the

---

[50] Labour Relations Act 1987 (NZ), s 227(c)(i). 'Compensation' was originally provided for by the Industrial Relations Act 1973 (NZ), s 117(7)(c).

[51] Employment Relations Act 2000 (NZ), s 113.

[52] *Geys* (n 11) 77.

[53] See David Cabrelli and Rebecca Zahn, 'The Elective and Automatic Theories of Termination in the Common Law of the Contract of Employment: Conundrum Resolved?' (2013) 76 MLR 1106.

Australian courts,[54] and which also represents the law in New Zealand.[55] Such a position is consistent with the contemporary approach to control of discretion:[56]

> the party who is in the wrong should not be permitted to benefit from his own wrong that is determinative. The timing of the repudiation may be crucial, and if the automatic theory were to prevail an employer may well be tempted to play this to his advantage – by getting in first before a rise in pay or pension entitlement takes place or, as in this case, a rise in the entitlement to bonuses.

The courts continue to see specific performance as inappropriate in the employment context. The position is less absolute than it once was, but only the bravest (or richest) of claimants would seek an order of this sort. The courts do acknowledge that a number of the traditional arguments no longer carry the same weight. For instance, it has long been said that it is inappropriate to grant specific performance where there is no longer mutual trust and confidence between the parties. It may be doubted whether this factor continues to have relevance, with the possible exception of employment by a small employer with a limited number of staff. In the Australian case of *Turner v Australasian Coal and Shale Employees Federation*, it was noted that this argument:[57]

> has lost a good deal of its relevance in present society. It is difficult to say that a relationship of mutual confidence must exist in the case of every person employed by a large corporate enterprise. There are many occupations in such enterprises where the precise identity of the employee performing a particular job is immaterial to the collective management of the corporation.

A further traditional argument against the granting of an order has been the difficulties that are said to arise from the need for continuing supervision. Developments in related areas of law cast doubt on the continuing force of this factor in employment cases. The change of practice in respect of commercial leases in some jurisdictions has not proved to be problematic:[58]

---

[54] *Automatic Fire Sprinklers Proprietary Ltd v Watson* (1946) 72 CLR 435.

[55] *Paper Reclaim Ltd v Aotearoa International Ltd* [2007] 3 NZLR 169.

[56] *Geys* (n 11) 537.

[57] *Turner v Australasian Coal and Shale Employees Federation* (1984) 55 ALR 635, 648. See *Gregory* (n 24).

[58] *Highland & Universal Properties v Safeway Properties (No 2)* 2000 [SC] 297, 310.

> Since that decision, orders of specific implement ad interim of the nature in issue have frequently been granted in the Court of Session, in *Retail Parks* and in numerous unreported decisions. The pursuer is, I consider, right to emphasise not only that this has frequently been done, but that it has apparently not given rise to any obvious difficulties of enforcement.

It should also be remembered that the courts always have a discretion in these matters. The increased willingness of the courts to grant injunctions against employers to prevent unlawful termination of the employment contract has cast considerable doubt over the validity of a number of the arguments used to justify the unavailability of specific performance.[59] Indeed, the injunction granted in *Powell v Brent London Borough Council* was, in substance, an order for specific performance, in that it obliged the employer to let the employee work as normal, pending the trial of the action.[60]

It might have been thought that the enactment of statutory remedies of reinstatement would have led to a more radical change of position at common law. Through the creation of a statutory version of specific performance, the legislature can be seen as rejecting the traditional arguments against the granting of such an order. Moreover, in the course of exercising their statutory jurisdiction, the courts have acknowledged that reinstatement is not at odds with the way in which employment relations are now conducted. In *Quinn v Overland*, it was said:[61]

> Dismissed employees are regularly reinstated into their former employments without apparent consequent difficulties. The long-standing nature of this remedy, and its acceptance as part of the industrial furniture, is a testament to the fact that as a matter of practice, a breakdown in confidence is not necessarily irreconcilable. What needs to be achieved by a reconciliation is a sufficient level of cooperation for a proper working relationship to resume; mutual affection and friendship are not essential.

However, it would be difficult to argue that statutory intervention has had a discernible impact on the common law, with the position in respect of interlocutory orders constituting a possible exception.

The biggest change in practice in the last 20 to 30 years has arisen in the context of disciplinary proceedings, where the courts have been willing to grant interlocutory orders, even in cases where the employer

---

59 See KD Ewing, 'Remedies for Breach of the Contract of Employment' [1993] CLJ 405.

60 *Powell v Brent London Borough Council* [1988] ICR 176.

61 *Quinn* (n 3) [98].

has sought to terminate the contract. The UK Supreme Court has acknowledged that an interim order may well be appropriate in the disciplinary context. Indeed, in *West London Mental Health NHS Trust v Chhabra*, the court offered a measure of guidance.[62] An order may be sought to restrain termination by means of an improper procedure. In *Robb v London Borough of Hammersmith*, the employer summarily dismissed the employee without going through the contractual disciplinary procedure.[63] The employee sought an injunction to restrain the employer from giving effect to the purported dismissal until the procedures had been complied with. Whilst the plaintiff was willing to agree to be suspended on full pay, the employer said that an injunction would be inappropriate because of their loss of trust and confidence. In considering whether to grant the injunction, Morland J placed great store on whether or not the order would be 'workable'. The employers' lack of confidence in the plaintiff's ability to perform the job was found to have no effect on the workability of the disciplinary procedures and, in consequence, the injunction was granted. In a similar vein, an interlocutory injunction was granted in *Irani v Southampton & South-West Hampshire HA*, to restrain the defendants from implementing a notice to terminate the contract before the appropriate procedure had been complied with.[64] The same willingness to promote procedural fairness at common law can be seen in Australia. Due process can prevent reputational damage that cannot adequately be compensated for by an award of damages. *Paras v Public Service Body* held that an interim order could be granted to restrain 'an employer treating a dismissal as valid or effective in circumstances where fair processes or natural justice have not been afforded to the employee in accordance with the contract of employment'.[65] *Robb* was influential:[66]

> If the employer and employee have lost faith and confidence in each other, that fact would be very relevant, but not necessarily fatal, to the grant of an injunction. Even where that is the case, injunctions have been granted where the employee's contract of employment requires a particular procedure to be followed as a precondition of dismissal, and that procedure has not been followed.

---

62 *West London Mental Health NHS Trust v Chhabra* [2013] UKSC 80, [2014] 1 All ER 943.

63 *Robb v London Borough of Hammersmith* [1991] ICR 514.

64 *Irani v Southampton & South-West Hampshire HA* [1985] ICR 590. See also *Jones v Gwent County Council* [1992] IRLR 521.

65 *Paras v Public Service Body* [2006] FCA 622, [39].

66 ibid [42].

On occasion, the courts have come close to granting specific performance; *Powell* is a prime example in this regard.[67] Again, in *Quinn*,[68] the court restrained the employer from acting upon directions given to the employee suspending them from work. The question remains as to why obtaining specific performance should still be almost impossible. It may be that, while the courts are content to ensure that due process takes place, they are reluctant to go further and insist that the employment relationship is maintained. The fact that an interlocutory order is granted in a disciplinary context does not mean that dismissal cannot take place when the appropriate procedures have been concluded.

The employer's interest tends to lie in making life difficult for the employee who wishes to jump ship.[69] The employer will argue that an injunction is necessary, as damages are an inadequate remedy. In *Evening Standard v Henderson*, it was said that:[70]

> If the defendant leaves the employment of the plaintiffs today, as he says he intends to do, and takes himself off straightaway or very shortly to the rival newspaper, the plaintiffs, in my judgment, will undoubtedly suffer damage but, as I have already said and the judge at first instance found, it will be almost impossible to quantify that damage.

In a number of judgments handed down in cases brought by employers, sanctity of contract is stressed in a way that it is not apparent where actions brought by employees are concerned. Indeed, if 'there were not adherence to such a principle, the conduct of private and commercial affairs would become an uncertain jumble'.[71] It is the case, however, that, in general, contract law sees damages as an adequate remedy. The employer will be unable to obtain an injunction where it would result in putting 'the employee in the position that he would either have to go on working for his former employers or starve or be idle'.[72] It is noteworthy that the law in this regard has been modernized to the benefit of the employer. It has been common practice for employers to meet the 'starvation' factor by giving an undertaking to the court as to remuneration that goes beyond the contractual obligation, in order that an

---

67 *Powell* (n 60).

68 *Quinn* (n 3).

69 See Joellen Riley, 'Sterilising Talent: A Critical Assessment of Injunctions Enforcing Negative Covenants' (2012) 34 Syd L Rev 617.

70 *Evening Standard v Henderson* [1987] ICR 588, 594.

71 *Seven Network (Operations) v James Warburton (No 2)* [2011] NSWSC 386, [3].

72 *Evening Standard v Henderson* [1987] ICR 588, 592.

injunction will be granted. Against a backdrop of judicial concern over the appropriate rights and duties of highly paid executives, the courts have taken a more robust approach and, in some circumstances, will not require the traditional undertaking.[73] In the United Kingdom, the courts start from the premise that the employee's difficulties are of their own making, given that the employment contract subsists but the employee does not wish to perform their obligations under it. In deciding whether or not to impose an undertaking, the court will consider 'whether the pressures on the employee will be such as to compel him to return to work'.[74] An undertaking may not be required in the case of, for example, a highly paid employee.

CONCLUSIONS

The common law takes a restrictive approach to the award of damages where employment is concerned; this is probably most marked in the United Kingdom. Developments in the law of contract more generally may not be taken on board, which may be to the detriment of the employee. The willingness, in the United Kingdom, to award damages for injury to feelings in an increasing range of situations apart from employment is a prime example. The position in New Zealand was more progressive prior to the abolition of actions for wrongful dismissal, in part, due to the timing of statutory consolidation of common law developments. In Australia and the United Kingdom, statutory reforms have had the potential to act as catalysts for change, but the courts have viewed statutory schemes as belonging to a separate world. In the United Kingdom, the compensatory award in the statutory law of unfair dismissal, subject to the ceiling on awards, is assessed in a manner akin to a personal injuries action, but this has not been regarded by the judiciary as an indicator that common law reform might be required. In Australia, the weakening of the 'least burdensome' principle is due to developments in the general law of contract, rather than the statutory scheme of protection against dismissal; and a much more purposive approach to reinstatement has been taken than in the United Kingdom. In *Blackadder v Ramsey Butchering Services Pty Ltd*, Kirby J declared that reinstatement under statute:[75]

---

[73] *Standard Life Health Care v Gorman* [2010] IRLR 233.

[74] *Sunrise Brokers v Rodgers* [2015] IRLR 57, [33].

[75] *Blackadder* (n 3) [29].

> is not to be frustrated or negatived because it conflicts with common law notions of freedom of contract or with other traditional legal rules respecting the personal character of the employment contract. All such rules must adapt to the statutory provisions which have been enacted for important social and industrial purposes.

Moreover, reinstatement requires the provision of actual work.[76] Such a wholesale embracing of what amounts to a form of statutory specific performance entails a categorical rejection of the validity of common law thinking, but has not resulted in a change of practice at common law. Where equitable remedies are concerned, the position has improved with respect to interlocutory orders but, beyond that, little has changed for the benefit of the employee.

Viewed in the round, the position in respect of remedies remains out of line with the needs of employees. In fact, in the United Kingdom, in some respects, the position has got worse – *Edwards v Chesterfield Royal Hospital NHS Foundation Trust*[77] extending the scope of *Johnson v Unisys Ltd*[78] to deny a claim for reputational damages arising from the breach of an express term providing for the disciplinary process. Collins has observed that 'express terms that limit dismissal to cases of gross misconduct or provide for an elaborate disciplinary hearing in the event of such allegations are designed to protect the employee against false allegations that will destroy employability'.[79] It may be that there is a concern that the burden on the employer would be too great:[80]

> What seems to have worried the courts most about such express terms is that the employer might end up being liable for damages representing career earnings, minus either some discount for the possibility of earlier termination of the contract on justifiable grounds by the employer or the employee resigning in order to take another job.

---

76 ibid.

77 *Edwards* (n 16).

78 *Johnson v Unisys Ltd* [2001] UKHL 13.

79 Hugh Collins, 'Compensation for Dismissal: In Search of Principle' (2012) 41 ILJ 208, 217.

80 ibid.

12. Conclusions

In Chapter 1, we noted the long-standing tendency of the common law to import the values of the law of master and servant.[1] As is conventional at this juncture, we referred to the content of implied terms such as the obligation to obey lawful and reasonable orders by way of evidence. Through the conduit of such key implied terms, the values of the law of master and servant continue to exercise an influence. Whilst this traditional perspective continues to carry validity, we sought to explore the extent to which the courts have seen fit to modernize the contract. In *Horkulak v Cantor Fitzgerald*, Newman J claimed that 'the notion of an employment contract giving rise to a "master and servant" relationship is now obsolete'.[2] Again, in a characteristically bold dictum in *Johnson v Unisys Ltd*, Lord Hoffmann expressed the view that much has changed:[3]

> Over the last 30 years or so, the nature of the contract of employment has been transformed. It has been recognised that a person's employment is usually one of the most important things in his or her life. It gives not only a livelihood but an occupation, an identity and a sense of self-esteem. The law has changed to recognise this social reality. Most of the changes have been made by Parliament. The Employment Rights Act 1996 consolidates numerous statutes which have conferred rights upon employees. European law has made a substantial contribution. And the common law has adapted itself to the new attitudes, proceeding sometimes by analogy with statutory rights.

It is only fair to acknowledge that Lord Hoffmann regards the legislature as the dominant actor, but what of his claim that 'the common law has adapted itself to the new attitudes'?

It would certainly be wrong to suggest that nothing has changed. In the United Kingdom, in *Spring v Guardian Assurance*, Lord Slynn drew attention to 'the changes which have taken place in the employer/employee relationship, with far greater duties imposed on the employer than in the past, whether by statute or by judicial decision, to care for the

[1] See Alan Bogg, 'Good Faith in the Contract of Employment: A Case of the English Reserve?' (2011) 32 Comp Lab L & Pol'y J 743.

[2] *Horkulak v Cantor Fitzgerald* [2003] IRLR 756, 760.

[3] *Johnson v Unisys Ltd* [2001] UKHL 13, [2003] 1 AC 518, [35].

physical, financial and even psychological welfare of the employee'.[4] Mutual trust and confidence is the most notable example, but it is also worth highlighting House of Lords decisions on disclosure of information and prevention of harassment.[5] New Zealand also adopted the implied term of mutual trust and went further than either Australia or the United Kingdom where remedies were concerned (those developments have been consolidated in statute). In Australia, mutual trust failed to take root, but it appears that implied obligations of the fair dealing type are still likely to offer a measure of assistance to employees.

Common law reform may be attributed, in part, to wider developments in the law of contract, such as the judicial recognition of relational contract scholarship and the increasing significance of norms of good faith. Judicial recognition of the realities of the employment relationship has also been hugely important. The judges have now come to accept the academic analysis in works such as Kahn-Freund's *Labour and the Law* that the employment relationship displays a marked disparity in bargaining power and that, in consequence, employees are vulnerable to oppressive treatment by employers.[6] This change of stance has had a cogent and conspicuous impact on doctrine. Discretionary powers, for instance, are now subject to judicial regulation at common law; abuse of power will be guarded against. The orthodox view had been that, where one party to a contract possesses an unambiguously worded express power, they may exercise it as they see fit. The Privy Council confirmed this as recently as 2002.[7] This view has now been discarded, and protectionism has become swiftly engrained. It is worthy of note that, in Australia, the demise of mutual trust and confidence appears to have had no impact on the existence of judicial control of the employer's discretion.[8] The courts have also begun to recognize (as we see from the dictum of Lord Hoffmann in *Johnson* referred to above) the importance to the employee of the non-pecuniary dimensions of the relationship. Job satisfaction and other intangible benefits may matter a great deal to the worker. The judges have begun to take some, albeit limited, cognizance of this. There have been tentative steps in the direction of an implied right to be given

---

4 *Spring v Guardian Assurance* [1994] UKHL 7, [1994] 3 All ER 129, [33].

5 *Scally v Southern Health Board* [1992] 1 AC 294; *Waters v Commissioner of Police* [2000] 4 All ER 934.

6 Paul Davies and Mark Freedland, *Kahn-Freunds' Labour and the Law* (3rd edn, Stevens and Sons 1983).

7 *Reda v Flag Ltd* [2002] UKPC 38, [2002] IRLR 747.

8 See Chapter 7.

actual work to do.[9] The common law is also more willing to grant an interlocutory order to preserve the employment contract in the face of the employer's breach, at least to ensure that due process is followed.[10]

It seems likely that the factors referred to in the preceding paragraph will continue to exert an influence on the content of the employment contract. Wider developments in the law of contract must also be considered. The contract of employment has been increasingly recognized by the judiciary as relational.[11] The extent to which this will have an impact on contractual doctrine remains to be seen. It is undoubtedly the case that a number of developments in the law of the employment contract (such as the emergence of the implied obligation of mutual trust and confidence[12]) are wholly consistent with relational contract theory. However, it will often be impossible to say to what extent, if any, there is a causal connection. Other drivers (and arguably more powerful ones), such as the norm of good faith, have played their part. In any event, it should not be assumed that any developments that produce greater affinity with relational contracting will be welcomed by employees. Commercial decisions have moved in the direction of more onerous disclosure requirements,[13] a move that would not be likely to be welcomed by employees.[14]

In contract law, as a whole, good faith has assumed much greater significance and there is growing acceptance that a norm of fair dealing is part and parcel of contracting in general. A steadily increasing weight of case law may lead to the emergence of an overarching principle of good faith. Against this backdrop, it is likely that the contract of employment will develop further dimensions of the good faith type. It was notable that, in *Commonwealth Bank of Australia v Barker*, it was said that:[15]

> The above conclusion should not be taken as reflecting upon the question whether there is a general obligation to act in good faith in the performance of contracts. Nor does it reflect upon the related question whether contractual

---

9 *William Hill v Tucker* [1999] ICR 291; *Blackadder v Ramsey Butchering Services Pty Ltd* (2005) 221 CLR 539.

10 See Chapter 11.

11 See e.g. *Braganza v BP Shipping* [2015] UKSC 17, [2015] 4 All ER 639.

12 It is worth noting that, in the United Kingdom, the emergence of mutual trust predated judicial recognition of relational contract scholarship.

13 *Yam Seng v International Trade Corp* [2013] EWHC 111 (QB).

14 See Chapter 8.

15 *Commonwealth Bank of Australia v Barker* (2014) 253 CLR 169; [2014] HCA 32, [42].

> powers and discretions may be limited by good faith and rationality requirements analogous to those applicable in the sphere of public law.

Australian cases since then suggest that, the caution expressed in the foregoing dictum notwithstanding, courts will regulate discretionary powers in the employment context on the basis of fair dealing; one such instance is *Romero v Farstad Shipping*.[16] The capacity of employers to contract-out of obligations implied by the courts may be restricted as a result of the growing influence of good faith. For instance, on traditional principles, it would be possible to contract-out of the implied obligation of trust and confidence, as the term is a default rule. This stands in contrast to the common position in a number of European systems, whereby 'the regulation of the content and the performance of contracts of employment ... more readily presents itself as *jus cogens* in character, its norms typically appearing to be inderogable, or derogable only in very limited circumstances'.[17] In Canada, the Supreme Court in *Bhasin v Hrynew* recognized that good faith constituted an overarching principle in the general law of contract.[18] The centrality of good faith in Canadian law led directly and decisively to a prohibition on contracting-out.

Good faith functions as a means of rationalization of the existing law, but also as a powerful catalyst:[19]

> The application of the organizing principle of good faith to particular situations should be developed where the existing law is found to be wanting and where the development may occur incrementally in a way that is consistent with the structure of the common law of contract and gives due weight to the importance of private ordering and certainty in commercial affairs.

Contracts of all types will change wherever good faith is recognized.

A common heritage notwithstanding, it is clear that there have been considerable differences in the way in which the common law has developed across the three jurisdictions. Statute has played a large part in this. In both Australia and New Zealand, employment relations have long been conducted within the four walls of a statutory framework, to a far greater extent than in the United Kingdom. This has meant that there has been far less scope for the common law to develop. Nevertheless, in New

---

16 *Romero v Farstad Shipping* [2014] FCAFC 177.

17 Mark Freedland and Nicola Kountouris, *The Legal Construction of Personal Work Relations* (Oxford University Press 2011) 182.

18 *Bhasin v Hrynew* 2014 SCC 71.

19 *Rodd v Alberta Health Services* 2015 ABQB 320, [66].

Zealand, in the 1980s, the courts modernized the employment contract in a number of ways. As a consequence, judicial acceptance of mutual trust and confidence emerged. In addition, *Addis v Gramophone*[20] was departed from and the position in respect of remedies improved. While this trend was reversed somewhat during the 1990s, statute has subsequently stepped in and consolidated and enhanced those developments. It would seem that further evolution will be likely to arise, in the main, in a statutory context. In Australia, the dominance of statute has engendered resistance to any common law development of an exceptional field of employment contract law, distinct from commercial contract law.

THE CENTRALITY OF MANAGERIAL PREROGATIVE

It would be wrong to create the impression that the employer's prerogative has been diminished to a material extent. The impact of common law reform on the life of the worker has clearly been limited. The extent of the employer's obligations to the workforce continues to be restricted and, for instance:[21]

> the scope of the rule of public policy in operation in these cases, and all cases of employers' liability, is to safeguard the health, safety and welfare of employees from the careless acts and omissions of their employers; and, in the event of breach, where personal injury is suffered to require the payment of compensation. The concepts of health, safety and welfare, properly understood, embody the notion of protection from personal injury and not from economic or financial loss suffered without personal injury.

It is arguable that the contract does not allocate the risks of employment in an equitable manner.[22]

Crucially, the scope of managerial prerogative remains extensive and judges are only prepared to take modest steps where amelioration is concerned. We have seen that questions of incorporation and construction tend to be approached from an employer-orientated perspective.[23] Again, the implied obligation of fidelity appears to be evolving in a way that is

---

20 *Addis v Gramophone Co Ltd* [1909] AC 488.

21 *Greenway v Johnson Matthey plc* [2016] IRLR 526, [36]; quoting *Greenway v Johnson Matthey plc* [2014] EWHC 3957 (QB), [47].

22 Douglas Brodie, 'Mutual Trust and the Values of the Employment Contract' (2001) 30 ILJ 84.

23 See Chapter 5.

more solicitous of the employer's interests.[24] The employer's dominant position is, perhaps, most in evidence at the point of entry into an agreement with the worker – where both the terms and nature of the contract are concerned. It is surely the case that the easiest way to contract-out of common law and statutory rights is to avoid the use of an employment contract. The courts reserve the right to determine the true nature of the relationship – a position reinforced by the emerging law on sham contracts. It should be said, however, that, in many contexts, it will be possible to construct the relationship on a basis that does not involve employment. Modern employers display great interest in other modes of working relationships. It has always been the case that employers have, at times, preferred to hire on the basis of self-employment, but the extent to which this occurs has increased greatly. Moreover, self-employment may place workers in a precarious position: 'Although they are classified as independent contractors, many have little actual control over the terms and conditions of work and many generate less income than employees'.[25] Self-employment has become only one of an array of contractual arrangements that govern working relations; franchises, for example, have become widespread. Employers will often act through an intermediary, and the use of agency workers has also become commonplace. The courts have found this reshaped landscape difficult to navigate. Judicial intervention is at the margins and is likely to remain that way. More radical changes are seen as a matter for the legislature. The dominance of neoliberal thinking on public policy cannot be discounted. Judges are aware that it is legitimate for an employer to look to the self-employed, agency workers and so on.

Whilst the issue of categorization remains troublesome, the common law (perhaps surprisingly) is also largely unchanged. It is fair to say that the most significant changes have come about where vicarious liability is concerned. This is not the case in New Zealand, where the statutory scheme of accident compensation serves to marginalize the common law. In the United Kingdom, however, the Supreme Court has accepted that employers should be responsible in law, not just for employees, but for those who are 'akin' to employees.[26] The Australian courts have yet to adopt this approach, though a finding of employment may be more likely

---

[24] See Chapter 7.

[25] See Kerry Rittich, *Vulnerability at Work: Legal and Policy Issues in the New Economy* (Law Commission of Canada 2004) 26.

[26] *The Catholic Child Welfare Society v Various Claimants* [2013] 2 AC 1.

in proceedings in tort.[27] In the United Kingdom, it now seems beyond doubt that a number of individuals who would be self-employed for other purposes are viewed as employees or 'quasi employees' and the employer is responsible in law as a result. The courts have resisted the suggestion that the employer should be vicariously liable for the self-employed. It was striking that the Court of Appeal, in *JGE v The English Province of Our Lady of Charity*, confirmed that employers are not liable for the activities of independent contractors, thereby denying the existence of the clearest analogy.[28] This conclusion was reached even though it was acknowledged that the endeavours of the self-employed may be just as central to the success of the enterprise as those of employees: 'the employer may have as close a connection with his regularly used independent contractor as he has with an employee who is but an anonymous member of his workforce'.[29] Nevertheless, judicial reform has been more radical where the interests of third parties are concerned. This may reflect a traditional freedom of contract approach, despite what has been said about recognition of disparity of bargaining power. The parties to the employment contract can, in theory, enter into an agreement on terms that protect their own interests, whereas the third party cannot.

THE VALUES OF THE EMPLOYMENT CONTRACT

In *Common Values and the Public-Private Divide*, Dawn Oliver suggested that the common law possessed certain core values, and that judicial vigilance is likely to be prompted by a threat to an individual's 'dignity, autonomy, respect, status or security'.[30] It is certainly the case that the employment contract has evolved in line with those values to some extent.[31] In 1971, in *Malloch v Aberdeen Corporation*, Lord Reid said that:[32]

---

27 There are indications, however, that the more expansive approach to vicarious liability that has emerged in the United Kingdom may be exerting an influence on the Australian courts: *Prince Alfred College v ADC* [2016] HCA 37.

28 *JGE v The English Province of Our Lady of Charity* [2011] EWHC 2871 (QB), [2012] 1 All ER 723.

29 ibid [61].

30 Dawn Oliver, *Common Values and the Public-Private Divide* (Cambridge University Press 1999) 60.

31 See Brodie (n 22).

32 *Malloch v Aberdeen Corporation* [1971] SC (HL) 85, [1971] WLR 1578, 1586.

> At common law a master is not bound to hear his servant before he dismisses him. He can act unreasonably or capriciously if he so chooses but the dismissal is valid. The servant has no remedy unless the dismissal is in breach of contract and then the servant's only remedy is damages for breach of contract.

This was, undoubtedly, the orthodox view at that time, but the law of the employment contract has moved on considerably since then and the common law is more willing to have regard to procedural fairness. The New Zealand courts have said that the obligation of mutual trust and confidence can be seen as 'an application of natural justice to contemporary industrial relations'.[33] The modern employment contract, particularly through the medium of implied terms, places greater weight on procedural fairness and displays strong affinities with natural justice. For instance, in *Crawford v Suffolk Mental Health Partnership NHS Trust*, it was said that 'it is particularly important that employers take seriously their responsibilities to conduct a fair investigation where, as is the case here, the employee's reputation or ability to work in his or her chosen field of employment is likely to be affected by a finding of misconduct'.[34] In the recent New Zealand case of *Rodkiss v Carter Holt Harvey*, the court held that the:[35]

> problem with that explanation, however, is that the issues identified were all matters that reflected adversely on Mr Rodkiss' performance and, as such, in terms of CHH's basic obligations of fairness and good faith, they should have been discussed with him and he should have had an opportunity to comment upon them before Mr Adams made his decision to implement the PIP [performance improvement plan].

The decision in *Johnson* is troublesome in terms of what it says about the values of the common law; in particular, that of natural justice and security. It holds that, whilst mutual trust may serve, in general, to constrain an employer's prerogative powers, that is not the case where termination is concerned. Yet again, managerial prerogative trumps other considerations. This is despite the fact that the need to assert control is

---

[33] *Auckland Shop Employees Union v Woolworths (NZ) Ltd* [1985] 2 NZLR 372, 376; and see Brodie (n 22).

[34] *Crawford v Suffolk Mental Health Partnership NHS Trust* [2012] EWCA Civ 138, [27].

[35] *Rodkiss v Carter Holt Harvey* [2015] NZEmpC 34, [99].

most acute where termination is concerned. Indeed, in *Johnson* itself, Lord Millett observed that:[36]

> In reality there was no comparison between the consequences for an employer if the employee terminated his employment and the consequences for an employee if he was dismissed. Many people build their lives round their jobs and plan their future in the expectation that they will continue. For many workers dismissal is a disaster.

THE FALL OF COLLECTIVE BARGAINING AND THE RISE OF HUMAN RESOURCE MANAGEMENT

Collective bargaining plays a much reduced role nowadays. Its decline may have influenced common law reform to some extent, given that the judiciary are clearly aware of the increased vulnerability of individual workers.[37] Whilst workplace relations are less likely to be regulated by collective bargaining, it is also the case that human resource management (HRM) has become very significant. The impact of this on the employment contract is difficult to assess, although it is conceivable that HRM will lend support to some of the recent changes at common law. Both HRM and the employment contract have a common interest in, and commitment to, procedural justice. HRM takes the view that a relationship underpinned by respect for procedural justice can evolve for the better. Lind writes that 'it is possible, by judicious choice and design of procedures, to enhance the quality of social life without increasing the external outcomes available for distribution under the procedures'.[38] This is of clear relevance to employment, where the employer's resources will be finite and subject to competing demands. Processes such as an annual pay review have considerable potential to give rise to tensions, disharmony and discontent with the substantive outcomes. If the employer's procedures are perceived to be fair, then employees are likely to believe that 'it is reasonable to expect long-term gains, even in the absence of short-term gains'.[39] A commitment to procedural justice may encourage a long-term view of self-interest and may be 'crucial to the long-term maintenance of positive social relationships within groups'.[40] Again, an

---

36 *Johnson* (n 3) [72].

37 See Brodie (n 22).

38 E Allan Lind, *The Social Psychology of Procedural Justice* (Plenum 1988) 26.

39 ibid 224.

40 ibid 226.

HR manager might also place importance on 'interactional justice' and the need to treat employees with respect and dignity:[41]

> When practices entail distributions, some will lose out on what is being distributed – jobs, promotions, opportunities, rewards. Focussing on dignity expands the distributive pie for those who end up worse off. They may be denied opportunities or have their jobs and lives disrupted, but attending to their dignity ensures that another good is distributed.

STATUTE AND THE COMMON LAW

The sheer extent of statutory intervention may mean that there is no, or very limited, scope for common law development. This may explain the limited amount of innovation in the Australian case law. It is also the case that specific statutory measures may have a discernible impact on common law development. *Johnson*[42] and *New South Wales v Paige*[43] are two instances of the 'natural' evolution of common law development being constrained by the existence of related statutory provisions. As is well known, the view was taken in both decisions that the creation of a right at common law would undermine the legislative scheme and was therefore impermissible. The fact that the claimants had sought to increase the rights of employees where job security was concerned is also of significance. Contemporary developments continue to leave very considerable scope to managerial prerogative.

It is also true to say that statute may serve to stimulate common law development. The way in which the statutory concept of constructive dismissal prompted the emergence of mutual trust and confidence offers the most graphic example. Again, where harassment is concerned, the Protection from Harassment Act 1997 (UK) has prompted the common law to accept that the employer should be vicariously liable for statutory torts.[44] A recent instance of statute acting as a catalyst is provided by *Romero v Farstad Shipping*, where the employer argued that the existence of legislation dealing with bullying militated against incorporation of a policy on 'Workplace Harassment and Discrimination', as employees

---

[41] Ashly Pinnington, Rob Macklin and Tom Campbell (eds), *Human Resource Management: Ethics and Employment* (Oxford University Press 2007) 244.

[42] *Johnson* (n 3).

[43] *New South Wales v Paige* (2002) 115 IR 283.

[44] *Majrowski v Guy's and St Thomas's Trust* [2006] UKHL 34, [2007] 1 AC 224.

were already adequately protected.[45] However, the legislation was seen as embodying the values of the employment relationship and incorporation was favoured: the parties should be encouraged to adopt 'a specific method as to the manner in which those statutory obligations are to be observed'.[46] It is also the case that the values underpinning statutory measures may influence the common law. The focus on procedural fairness in statutory schemes offering protection against unfair dismissal has served to encourage greater recognition of natural justice at common law.

The common law may also take on a gap-filling role. In *Scally v Southern Health Board*, the claimants sought damages in respect of the employer's failure to inform them of rights arising under the rules of their pension scheme.[47] The House of Lords held that the failure of the employer to provide written particulars did not give rise to an action for breach of statutory duty. Such an outcome was regarded as unnecessary, given that statute already provided a remedy. Nevertheless, the failure to provide the requisite information was found to amount to a breach of the employer's implied contractual obligations.

Viewed in the round, the relationship between statute and common law is not as symbiotic as it might appear. Developments in the law of remedies under statute have not served to empower the common law, which continues to be inadequate from the perspective of the employee. In the field of employment law, statute and the common law tend to stand apart. This appears to be less true in some other jurisdictions. Turning to the United States, we find a body of case law where outcomes have been determined by gauging the merits of a claim for judicial innovation against the demands of public policy, as expressed in the relevant statute. Thus, common law remedies have been devised to supplement those contained in discrimination legislation: further exceptions to the employment-at-will doctrine are justified, as discrimination is viewed as contrary to public policy.

CONCLUSIONS

Our study of the evolution of the common law of employment in the three jurisdictions of the United Kingdom, Australia and New Zealand confirms the continuing importance of the employment relationship as

---

45 *Romero* (n 16).
46 ibid [53].
47 *Scally v Southern Health Board* [1992] 1 AC 294.

one of Marsden's two pillars of modern business enterprise.[48] The different post-colonial histories of Australia and New Zealand have generated some variations in the features of the regulation of employment from the United Kingdom, largely as a consequence of the development of indigenous systems of conciliation and arbitration of industrial matters. In more recent times, the dismantling of aspects of those systems has restored a focus on individual employment relationships, and encouraged greater resort to contract law to resolve the challenges presented by contemporary economic, technological and social developments. The commonality of those contemporary challenges, and continued reference by a largely conservative judiciary to a common repository of core common law values and principles, has preserved a broad compatibility between the jurisdictions, notwithstanding differences in detail.

48 See Chapter 1 (n 1).

Index